Macs For Dummies,®
8th Edition

Cheat Sheet

D0520094

What've You Got There?

To find out how much memory your Mac has and what system-software version, choose About This Mac from the menu. (This book assumes that you have Mac OS X 10.3 or later.) Write the answers down here.

Your Mac OS version: 10.4.8

Memory: _____

The Dock

The Dock keeps your favorite programs, documents, folders, and disks handy for quick access. (Point to an icon without clicking to see its name.)

To add an icon to the Dock, drag it there with the mouse (programs go on the left side of the Dock's white divider line, everything else on the right). To remove something from the Dock, drag its icon up and away. To rearrange Dock icons, just drag them sideways with the mouse.

Surviving the First Half Hour

You may only need this information at the very beginning of your Mac career — but you'll really need it.

Turning on the Mac

Press the power button. For most Macs, it's a round, flat button on the front or top panel (Chapter 1).

Turning off the Mac

Truth is, you don't need to think about turning off the Mac. After about half an hour, it goes to "sleep" on its own, consuming only a night-light's worth of electricity, ready to wake up when you touch a key or the mouse.

But if you want it all the way off, open the menu and choose Shut Down, or just press the power key again. Click the Shut Down button that appears.

Troubleshooting Keystrokes

One of your programs is frozen, but the cursor moves: From the menu, choose Force Quit. Click the name of the program that seems to be frozen, and then click the Force Quit button. You can keep on working in your other programs, and even re-open the one that acted up before.

The Mac has completely frozen: This hardly ever happens — but if it does, press the Power button for six seconds to turn the machine off. Then press it again to turn the machine on again.

A CD is stuck in the machine: Restart the computer. As it's turning on, hold down the mouse button continuously until the CD spits out.

You're panicking: Call Apple's hotline: 800-500-7078.

Working with Icons
Renaming a file

1. **Click an icon (once). Press Return.**
2. **Type a new name; then press Return.**

A file's name can be up to 255 letters long.

To insert a CD or DVD

Hold the disc by the edges (or the hole), label side up. If your Mac has a felt-lined slot for discs, just put the disc into it far enough for the Mac to slurp it in. Some Macs have a CD *tray* instead; hold down the ▲ key on your keyboard to make it come out, put the CD or DVD into it, and then push the ▲ key a second time to make the tray close.

The disk's icon appears on the screen.

Ejecting a disk

Hold down the ▲ button on your keyboard. Or drag the disk's icon onto the Trash icon (at the end of the Dock).

Copying files onto a blank CD

Insert a blank (called a CD-R disc) into your Mac, type a name for it when requested, and click OK. Then drag the files you want to copy onto the CD's icon, like this:

To finish burning the CD, choose Burn Disc from the File menu.

For Dummies: Bestselling Book Series for Beginners

Macs For Dummies,®
8th Edition

Cheat Sheet

What All These Little Controls Do

They call this box a *dialog box* because the Mac is asking questions it needs answered. Here are the elements of a typical dialog box.

Radio buttons

Named after the pushbuttons on a car radio, where only one can be pushed in at a time. Likewise, only one Mac radio button can be selected at a time.

Check boxes

Used to indicate whether an option is on or off. Click once to place the checkmark in the box; click again to remove the checkmark (and turn off the option).

Text fields

You're supposed to type into these blanks. To move from one blank to another, either click with the mouse or press the Tab key.

Pop-up menus

When you see this, you're seeing a *pop-up menu*. Point to the text, hold down the mouse button, and make a selection from the minimenu that drops down.

Buttons

Every dialog box has a clearly marked button or two (usually OK and Cancel) that make the box go away — your escape route.

Click OK (or Print, or Proceed, or whatever the button says) to proceed with the command you originally chose from the menu. Click Cancel if you want to back out of the dialog box, as though you'd never issued the command.

See the Next button above? If you could see the *real* Next button on your screen, you'd see that it's blue and pulsing. Whenever you see a blue, pulsing button, you don't have to use the mouse to click it. Instead, you can press either the Return or Enter key on your keyboard — a few precious seconds saved.

Working with Several Programs

The Mac lets you run more than one program at once. Here are some pointers.

Determining what programs are running

Look for the tiny triangles underneath your Dock icons. These are the programs that are currently open.

Hiding or quitting programs

Many Mac fans *never* quit their programs; instead, they just *hide* the ones they're not actively using (from the menu next to the menu, choose Hide TextEdit, or Hide Mail, or Hide whatever). But if you're really, truly finished with a program for the day, you can choose Quit TextEdit, or Quit Mail, or Quit whatever, from the menu that bears the program's name (next to the menu).

Opening or Closing a Window

Every window was once an *icon* that you double-clicked to see what was inside.

1. Double-click any icon to open its window.

2. To get rid of a window, click the *close button* in the upper-left corner.

For Dummies: Bestselling Book Series for Beginners

MACINTOSH METHODOLOGIES IN THEORY AND PRACTICE

A technical guide for experienced users

formerly *Macs For Dummies*

BY D. WELCH POGUE

Includes advanced treatment of these topics:

◆ Invoking the commencement of A/C 120V electric power to the CPU unit

◆ Propelling the cursor-control module on a horizontal plane

◆ Insertion and removal of optical data storage media

Look, we use the word *Dummies* on the cover with affection and a twinkle in the eye. Still, we understand if you're not thrilled about leaving a book on your desk called *Macs For Dummies*.

We hear you. And we've got the perfect solution: Just rip off the real cover of the book! This phony cover will be all that's left. Leave it on your desk in plain sight, so everybody will know what a computer whiz you are.

Macs FOR DUMMIES® 8TH EDITION

by David Pogue

WILEY

Wiley Publishing, Inc.

Macs For Dummies®, 8th Edition

Published by
Wiley Publishing, Inc.
111 River Street
Hoboken, NJ 07030-5774

Copyright © 2004 by Wiley Publishing, Inc., Indianapolis, Indiana

Published by Wiley Publishing, Inc., Indianapolis, Indiana

Published simultaneously in Canada

For general information on our other products and services or to obtain technical support, please contact our Customer Care Department within the U.S. at 800-762-2974, outside the U.S. at 317-572-3993, or fax 317-572-4002.

Wiley also publishes its books in a variety of electronic formats. Some content that appears in print may not be available in electronic books.

Library of Congress Control Number: 2004102348

ISBN: 0-7645-5656-8

Manufactured in the United States of America

10 9 8 7 6 5 4 3

8O/SR/QU/QU/IN

WILEY

About the Author

David Pogue, Yale '85, is the weekly personal-technology columnist for the *New York Times* and technology correspondent for *CBS News Sunday Morning*. With nearly 3 million books in print, he is also one of the world's bestselling how-to authors, having written or co-written seven books in the *For Dummies* series (including *Macs, Magic, Opera,* and *Classical Music),* several computer-humor books, and even a techno-thriller, now out of print, called *Hard Drive.*

David is also the creator and primary author of the Missing Manual series of funny intermediate computer books (*www.missingmanuals.com*). The series includes books on Mac OS X, iMovie and iDVD, iPhoto, iPod and iTunes, Office X for Macintosh, Dreamweaver, and many others.

With his madly adored wife Jennifer, son Kelly, daughter Tia, and Bullwinkle the Wonderdog, he lives in Connecticut, where he does magic tricks and plays the piano. The family photos lurk on the World Wide Web at *www.davidpogue.com.*

Author's Acknowledgments

This book was made possible by the enthusiasm and support of Project Editor Mary Goodwin, Acquisitions Manager Bob Woerner, and everyone else in the sprawling universe of Wiley & Sons voicemail. Thanks, too, to technical editor Dennis Cohen.

Above all, my gratitude and love go to the lovely Jennifer, Kelly, and Tia, who stood by me (or crawled by me, as the case may be) during the writing of this book.

Publisher's Acknowledgments

We're proud of this book; please send us your comments through our online registration form located at www.dummies.com/register/.

Some of the people who helped bring this book to market include the following:

Acquisitions, Editorial, and Media Development

Project Editor: Mary Goodwin

Acquisitions Manager: Bob Woerner

Technical Editor: Dennis Cohen

Editorial Manager: Carol Sheehan

Media Development Manager: Laura VanWinkle

Media Development Supervisor: Richard Graves

Editorial Assistant: Amanda Foxworth

Cartoons: Rich Tennant (www.the5thwave.com)

Production

Project Coordinator: April Farling

Layout and Graphics: Andrea Dahl, Lauren Goddard, Stephanie D. Jumper, Michael Kruzil, Lynsey Osborn, Heather Ryan, Jacque Schneider

Proofreaders: Andy Hollandbeck, Betty Kish, Carl Pierce, Brian H. Walls

Indexer: Steve Rath

Publishing and Editorial for Technology Dummies

Richard Swadley, Vice President and Executive Group Publisher

Andy Cummings, Vice President and Publisher

Mary C. Corder, Editorial Director

Publishing for Consumer Dummies

Diane Graves Steele, Vice President and Publisher

Joyce Pepple, Acquisitions Director

Composition Services

Gerry Fahey, Vice President of Production Services

Debbie Stailey, Director of Composition Services

Contents at a Glance

Table of Contents

Introduction

• •

*I*f you bought a Mac, you're unbelievably smart (or lucky). You've neatly eliminated much of the hassle, frustration, and annoyance that normally comes with buying a computer. You have a computer that doesn't just look a heck of a lot better than other kinds of computers — it works better, too, because both its hardware and its software were designed by a single company. And not a single computer virus has yet surfaced that can affect the Mac's operating software. (You know how your friends and your newspaper are always going on about viruses and hackers? They're talking about Windows computers. The Mac doesn't do Windows.)

The Mac also has everything you need built in: a modem (so you can use the Internet and e-mail), a CD burner (great for making backups), or even a DVD burner (for preserving your home movies on DVD), and a huge assortment of free programs.

Who Needs a Mac Book?

If the Mac is so simple, then who needs a book about it?

Well, despite all the free goodies you get with the Mac, a *manual* isn't among them. You need somewhere to turn when things go wrong, when you'd like to know what the add-on software does, or when you want to stumble onto the Internet for the first time.

By the way, of *course* you're not a dummy. Two pieces of evidence tell me so: For one thing, you're learning the Mac, and for another, you're reading this book! But I've taught hundreds of people how to use their Macs, and an awful lot of them start out saying they *feel* like dummies when it comes to computers. Society surrounds us with fast-talking teenagers who grew up learning English from their Nintendo sets; no wonder the rest of us sometimes feel left out.

But you're no more a dummy for not knowing the Mac than you were before you knew how to drive. Learning a Macintosh is like learning to drive: After a lesson or two, you can go anywhere your heart desires.

So when we say *Dummies,* we're saying it with an affectionate wink. Still, if the cover bothers you even a little — I'll admit it, you wouldn't be the first — please rip it right off. The inner cover, we hope, will make you proud to have the book out on your desk.

How to Use This Book (Other Than as a Mouse Pad)

Start with the very basics in Chapter 1; turn to Chapter 16 in times of trouble; and consult the other chapters as the spirit moves you.

Macintosh conventions

Macintosh conventions? Sure. They're called Macworld Expos, and there's one in Boston and one in San Francisco each year.

Conventions in this book

Oh, *that* kind of convention.

So that we'll be eligible for some of the more prestigious book-design awards, I've marked some topics with these icons:

Nerdy stuff that's okay to skip but will fascinate the kind of people who read Tom Clancy novels.

The Macintosh is the greatest computer on earth, but it's still a computer. Now and then it does unexplainable stuff, which I'll explain.

A shortcut so you can show off.

Denotes an actual You-Try-It Experience. Hold the book open with a nearby cinder block, put your hands on the computer, and do as I say.

Points out something really cool that your Mac can do that mere mortal computers can only eye jealously.

The cult of Macintosh

You may already be aware that less than five percent of computers sold in the U.S. are Macs. The rest are primarily what are known as PCs: personal computers whose operating-system software is Microsoft Windows.

This statistic may boggle your mind. If the computers that appear in TV shows or in the movies were any indication, you'd think that the situation was reversed. (Hollywood *loves* Macs.)

You'd also be shocked if you work in just about any creative business — publishing, music, art, film, Web design, science, and so on — all of which are fields where the Mac dominates. The Mac's market share is much higher in many overseas countries, too.

One place where the Mac does *not* dominate is in the corporate offices of America, where a single buyer may order up 500 computers at a time. Those gigantic corporate purchases are one huge factor in making the Mac's presence seem puny. ("Corporations buy PCs; people buy Macs," I always say.)

But five percent is still enough to constitute 20 million people; still enough to keep Apple profitable and thriving (even through the tech recession of 2000–2003, when other computer companies were hurting); and most importantly, still enough to attract software companies to write cool and useful software that runs on the Mac. The number of programs available for the Mac continues to rise, month after month.

None of this may seem to matter to you, though, when the inevitable confrontation occurs. You'll be at some party, some meeting, and somebody, sooner or later, will put you down for being a Mac fan. They'll tell you that Apple is doomed because its market share is so small, or that none of the really good games are available for the Macintosh, or that Macs cost too much.

Whether you choose to dignify these sorts of remarks with a response is up to you. But if you need ammunition, here are a few points to remember:

- ✔ There are no viruses for Mac OS X, the operating system you use. There are *monthly* national crises for Windows computers.
- ✔ A single company — Apple — makes both the hardware and the software of a Macintosh. That's why everything seems to work well together. (In the Windows world, you use hardware from one company — like Dell or IBM — that runs operating-system software from another — Microsoft.)

✔ Apple may be small, but it's incredibly influential. Apple either invented or standardized just about every aspect of modern computing, including the mouse, the floppy disk, the CD drive, the DVD burner, the digital camera, the laser printer, the wireless network, the non-beige computer, and so on.

✔ Apple takes in $6 billion a year, has $5 billion in cash, and sells about a million computers a year. If you call that doomed, then Dell and Microsoft must *really* be in trouble.

✔ Desktop Macs usually do cost more than desktop Windows computers. But *laptop* Macs, feature for feature, usually cost *less*.

Or you can just say nothing at all. A quick demonstration of an amazing program like GarageBand, iMovie, iPhoto, iDVD, or iTunes (all described in this book) is usually all it takes to turn naysayers into dropped-jaw admirers.

Part I
For the Absolute Mac Virgin

The 5th Wave   By Rich Tennant

"Fortunately at this grade level the Mac is very intuitive for them to use. Unfortunately so is sailing mousepads across the classroom."

In this part . . .

There are three ways to learn how to use a new computer: You can consult the manual; unfortunately, your Mac didn't come with one. You can take a course (like you've got time for that?). Or you can read a book.

In these opening chapters, you'll learn, as kindly and gently as possible, how to get up and running on your Mac — and nothing else.

Chapter 1

How to Turn On Your Mac (and What to Do Next)

● ●

In This Chapter

▶ How to turn the Mac on (and off)

▶ New meanings for old words like *mouse, menu,* and *system*

▶ Doing windows

▶ Mindlessly opening and closing folders

● ●

*O*nce you've paid for your Mac, the hard part is over. Take it home, open the carton, and haul it out of its sculptured Styrofoam blocks.

Now you should set aside, oh, a good two minutes for getting it all plugged in (see Chapter 20).

At this moment, then, you should have a ready-to-roll Mac on your desk, in all its gorgeous glory, and a look of fevered anticipation on your face.

Switching On the Mac

In this very first lesson, you'll be asked to locate the On button. It's round, it's on the front, side, or top of the computer, and it bears the universal symbol for Mac On-Turning, like this:

On button

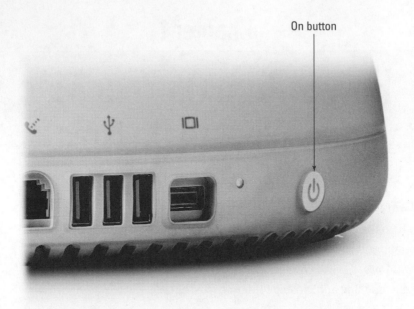

Try pushing this button now. If the Mac responds in some way — a sound plays, the screen lights up, missiles are launched from the Arizona desert — then your machine is working.

If pressing that button doesn't do anything, then your Mac isn't plugged into a working power outlet. I'll wait here while you get that problem sorted out.

If your On-button experiment was successful, you hear a chord, and after a few seconds, an image appears on the screen. Now you're treated to the famous Apple logo, revered by millions. It looks like this:

(In the rare event that your Apple logo appears like this —

— your screen is upside-down.)

As the startup process proceeds, a progress bar inches its way across the screen as it fills with what looks like shimmering blue water. It telegraphs how much longer you have to wait.

What Happens Next

Life is never easy for computer-book authors (except for the screaming mobs of attractive fans in bookstores, of course). Pity the guy who has to explain what happens once you've turned on the Mac.

The truth is, you may encounter any of three things at this point. If the machine is fresh out of the box, you're guided through an interview in which you set the computer's clock and perform other digital paperwork. If it's already been set up, you might be asked to choose your name from a list before gaining access. And you may go straight to the swirling blue of the Mac *desktop* picture, ready for work. The following pages tell you what to do in each of these three situations.

All three situations, by the way, require your mastery of the *mouse*. If you've never used the mouse before, read the sidebar called "Mouse College."

The Setup Assistant

If you are the first person ever to turn on the Mac, the computer takes this opportunity to interview you, one question per screen. It's kind of unfortunate that your computing experience has to begin with paperwork instead of, say, blasting aliens, but that's life in the fast lane.

In any case, this setup program asks you what country you're in (twice), what your name and address are, and whether or not you want to get junk mail. Fill in the answers by clicking the multiple-choice buttons with the mouse and typing into the empty boxes with the keyboard. When you're finished with each screen, click the Continue button with your mouse.

Mouse College

The *mouse* is the transparent, capsule-like thing on the desk beside your keyboard. Having trouble visualizing it as a rodent? Think of the cord as its tail and (if it helps you) draw little eyeballs on the domed surface facing you.

To use the mouse, keep it turned so that the cord *always* points away from you.

Now then, scrape the mouse across the desk (or mouse pad). See how the arrow pointer moves across the screen? For the rest of your life, you'll hear that pointer called the *cursor*. And for the rest of your life, you'll hear moving the mouse called *moving the mouse*.

Try lifting the mouse off the desk and waving it around in midair like a remote control. Nothing happens, right? The mouse controls the cursor only when it's on a flat, opaque surface. (An electronic eye on the bottom of the mouse is constantly scanning the table surface. That's how it knows when you're moving it. That's also why dragging it across a glass or mirrored surface is a mean prank to play on this helpless little gadget.)

You can pick up the mouse when you run out of desk space, but the cursor will stay in place on the screen. Only when you set the mouse down and begin to roll it again will the cursor continue moving.

Now put your index finger on the far end of the mouse and briefly press down (and then release). If all goes well, you should feel the mouse *click*.

Congratulations — you've learned how to *click the mouse*. You'll encounter that instruction over and over again in your budding computing life.

Oh — and if you have a laptop (an iBook or PowerBook), you don't have a mouse. Studies have shown that rolling an ovoid plastic box across the thigh of the guy next to you on the plane can have unpleasant results, ergonomically and socially speaking. Therefore, you've been given, instead, a *trackpad*. The principle is the same: Stroke the pad away from you, and the cursor moves up the screen. Instead of a mouse button, you have a broad, clicky button nestled against the pad.

I won't mention this distinction again, because if you're smart enough to have bought a laptop, you're smart enough to translate future references to the mouse into trackpad terms.

Eventually, you arrive at a Create Your Account screen. It's somewhat technical looking, but as computer screens go, this one is pretty important.

This is where you identify yourself to the Mac. Fill in the boxes called Name (example: *Huckleberry Finn*), Short Name (example: *Huck*), Password (*don't forget it!*), and Password Hint (which the Mac will show you if you ever *do* forget your password).

If this is your own personal Mac that nobody else uses, count your blessings: You'll only rarely need to type in this password. If you share the computer with other people in your family, school, or office, you'll be grateful that that little password keeps your own stuff safe from the inquiring minds of your comrades. (Details on this *user accounts* feature in Chapter 13.)

When you click Continue again, you're asked how you want to get onto the Internet.

- ✔ If you don't have an Internet account, click "I'd like a free trial account with Earthlink." (When you click an option like this, you can click *either* the little round button *or* the sentence itself.) When you click Continue, you'll be guided through the process of getting an account with Earthlink, one of the biggest Internet service companies. It won't let you into its hallowed halls, however, without your credit-card number, even though the first month is free. (Your Mac will actually dial into the Internet during this process, so make sure that you've connected a phone wire from the Mac's phone jack to a wall phone jack.)

- ✔ If you already have an Internet account, choose "I'll use my existing Internet service." When you click Continue, you'll be asked what kind of connection you have (telephone modem, cable modem, and so on), and then asked for a lot of technical parameters like IP addresses and DNS addresses. Unless you're some kind of competent Internet guru, skip this option and set up your account later, as described in Chapter 6.

- ✔ If all of this red tape is giving you a tension headache, you can always confront the Internet later. In that case, choose "I'm not ready to connect to the Internet" and click Continue. You can set up an Internet account when you're reading Chapter 6.

The interview continues. You'll be asked to register (click Register Later, unless you're a real fan of junk mail). You'll be shown a map of the world, which you can click to specify your time zone. You'll be asked to set the Mac's clock. You're invited to sign up for Apple's $100-a-year *.Mac account* (see Chapter 6; decline for now).

Finally, the Mac thanks you for your bureaucratic efforts. Click the Done button.

At last, the colored full-screen pattern, called the *desktop,* appears. Congratulations! You've arrived.

(If you saw anything else during the startup process — a blinking question-mark icon, a strange error message, or thick black smoke — you've just met your first computer problem. Proceed directly to Chapter 16, which is all about troubleshooting.)

The Welcome screen

If turning on the Mac produces a list of people's names, like this —

— then you're not the first person to use this machine. Somebody has beat you to the setup process. Click your name, if you see it; type your password, if you've been given one; and then read on.

In any case, you'll find an explanation of this name-and-password signing-in process at the end of Chapter 13.

The desktop and menu bar

For some people, turning on the Mac takes you directly to the *desktop,* as shown in the upcoming illustration.

You also wind up here *after* encountering the Setup Assistant or list of names described in the previous pages. In any case, the machine is officially on now, and ready to do work for you.

Let's try some real computing here. Move the cursor up to the lightly striped strip at the top of the screen. It's called the *menu bar,* named after a delightful little pub in Silicon Valley. Touch the arrow on the logo at the upper-left corner of the screen. (The *tip* of the Mac's arrow is the part you need to worry about. Same thing with real-life arrows, come to think of it.)

Pointing to something on the screen in this way has a technical term: *pointing.* (Think you're going to be able to handle this?)

The big turn-off

Before we get into 3-D color graphs, space-vehicle trajectories, and DNA analysis, I guess I should tell you how to turn the Mac *off.*

In a pinch, sure, you can just yank the power cord out of the wall. But regularly turning off the Mac by chopping off its power can theoretically invite technical problems with the hard drive.

Instead, you're supposed to turn off your Mac using one of the commands listed in the menu that you opened just a moment ago. Click the logo; when the list of commands appears, roll the mouse downward so that each successive command turns dark. When each menu command turns dark, it's said to be *highlighted.*

(The only commands that don't get highlighted are the ones that are dimmed, or *grayed out.* They're dimmed because they don't make any sense at the moment. For example, if no disc is in the CD-ROM drive, choosing Eject wouldn't make any sense. So the Mac makes that command gray, which means it's unavailable to you.)

If you've had enough of a computer lesson for now, let the cursor come to rest on the *Shut Down* command — and then click the mouse again. The computer promptly shuts itself off. See? This thing's no harder than a toaster.

(Another way to turn off the Mac: Press the power button again. This box appears:

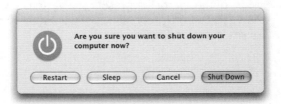

Click Shut Down with the mouse, or press the Return key, which triggers the blue, pulsing button in any box on the screen.)

If you're ready to read on, though, confident that you now know how to turn this thing off, move the mouse cursor away from the menu and click anywhere else on the screen. The Mac, amazingly, does nothing at all but continue looking extremely cool.

Why not to turn off the Mac

Believe it or not, many Mac owners *never* turn the machine off. Instead, whenever they're not using it, they let the Mac drift off to *sleep*.

When the Mac is asleep, the screen is dark, the components inside stop whirring, all activity stops, and electricity consumption slows to a trickle. When you press a key later, the computer brightens right up. Whatever was on the screen is still there, ready for you to begin working again.

When you first buy a Mac, it's set to sleep automatically several minutes after you've stopped using it. But you can also make the machine sleep instantly, on your command, which is useful when you're browsing the "Survivor" Web site at work just as the boss walks by.

To do so, open the menu again and then click the Sleep command. The Mac blinks right off to sleep. (Or press the power button; in the resulting box on the screen, click the Sleep button.)

While it's dozing, a little white or bluish light near the screen (or on the edge, if it's a laptop) stays on, slowly "breathing" on and off, your cue that the machine isn't entirely off. It makes a handy night light for the office (well, if your office is about one inch wide).

Desktop, Dock, and Icons

Take a look around the screen. At the bottom is a row of icons called the *Dock*. Most of these icons represent the various programs that came with your Mac. (To find out their names, try pointing to them without clicking.) The Dock is described in Chapter 3.

Menu bar   Desktop   Hard-drive icon

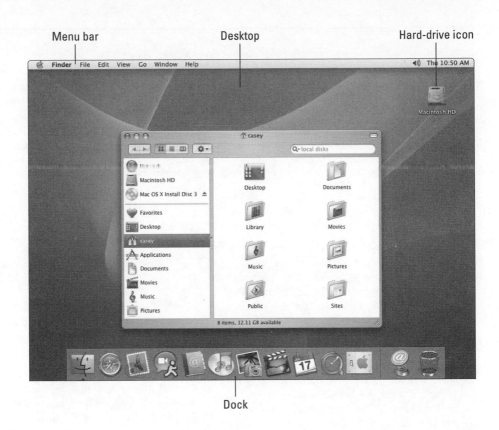

Dock

Near the upper-right corner of the screen, you see an *icon,* a little, inch-tall, symbolic picture. Unless you've changed it, that icon is called *Macintosh HD.*

Icons represent everything in the Mac world. They all look different: One represents a letter you wrote, another represents the Trash can, another represents a CD you've inserted. Here are some examples of icons you'll probably be seeing before long:

A CD   A hard drive   A folder   A picture   A program

All systems are go

An *operating system* is the behind-the-scenes software that runs your computer. But because everyone's in such a hurry these days, people now just call it the *OS.* (Say it "O. S.," not "oss.") Your computer, in fact, runs one of the most advanced and beautiful operating systems on earth: Mac OS X.

(That X is supposed to be a roman numeral 10. Say "Mac Oh Ess Ten." Don't say "Mack Ossex," unless you want people to look at you funny.)

Just like car companies, Apple Computer piles on a few new features to Mac OS X every year. It distinguishes one version from the previous by tacking on additional decimal points. Your Mac may run Mac OS X version 10.1, or 10.2.8, or even 10.3-point-something.

Want to find out what you've got? Get a pencil.

Remember the logo in the upper-left corner of the screen? Point your arrow cursor tip on the apple and click the button to open the menu. Click the first command here, About This Mac. A window appears, like the one shown here, revealing what version of Mac OS X you have.

The version is a number you'll need to know later in this book and later in your life. Therefore, take this opportunity to write it onto your Cheat Sheet (the yellow cardboard page inside the front cover of this book). You'll find a little blank for this information in the upper-left corner of your card, where it says, "Your System version."

But write it in pencil, because as Apple improves its software, fixes bugs, and dreams up speed enhancements, it will send them to your Mac automatically the next time you connect to the Internet. One day, you'll wake up to discover that your 10.3.1 machine now runs 10.3.2, or whatever. Strange, useful — and freaky.

(The instructions and pictures in this book, by the way, depict Mac OS X 10.3-point-whatever, nicknamed Panther.)

When you're finished with this little piece of homework, close the About This Computer window by clicking the little, round, red button in the upper-left corner — the Close button.

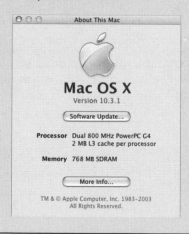

About This Mac

Mac OS X
Version 10.3.1

[Software Update...]

Processor Dual 800 MHz PowerPC G4
2 MB L3 cache per processor

Memory 768 MB SDRAM

[More Info...]

TM & © Apple Computer, Inc. 1983–2003
All Rights Reserved.

You can move an icon by dragging it. Try this:

1. **Point to the Macintosh HD icon.**
2. **Press and then hold down the mouse button continuously — and, while it's down, move the mouse to a new position.**

   This sophisticated technique is called, by the way, *dragging*. You're dragging the hard drive icon now.

3. **Let go of the mouse button.**

Other than the fact that there's a Trash can near the bottom of the screen, nobody's really sure why they call this main screen the *desktop*. It has another name, too: the *Finder*. It's where you file all your work into little electronic on-screen file folders so that you can *find* them again later. The word *Finder* even appears at the top of the screen, next to the menu.

Macintosh syntax

Point once again to the hard-disk icon in the upper-right corner of the screen, like this:

This particular icon represents the giant disk inside your Mac, known as the *hard drive* or *hard disk,* which serves as your filing cabinet. It's where the computer stores all your work, all your files, and all your software.

So how do you see what's in your hard drive? Where do you get to see its table of contents?

It turns out that you can *open* any icon into a window, where you'll see every item inside listed individually. The window has the same name as the icon you opened.

Before we proceed, though, it's time for a lesson in Macintosh syntax. Fear not; it's nothing like English syntax. In fact, everything that you do on the Macintosh has this format: *noun-verb*. Shakespeare it ain't, but it's sure easy to remember.

Let's try a noun-verb command, shall we?

1. **Click the hard-disk icon in the upper-right corner of the screen.**

   The icon turns black, indicating that it's *selected*. Good job — you've just identified the *noun*.

2. **Using the mouse, click the File menu, and choose Open.**

You guessed it — Open is the *verb*. And, sure enough, your hard disk opens into a window, where you can see its contents. (If another window was already on your screen, it immediately disappears to make way for the Macintosh HD window.)

In the world of Macintosh, you always specify *what* you want to change (using the mouse) and then you use a menu command to specify *how* you want it changed. You'll see this pattern over and over again: *Select* something on the screen and then *apply* a menu command to it.

The complete list of window doodads

Look over the contents of your hard-drive window, as shown in the following figure. (Everybody's got different stuff, so what you see on your screen may not exactly match the illustration.)

Better yet, look over the various controls and gadgets around the *edges* of this window. Using these controls and buttons, you can do all kinds of neat things to a window: stretch it, move it, or make it go away. These various gadgets are worth learning about — you're going to run into windows *everywhere* after you start working.

Close Button – Click here to close the window.

Minimize Button – Click the yellow glob to hide the window.

Title Bar Icon – Click and hold, and then drag, to move the entire window to the Trash, to another disk, or to another window.

Zoom Button – Click to make the window just big enough to show all its contents.

Title Bar – Drag anywhere in this striped area to move the whole window.

Toolbar Button – Click to hide (or bring back) the toolbar and the Sidebar.

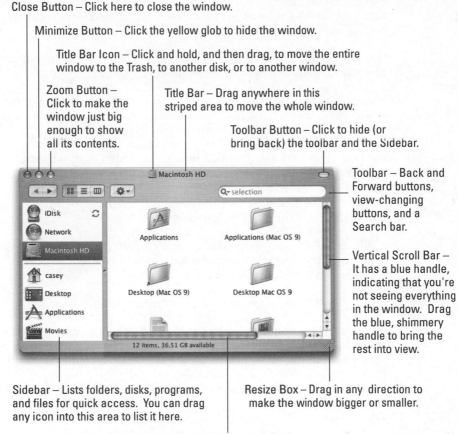

Toolbar – Back and Forward buttons, view-changing buttons, and a Search bar.

Vertical Scroll Bar – It has a blue handle, indicating that you're not seeing everything in the window. Drag the blue, shimmery handle to bring the rest into view.

Sidebar – Lists folders, disks, programs, and files for quick access. You can drag any icon into this area to list it here.

Resize Box – Drag in any direction to make the window bigger or smaller.

Horizontal Scroll Bar – If there's no blue handle, you're seeing everything in the window (left to right, anyway).

Try out some of the little boxes and scroll bars. Click them. Tug on them. Open the window and close it again. No matter what you do, *you can never hurt the machine by doing "the wrong thing."* That's the wonderful thing about the Mac: It's the Nerf appliance.

Double-clicking in theory and practice

So far, all of your work in the Finder (the desktop) has involved moving the mouse around. But your keyboard is useful, too. For example, do you see the System folder, the one with a big X on it? Even if you don't, here's a quick way to find it: Quickly type **SY** on your keyboard.

Presto, the Mac finds the System folder (which happens to be the first thing that begins with those letters) and highlights it, in effect dropping it in front of you, wagging its tail.

Now try pressing the arrow keys on your keyboard — right, left, up, down. The Mac highlights neighboring icons as you do so.

Suppose you want to see what's in the System folder. Of course, using your newfound noun-verb method, you could (1) click the System folder to select it and then (2) choose Open from the File menu.

But that's the sissy way. Try this power shortcut: Point to the System folder icon so that the tip of the arrow cursor is squarely inside the picture of the folder. Keeping the mouse still, click twice in rapid succession. With stunning originality, the Committee for the Invention of Computer Terminology calls this advanced computing technique *double-clicking*.

If all went well, your double-click opened a different window, showing you the contents of the System folder. (If it didn't work, you probably need to keep the mouse still or double-click faster.)

Remember this juicy golden rule: *Double-click means "open."*

In your Mac life, you'll be asked (or tempted) to click many an item on-screen: buttons that say "OK"; tools that look like paint brushes; all manner of multiple-choice buttons. In every one of these cases, you're supposed to click *once*.

The only time you ever *double*-click something is when you want to *open* it. Got it?

One window

Now you have the System window open. Well, that's just great, but what happened to the hard drive window?

The Mac tries to keep your life simple by showing you only one window at a time. When you open one folder, its window *replaces* whatever window you were just looking at. It works like a TV: You can change channels, but the frame around your screen always looks the same.

That's all great, but what if you want to backtrack? What if, now that you've savored the System folder for a moment, you want to return to the Macintosh HD window that you opened first?

That's what the Back button is for. Just click the button to go back to whatever window you had open before. In fact, if you'd opened several folders in succession, you can click the Back button *repeatedly* for a little reverse slide show of the windows you've recently opened.

Multiple windows

This business of keeping only one window before you at all times is fine for timid beginners, and it certainly keeps your screen tidy. But sooner or later, you're going to wish you could open two windows simultaneously — when you want to move a picture or a chapter from one window into another.

Try this: From the File menu, choose New Finder Window. Presto: A second window appears. (It's probably the window where you're supposed to keep all your stuff, the one that bears your name — your *Home folder*. Details in Chapter 2.)

You can tell that this window is in back, because it looks sort of faded. Click anywhere in the window to bring it to the front.

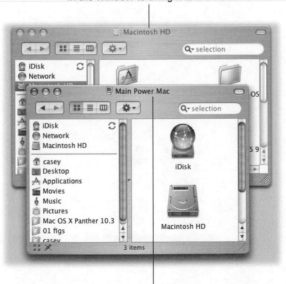

You can tell that this window is in front, because its title bar is bright and bold.

Windows on a computer are like pieces of paper on a desk: There may be a whole pile of them, but only one can be on top. And on a Mac, you bring a window to the top just by clicking it.

Take a stress-free moment to prove the point, using the two windows now before you: Click the back one to bring it forward; then click the one that was in front to bring it to the front again. To move a window, drag it with the mouse, using anything that looks like brushed metal as a handle (like the strip at the top — the title bar).

When you're finished goofing around, close each window by clicking its Close button (the little red glob of Colgate Very Berry Gel in the upper-left corner).

Where to Get Help

It's true that your Mac didn't come with a printed manual. If you're cynical, you might guess that Apple was hoping to save a few bucks. If you're idealistic, you might assume that Apple is simply concerned about global deforestation.

In any case, your computer does come with a manual, of sorts — an electronic one. It's very terse, somewhat incomplete, and contains no jokes whatsoever, but it's there. To find it, open the Help menu, and choose Mac Help. You get a window that looks something like this:

You can use this Help Center in two ways. First, you can type a Help topic into the blank at the top of the window (such as *naming files* or *dialing the Internet*) — and then press the Return key. If you're having a good night, the window will then show you a list of Help pages that might contain the answer you're looking for; click the name of the topic that seems to hold some promise, as shown here:

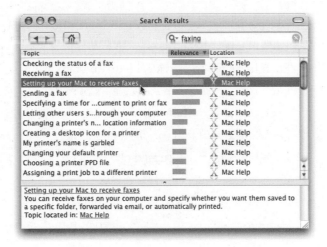

Second, you can click your way through this little Help program. In the previous illustration, see the heading called Browse Mac OS Help?

By clicking that headline, and then (on the next screen) by clicking the topic you want, you can often home in on the precise Help article you're interested in.

Pit stop

Shut the Mac down now, if you want (flip back a few pages to the section "The big turn-off" for complete instructions). Or just walk away, confident that it will put itself into an energy-saving Sleep mode after half an hour.

Chapter 2 shows you how to harness your new mastery of icons and windows to begin organizing the clutter of your life.

Top Ten Similarities between You and Your Mac

Before you move boldly forward to the next chapter, ponder the following frightening similarities between a Mac and its owner:

1. Each is pulled out of a very special container on Day One.

2. Each is most attractive when it's young.

3. Each has slots to provide adequate ventilation.

4. Each reacts to sudden movements of mice.

5. Each may crash when asked to do too much at once.

6. Each has a button in (or on) its abdomen.

7. Each lights up when turned on.

8. Each occasionally enjoys a good CD.

9. Each may be connected to a phone line for days at a time.

10. Sooner or later, each goes to sleep automatically.

Chapter 2

Windows, Icons, and Trashes

- -

- -

Becoming Manipulative

All of the clicking and dragging and window-shoving you learned in Chapter 1 is, in fact, leading up to something useful.

Meet the hard drive

See the Macintosh HD icon in the upper-right corner of your screen? It represents your *hard drive,* which is a furiously spinning disk inside every Mac. The concept of a hard drive confuses people because it's hidden inside the Mac's case. Since you can't see it or touch it, it's sort of conceptual — like beta-carotene or God, I guess. But it's there, spinning quietly away, and a hefty chunk of your Mac's purchase price paid for it.

A hard disk is where your life's work is going to live when the computer is shut off. You will, like it or not, become intensely interested in the overall health of your computer's hard disk.

Foldermania

As you now know, your hard disk is like the world's biggest filing cabinet. It's where you store all your stuff. But a filing cabinet without filing *folders* would be about as convenient to handle as an egg without a shell.

The folders on the Mac screen don't occupy any space on your hard drive. They're electronic fictions whose sole purpose is to help you organize your stuff.

Mr. Folder

Your Home folder

As far as you're concerned, the most important folder on the Mac is your *Home folder*. It's the one that will soon contain all of your work, store all your e-mail, remember all of your favorite Web pages, keep track of your preference settings in every program you use, and so on.

But the Home folder isn't just a convenient folder that offers one-stop shopping for all your stuff. It's also a security feature. Nobody else who uses this Mac is allowed to see, mess with, or delete anything in the folders here (assuming all of you sign in using the *accounts* feature described at the end of Chapter 13).

In short, the Home folder, gentle reader, is your new digital home.

Because this folder is so important, Apple has equipped your machine with a long list of ways to get there. For example:

- ✔ Open the Go menu. Choose Home.
- ✔ Press Shift-⌘-H. (That's a three-key combination. Instructions on deciphering this kind of instruction in a moment.)
- ✔ Click the Home icon in the Sidebar (the left-side panel) of any open window, like this:

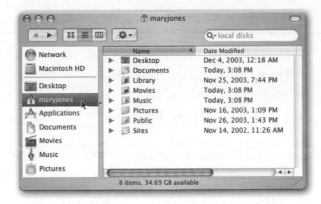

In any case, your Home folder now appears, filled with folders that you'll grow to know and love.

Leave it open for the following exercise. As a matter of fact, you might even want to make it a little bigger by tugging its lower-right corner handle.

Folder factory

The Mac provides an infinite supply of folders. Want a folder? Do this:

From the File menu, choose New Folder.

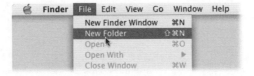

Ooh, tricky, this machine! A new folder appears. Notice that the Mac gracefully proposes "untitled folder" as its name.

Notice something else, though: The name is *highlighted* (shaded with a color). Remember our earlier lesson? Highlighted = selected = ready for you to *do* something. When *text* is highlighted, the Mac is ready for you to *replace* it with anything you type. In other words, you don't even have to backspace over the text. Just type away:

1. **Type *USA Folder* and press the Return key.**

   The Return key tells the Mac that your naming spurt is over.

   Now, to see how folders work, create another one.

2. **From the File menu, once again choose New Folder.**

   Another new folder appears, once more waiting for a title.

3. **Type *Ohio* and press Return.**

You're going to create one more empty folder. But by this time, your wrist is probably weary from the forlorn trek back and forth to the File menu. Don't you wish you could make a folder faster?

You can.

Keyboard shortcuts

Open the File menu, but don't select any of the commands in it yet. See those weird notations to the right of some commands?

File	
New Finder Window	⌘N
New Folder	⇧⌘N
Open	⌘O
Open With	▶
Close Window	⌘W
Get Info	⌘I
Duplicate	⌘D
Make Alias	⌘L
Show Original	⌘R
Add To Favorites	⇧⌘T
Create Archive of "tax advice.doc"	

Get used to 'em. They're *keyboard shortcuts,* and they appear in almost every menu you'll ever see. Keyboard shortcuts let you select certain menu items without using the mouse.

Some people love keyboard shortcuts, claiming that if you're in a hurry, pressing keys is faster than using the mouse. Other people loathe keyboard shortcuts, pointing out that using the mouse doesn't require any memorization. In either case, here's how keyboard shortcuts work.

When you type on a typewriter, you press the Shift key to make a capital letter, right? Computer nerds call the Shift key a *modifier key* because it turns ordinary, well-behaved citizen keys like 3 and 4 into madcap symbols like # and $.

Menu Symbols Unlimited

Besides the little keyboard-shortcut symbols at the right side of a menu, you'll occasionally run into a little downward-pointing arrow, like this:

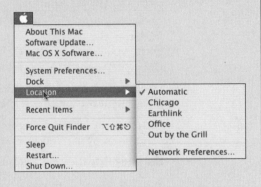

That arrow tells you that the menu is so long, it doesn't even fit on the screen. The arrow is implying that still more commands are in the menu that you're not seeing. To get to those additional commands, carefully roll the pointer down the menu all the way to that down-pointing triangle. Don't let the sudden jumping scare you:

The menu commands will jump upward, bringing the hidden ones into view.

And then there are the little black triangles pointing to the *right*. These triangles indicate that, when selected, the menu command won't do anything except offer you several *other* commands, which pop out to the side:

Welcome to the world of computers, where everything is four times more complicated. Instead of having only *one* modifier key, the Mac has *four* of them! Look down next to your spacebar. There they are: In addition to the Shift key, one says Option, one says Control, and another has a little ⌘ symbol on it.

It's that little cloverleaf — the *command key* — whose symbol appears in the File menu. Next to the New Folder command, you see ⌘-N. That means:

1. **While pressing the Shift and ⌘ keys, press the N key and then release everything.**

   Bam! You've got yourself another folder. (Sometimes you might see *two* symbols next to a menu command, like the ones next to Computer in the Go menu. That means press *both* the Shift and ⌘ keys as you type the specified letter.)

2. **Type *Michigan* and press Return.**

   You've just named your third folder. So why have you been wasting a perfectly good afternoon (or whatever it is in your time zone) making empty folders? So you can pretend you're getting organized.

3. Drag the Ohio folder on top of the USA Folder.

Make sure that the tip of the arrow actually hits the center of the USA Folder so that the folder becomes highlighted, and its icon resembles an *open* file folder. The instant it darkens and changes, let go of the Ohio folder — and watch it disappear into the USA Folder. (If your aim wasn't good, you'll now see the Ohio folder sitting next to the USA Folder; try the last step again.)

4. Put the Michigan folder into the USA Folder in the same way — by dragging it on top of the USA Folder.

As far as you know, though, those state folders have *disappeared*. How can you trust me that they're now neatly filed away?

5. Double-click the USA Folder.

Yep. Opens right up into a window, and there are your two darling states, nestled sweetly where they belong.

Okay, so how do you get these inner folders *out* again? Do you have to drag them individually? That would certainly be a bummer if you had all 50 folders in the USA Folder.

Turns out there are several ways to select more than one icon at a time.

6. Click above and to the left of the Michigan folder (Step 1 in the upcoming picture) and, without releasing the mouse, drag down and to the right so that you enclose both folders with a light gray rectangle (Steps 2 and 3).

Release the mouse button when you've got both icons enclosed.

Now that you have several folders selected, you can move them en masse to another location.

7. **Drag the Ohio folder outside the USA Folder window — onto the blue desktop, for example.**

   The Michigan folder goes along for the ride.

   This was a somewhat unproductive exercise, of course, because you were only working with empty folders. It gets much more exciting when you start working with your own documents, as you will in the following chapters. All of these techniques work equally well with folders and with documents.

The Sidebar

You already know that the hard drive stores everything in your computer world, and that *folders* make it easier to organize your stuff into related puddles of information.

But it occurred to somebody at Apple that not all folders are created equal. Your *Urgent Life Projects* folder, the one you work in every day, is somewhat more important than your *Drugstore Receipts, 1980–1985* folder. And it should therefore hold a more prominent position on your screen.

That's why the latest Macs have something called the *Sidebar* at the left side of every desktop window, where you can park your most beloved icons so that you don't have to go digging for them ten times a day.

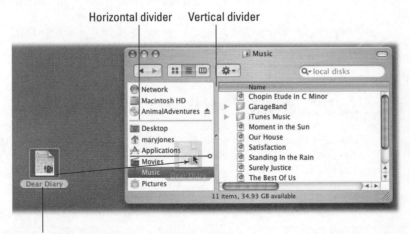

Drag an icon into the Sidebar to install it there.

Above the horizontal divider, the Sidebar lists places where you might look for files and folders — that is, disks, folders, and network disks. Below the divider, you can stick the icons of anything else you use often: files, programs, folders, or whatever.

Each icon is a shortcut. For example, click the Music icon to view the contents of your Music folder in the main part of the window, as shown here. And if you click the icon of a file or program, it opens.

The beauty of this little icon parking lot is that it's so easy to set up with *your* favorite places. For example:

- **Remove** an icon by dragging it away from the window entirely. It vanishes with a little puff of cartoon smoke. (You haven't actually removed anything from your *Mac;* you've just removed its button from the Sidebar.)

- **Rearrange** the icons by dragging them up or down in the list.

- **Install a new icon** by dragging it off of your desktop (or out of a window) into any spot in the appropriate half of the Sidebar: disks above the divider bar, everything else below.

- **Adjust the width** of the Sidebar by dragging the vertical divider bar (marked by the dot in its center) right or left. You'll "feel" a snap when the divider hits the spot where you're seeing all of the icon names but not wasting any extra white space to their right.

- **Hide the Sidebar entirely** by double-clicking the vertical divider. The main part of the window expands to exploit the freed-up space. (To bring the Sidebar back, double-click the left edge of the window.)

Then again, why would you ever *want* to hide the Sidebar? It's one of the handiest navigational aids since the invention of the map.

Icon, List, and Column Views

The first time you visit your Home folder, you see attractive little pictures that represent the files and folders inside. In other words, you're viewing this window in *icon view* — a fact that you can confirm by opening the View menu. See the check mark next to "as Icons" in the View menu?

But lovely though icon view may be, it's not ideal for every folder. What if you had a folder containing 250 pictures from a digital camera? You'd go nuts trying to swim through 250 little icons in random order.

Fortunately, Mac OS X lets you call up any of three different views for any window you're perusing: icon, list, or column. You switch among them either by choosing "as Icons," "as List," or "as Columns" from the View menu — or just by clicking the corresponding buttons in your toolbar, shown here:

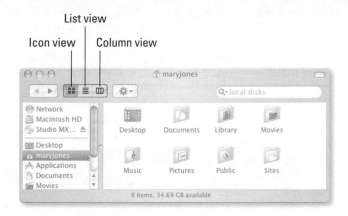

Each view is appropriate for different kinds of windows, as you're about to find out.

Bonus technique for extra credit

The method of selecting several icons by dragging a rectangle around them is fine if all the icons are next to each other. But how would you select only the icons that begin with the letter A in this picture? You can't very well enclose each A by dragging the mouse — you'd also get all the *other* icons within the same rectangle.

The power-user's secret: Click each icon *while pressing the ⌘ key*. As long as you're pressing Shift, you continually add additional, nonadjacent icons to the selection. (And if you ⌘-click one by accident, you can deselect it by ⌘-clicking *again*. Try it!)

Icon view

Icon view is ideal for windows that contain only a few icons — your Home folder when you're just starting out, for example.

Icon view is also by far the most fun view. Play your cards right, and just fiddling with icon-view options can provide hours of hilarity for the whole family.

For example, all those attractive little folders don't have to be attractive *little* folders. You can make them as large or small as you like. For proof, open the View menu and choose View Options. As you can see here, the resulting dialog box contains a slider that lets you make your icons minuscule, gigantic, or anything in between:

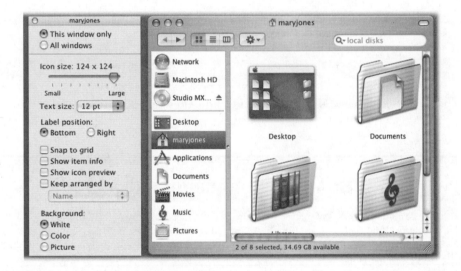

See the controls at the bottom of this dialog box? If you click Color and then the small rectangular button that appears beside it, you're offered a color wheel. Use it to choose a solid color for the background of an icon-view window — just the ticket when you feel the urge to interior-decorate your Home folder in a soothing sea green.

In fact, the wallpaper for an icon-view folder can even be a photo. If you click Picture, and then Select, the Mac offers you its Open File dialog box, which lets you navigate your hard drive in search of the perfect photo background. (More on the Open File dialog box in Chapter 4.)

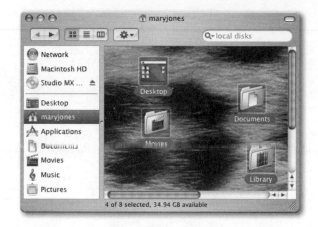

List view

The second standard view for folder windows will make Type A personalities wriggle with delight: a list, sorted alphabetically, chronologically, or any way you like. This is the perfect view for windows that hold more than a handful of icons.

Drag a column heading sideways to rearrange the columns.

Click a column heading to sort the list that way.
(Click again to sort the opposite way.)

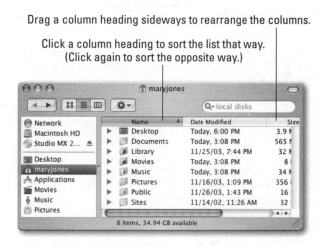

Once a window's contents are in a list, each folder *within* the window is marked by a tiny triangle. You can open one of these folders-within-a-folder in the usual way, if you wish — by double-clicking. But it's much more satisfying for neat freaks to click the *triangle* instead. In the following figure, the before-and-after view of the Library folder (inside your Home folder) shows how much more organized you can be.

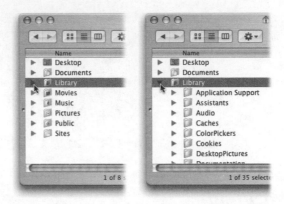

When you click the triangle, in other words, your window contents look like an outline. The contents of that subfolder are indented. To "collapse," or close, the folder, click the downward-pointing triangle.

Column view

As noted in Chapter 1, you usually see only one window at a time. When you open folder B, folder A's window closes automatically. Apple's trying to keep your life tidy.

In column view, however, you see exactly where you're going, and where you've come from, as you burrow through folders-within-folders on your hard drive.

That's because column view divides your window into several vertical panes. The Sidebar (the panel at the far left) shows all the icons of your disks, including your main hard drive.

How column view works

When you click your Macintosh HD icon — or, indeed, *any* disk or folder icon in the Sidebar — the second pane shows a list of all the folders on it. When you click one of those folders, the third pane shows all the folders inside *it*.

And so on. Each time you click a folder in one pane, the pane to its right shows what's inside; the other panes slide off to the left. (Use the horizontal scroll bar to bring them back, if you like.)

You can keep clicking until you're actually looking at the file icons inside the most deeply nested folder. If the file is a picture, movie, or sound file, you can even watch it or listen to it right there in the window (see the little triangle Play button here?).

Click a disk or folder here to begin your journey through folders inside of folders.

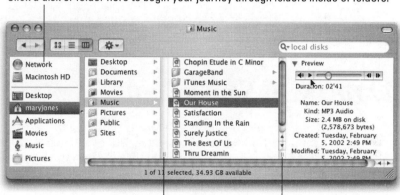

Drag one of these handles to make a column wider or narrower.

If you discover that your hunt for a particular file has taken you down a blind alley, you can easily backtrack, thanks to the trail of folders that's still visible on the screen. Just click a different folder in one of the earlier panes to start burrowing down a different rabbit hole.

In short, column view not only keeps your screen tidy (by showing several windows' worth of information in a single window), but you're less likely to get lost, wondering what folder you're in and how you got there. Your trail of digital breadcrumbs is visible at all times.

Manipulating the columns

Every now and then, the column widths in column view aren't ideal. You may have a list of files with very short names, wallowing in space in very wide columns. Or maybe your files have very *long* names, and the columns are far too narrow to show the full names.

You have considerable control in these situations. For example:

✔ To make a single column wider or narrower, drag the handle at the bottom of the column (see the previous illustration).

✔ You can make all the columns wider or narrower simultaneously by dragging any of the small handles at the bottom of the columns while pressing the Option key.

✔ To read a file name that's too long to fit in its column, just point to it without clicking. After a moment, you'll see a yellow, rectangular balloon pop up at your arrow tip, revealing the full name.

✔ If you'd like to see more columns at once, make the window wider (drag the resizing handle at its lower-right corner).

How to Trash Something

Of all the computers on earth, the Mac is probably the most conducive to helping you be productive and creative. But even Mozart crumpled up the occasional half-finished overture and threw it into the fireplace.

You, too, can throw away files or folders you no longer need. You might decide to throw away that USA Folder you made in your Home folder, for example. (If the Home folder isn't on the screen right now, choose its name from the Go menu. Put the window back into icon view, if you like.)

To do so, just point to the USA Folder (or whatever you're trying to delete). Then, carefully keeping the far end of the mouse "clicked down," drag the folder down and to the right, until it's right on top of the Trash can at the right end of the Dock.

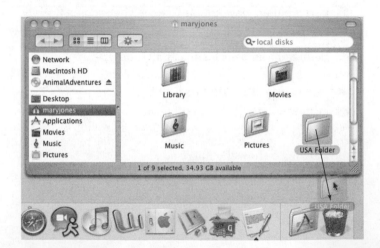

Don't let go until the Trash icon actually turns black (when the tip of the arrow cursor is on it). When you do let go, notice how the Trash icon changes from a wastebasket to a wastebasket-filled-with-crumpled-up-papers, to let you know there's something in there.

That's how you throw things out on the Mac: Just drag them onto the Trash. (There's even a keystroke for this: Highlight an icon and then press ⌘-Delete. The chosen icon goes flying into the Trash as though it's just been drop-kicked.)

What's really hilarious is how hard Apple made it for you to get rid of something. Just putting something into the Trash doesn't actually get rid of it; technically, you've only put it into the Oblivion Waiting Room. It'll sit there forever, in an overflowing trash basket. To rescue something, you just double-click the Trash basket to open its window, and then drag whatever-it-was right back onto the screen.

So if putting something into the Trash doesn't really delete it, how *do* you really delete it? You choose Empty Trash from the Finder menu.

But even *then* your stuff isn't really gone. You get a final warning like this:

Only when you click OK is your file is finally gone.

In fact, even *then* it can theoretically be recovered — by an expert using a data-recovery program like Norton Utilities.

Now you can understand why you never hear Mac owners complain of having thrown away some important document by accident — a Mac won't *let* you get rid of anything without fighting your way through four layers of warnings and red tape.

(P.S. — If you're throwing away something important — that is, if it's important to you that nobody can *ever* resurrect it — choose Secure Empty Trash from the Finder menu instead of Empty Trash. The Mac scrubs over that file's spot on the hard drive with invisible gibberish to make sure that it's really gone for good.)

Top Ten Window and Icon Tips

Staggering through the basics of using your Mac unattended is one thing.
Shoving around those on-screen windows and icons with grace is quite
another. Master the following, and then invite your friends over to watch
some evening.

1. To rename an icon, click carefully on its name. Wait for a second or so,
   until a rectangle appears around the name. That's your cue to type away,
   giving it a new name. (You can type really long names, too, like *The chapter I started on Saturday night after "When Harry Met Sally" on TV but
   stopped when I got to the part about the vampire's wedding, because Chris
   came over with pizza and who could possibly work under those circum-
   stances?*) Press Return when you're done.

2. To make a copy of a file the traditional way, click the icon and then
   choose Duplicate from the File menu. Or, while pressing the Option key,
   drag the icon into a new window or folder.

3. To move some files from one window into another the modern way, start
   by selecting them (click them — or ⌘-click them, if there's more than
   one). Then, from the Edit menu, choose Copy.

   You've just socked them away onto the Mac's invisible Clipboard storage
   area.

   Now click the folder, or click inside the window, where you want the
   copies to appear. From the Edit menu, choose Paste. As though by
   magic, the icons you copied reappear in their new home.

4. Every time you choose Empty Trash from the Finder menu, the Mac asks
   you if you're absolutely sure. If you're *always* sure, you can make it stop
   asking you that. To do so, open the Finder menu and choose
   Preferences. In the dialog box, click the Advanced button, and then turn
   off "Show warning before emptying the Trash." Close the window and
   savor the resulting time savings.

5. If you have a very important document, you can prevent it from getting thrown away by accident. Click its icon. From the File menu, choose Get Info. Turn on the Locked check box. Now, the Mac won't even let you put it into the Trash, let alone empty it.

6. Isn't it frustrating to open a window that's too small to show you all its contents (shown below at left)?

   Of course, you could spend a weekend fussing with the scroll bars, trying to crank the other icons into view. Or, by using trial-and-error, you could drag the lower-right handle (the resize box) to make the window bigger.

   There's a much quicker solution. Click the green *zoom button* in the upper-left corner of the window (shown below at left by the cursor). The Mac automatically makes the window exactly large enough to show all of the icons.

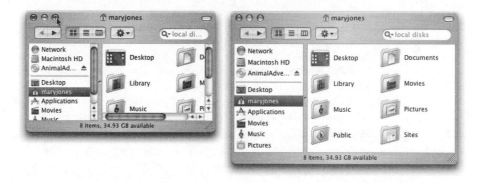

7. In column view, you can press the arrow keys to navigate the different panes. Press the left and right arrow keys to jump from pane to pane, or the up and down arrow keys to "walk" up or down the list of files and folders in it.

8. Try this sneaky shortcut: While pressing the Control (Ctrl) key, point the cursor tip on an icon, disk, or the inside of a window. Keep the Control key pressed; if you now hold down the mouse button, a pop-up menu appears at your cursor tip, listing commands that pertain only to that icon, disk, or window.

For example, if you Control-click a disk or CD, you'll be offered commands like Eject, Get Info, and Open. If you Control-click an icon, you get commands like Show Info, Duplicate, and Move To Trash. And if you Control-click anywhere inside a window — but *not* directly on an icon — you're offered New Folder, Help, and Show Info. (The geek term for this phenomenon is *contextual menus,* because the menu is different depending on the context of your click.)

9. When your life overwhelms you with chaos and random events, at least your Mac can give you a sense of control and order.

   Using the contextual menus described above, you can tag your icons with any of seven different *color labels,* like this:

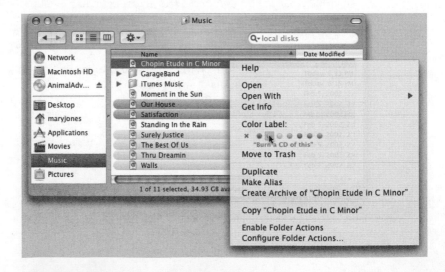

After you've applied labels to icons, you can perform some unique file-management tasks — in some cases, on all of them simultaneously, even if they're scattered across multiple hard drives. For example, you can use the Find command described in Chapter 4 to round up all icons with a particular label. Thereafter, you can copy them en masse to a backup disk, for example.

You might also use different color labels to track the status of files in a certain project. The first drafts have no labels at all. Once they've been edited and approved, make them blue. Once they've been sent to the home office, they turn purple.

And once they start making money, you can color them green.

(P.S. — At first, the seven labels are named Red, Orange, Yellow, and so on. Fortunately, you can rewrite these labels, tailoring them to your purposes. From the Finder menu, choose Preferences. Click the Labels button. Now you can edit the text of each label. Make them say, "Overdue," "Hot Prospects," or whatever.)

10. You don't have to clean up your windows before you shut down the computer. The windows will be right where you left them the next time you turn on the Mac.

Chapter 3

Actually Accomplishing Something

*T*he Mac, if you think about it while squinting, is like a DVD player. The software programs you install on the Mac are like the DVDs you slip into your player. Without DVDs (software), the DVD player (Mac) is worthless. But with DVDs (software), your DVD player (Mac) can take on any personality.

A DVD player might let you watch a Western one night and a seven-hour Kevin Costner vanity project the next. In the same way, your Mac can be a typing instructor, a checkbook balancer, or a movie-editing machine, depending on the software you use. Each piece of software — called a *program* or an *application* — is like a different GameBoy cartridge: It makes the Mac look, feel, and behave differently. The average Mac user winds up using about six or seven different programs regularly.

In the next chapter, you're going to do some word processing. This chapter is the warm-up. It tells you where to find the programs that came with your Mac, explains how to use the Dock that dishes them up, and illustrates some of the basic principles of using programs on the Mac.

Your Software Collection

The Mac comes with a handsome bonus gift of software preinstalled on the hard disk. That's fortunate, because software, for the most part, is expensive.

These 50 or so programs include programs called iTunes, iPhoto, and iMovie (Chapters 9, 10, and 11), which turn the computer into what Apple calls a "digital hub" — a headquarters for music players, digital cameras, and camcorders. You also have an e-mail program (Chapter 8), a Web browser (Chapter 7), and a whole raft of cute little accessory programs (see the end of this chapter).

Getting more software

Some people are set for life with the programs that came on the Mac.

But if you deal with anyone in the business world, you'll probably wind up buying something called Microsoft Office X for Macintosh — a single CD that contains Microsoft Word (the most popular word-processing program), Excel (a spreadsheet, for number crunching), PowerPoint (a slide-show program for making pitches around a board-room table), and Entourage (a calendar/e-mail program). (You can also buy these programs individually.)

Obsolescence therapy

Your relationship with a software company doesn't end when you buy the program. First, the company provides a technical help staff for you to call when things get rocky. Some firms are great about this relationship — they give you a toll-free number that's answered immediately by a smart, helpful, customer-oriented technician. More often, though, sending out an SOS is a long-distance call . . . and a long-distance ten-minute wait before somebody can help you.

Like the computers themselves, software programs are continually being improved and enhanced by their manufacturers. Just as in owning a computer, owning a software program isn't a one-time cash outlay. Each time the software company comes out with a new version of the program, you'll be offered the chance to get it for a small "upgrade fee" of $49 or $99, for example.

You'd think people would get fed up with this endless treadmill of expenses and just stick with the version they've got, refusing to upgrade to successive versions. Some manage it. Most people, however, succumb to the fear that somehow they'll be left behind by the march of technology and wind up forking over the upgrade fees once a year or so. Let your budget and sense of independence be your guide.

El cheapo software

Once you've read Chapter 6, and you've decided it might be fun to plug your Mac into the telephone line or TV cable to dial up faraway computers, you may stumble onto another kind of software: *shareware*. These are programs written by individuals, not software companies, who make their programs freely available on the Internet. You can grab them, via telephone, and bring them to your own Mac. And get this: Only the honor system (and on-screen nagging boxes) compels you to pay the authors the $15 or $20 they're asking for.

Sure, shareware often has a homemade feel to it. On the other hand, some of it's really terrific. You can search for the kind of shareware program you want (and also for acres of sounds, pictures, clip art, and games) on America Online and on the Internet (such as at *www. macdownload.com* or *www.versiontracker.com*).

Want a database for handling order forms, tracking phone calls, and creating form letters? Check out the fantastic FileMaker Pro (around $200). Try, *try* not to focus on the fact that what you *get* for that money is a 50-cent CD and a $2 manual.

Where to buy it

There are two places to buy software: via mail order and at a store. Unfortunately, as you'll quickly discover, today's computer stores generally offer a pathetically small selection of Macintosh software. (One exception: Apple Stores, which are cropping up in affluent cities all over America.)

On the other hand, mail-order companies like *www.buy.com,* *www.macmall.com,* and *www.macwarehouse.com* offer thousands of choices, give much bigger discounts, take returns after you've opened the box, and generally don't charge sales tax. And, of course, you don't have to fire up the old Toyota.

Overnight mail-order companies like these are bright spots in the computer world. You can call some of them until midnight, in fact, and get your new programs by midmorning, only hours later. After ordering from these companies, you'll start to wish there were overnight mail-order grocery stores, gas stations, and dentists.

All right, maybe not dentists.

The Dock

Every program you'll ever use on your Mac is conveniently parked in a single place: the Applications folder. Want to see this impressive list of software tools? You can get to it by choosing Applications from the Go menu, or by pressing Shift-⌘-A, or just by clicking the Applications icon on your Sidebar.

In general, though, that's a lot of hassle, especially for the programs you wind up using often. Fortunately, Apple has provided you with a much more convenient shelf that puts your favorite programs only a click away: the Dock.

How the Dock works

See the fine dark line running down the Dock in this picture?

Point to an icon to see its name.

Programs on this side   Files, folders, disks on this side

That line separates all your favorite *programs,* on the left side, from your favorite everything-else (files, documents, folders, and disks), on the right.

As you've probably noticed, none of these icons are identified by name, at least not until you point to a Dock icon without clicking. Then the name appears just above the icon.

To open an icon that's on the Dock, just click it. If you click a program, its icon hops up and down excitedly during the time it takes that program to start up — you can't help share its enthusiasm — and then finally settles down with a little triangle underneath it, as shown in the previous picture.

Adding your own icons

Apple starts off the Dock with the icons of some built-in Mac programs — but that's just a tease. The Dock won't truly win your heart until your *own* favorite icons are on it.

Doing so couldn't be easier: Just *drag* any icon onto the appropriate half of the Dock. (Remember: Programs go on the left.) For example, you might open your Applications folder and drag, say, the Calculator from there onto the Dock, like this:

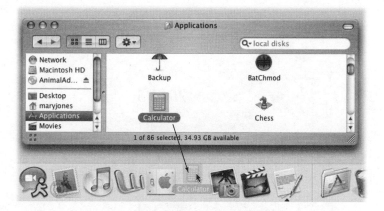

The other Dock icons politely scoot aside to make room.

It won't take you long to guess how you *remove* an icon from the Dock, either: You just drag it up and away. Once your cursor has cleared the Dock, let go of the mouse. A cheerful little puff of cartoon smoke appears, as your icon vanishes to the Great Mac in the Sky. The other Dock icons slide together to close the gap. (You can't ever ditch the Finder, the Trash, or a program or document that's currently open.)

Minimizing a window

The Dock isn't only a parking place for favorite Mac goodies. It can also be a handy shelf for windows you'd like to get out of your way temporarily.

Try this: Open up some window — your Home folder, let's say. (From the Go menu, choose Home.) Now suppose that you'd like to see what's behind it.

You could just close the window, of course. But if you want to return to it momentarily, there's a better way: You can *minimize* it. To do that, click the button that looks like a round, yellow glob of gel in the window's upper-left corner — the *minimize* button, as it's called. (Alternative-lifestyle fans may prefer to choose Minimize Window from the Window menu, or just press ⌘-M, to achieve the same effect.)

As you can see here, the entire window collapses, shrinking like a genie through a transparent funnel, to the right end of the Dock:

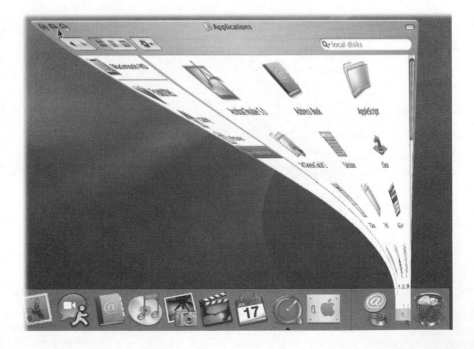

The window isn't gone; it hasn't actually closed. It's just out of your way for the moment, as though you've set it down on a shelf. When you want to bring it back, click the newly created Dock icon. The window genies its way right back to its original position on the screen.

Minimizing a window in this way is a great window-management tool. In the Finder, doing so lets you see whatever icons are covered by a window. In a word processor, this technique helps you type up a memo that requires frequent consultation of a spreadsheet behind it.

Four fancy Dock tricks

If your Mac were a Thanksgiving dinner, the Dock would be the turkey. All right, maybe that's not the best analogy, but the Dock *is* the centerpiece of the Mac, and a very big deal. You'll spend a lot of time with it.

In fact, you may as well start spending time with it right now. Put it through the paces with these stunts:

- The Dock doesn't have to sit at the bottom of the screen like some kind of muck-eater. It's just as happy on either *side* of your screen. Considering the fact that your screen is wider than it is tall, in fact, the side of the screen might be a less space-hogging position for it.

  To put it there, open the menu, mouse down to the Dock command, and choose "Position on Left" or "Position on Right" from the submenu.

  When you position your Dock vertically, the "right" side of the Dock becomes the bottom. In other words, the Trash now appears at the bottom of the vertical Dock.

- You can also hide the Dock completely, which can come in very handy when it's overlapping some window that you're trying to read. From the Dock command in the menu, choose Turn Hiding On. (Or just press Option-⌘-D.) The Dock disappears promptly, sliding off the screen into oblivion.

  That doesn't mean you have to do without it altogether. You can bring it back, either by pressing the same keys again or by moving your cursor to the Dock's edge of the screen. Presto: It slides back into view. Click whatever it is you were intending to click on the Dock — and then move the cursor back to the middle of the screen. The Dock slithers out of view once again.

✔ As you may eventually notice for yourself, the icons on the Dock get smaller as the Dock gets more crowded. (If they didn't, the icons would have to extend beyond the edges of your screen, a condition definitely not covered by your warranty.)

Once they reach that point, you may run into a small problem: How are you supposed to make out the pictures on the icons when they're the size of atoms?

Easy: Just tell the Mac to enlarge them as your cursor passes across them. To turn on this strange and wonderful feature, open the menu, slide down to the Dock command, and choose Turn Magnification On from the submenu.

Now your Dock icons puff up bigger as your cursor passes over them, as shown here — an effect whose novelty takes *minutes on end* to wear off.

The First Tutorial

This handy lesson involves two of the Mac's freebie programs: the Calculator, whose function you can probably guess, and Stickies, whose function you probably can't. The trouble is, they're not on your Dock yet, so the only way to find them is to open your Applications window.

Remember how to do that? From the Go menu, choose Applications. (Or click Applications in your Sidebar.)

Once the Applications window opens, finding the Calculator shouldn't be very hard. (If it's not staring you in the face, type *CA* quickly to highlight its icon.) If you occasionally perform little calculations at your desk, install the Calculator onto the left side of your Dock by dragging it there from your Applications window.

Let's start simple. If you have indeed put the Calculator icon onto your Dock, click it. Otherwise, find the Calculator icon in your Applications window and double-click it. Either way, the Calculator pops up in a window of its own.

The Calculator

Using the mouse, you can click the little Calculator buttons. The Mac gives you the correct mathematical answer, making you the owner of the world's most expensive pocket calculator.

What's neat is that you can also type the number keys on your keyboard. As you press these real keys, you can watch the on-screen keys in the Calculator window get punched accordingly. Try it out!

Take a moment to reinforce your love of windows: By dragging the *title bar* (above the "readout" that shows your calculations), move the Calculator window into a new position. If you were tired of looking at it, you could also make the Calculator go away by clicking its close box (the little red dot in the upper-left corner, like on all windows).

But don't close the Calculator just yet. Leave it open on the screen.

Stickies

For your next trick, you'll need another freebie Mac program called Stickies. Once again, you'll find it in your Applications window. (Click in the Applications window to bring it to the front, and then type *ST* to jump to Stickies.)

Once again, you can install it onto your Dock to make it easier to get to in the future. Try opening Stickies right now (click its icon on the Dock, or double-click its icon in the Applications window).

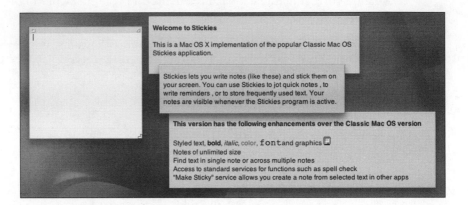

Stickies is the electronic version of those little yellow sticky notes that people stick all around their computer screens. Frankly, the Mac is much too beautiful a machine to junk up with little scraps of gluey paper, so Apple has created an electronic version of the same thing.

You can use Stickies to type quick notes and to-do items, paste in phone numbers you need to remember, and so on. All of your Stickies appear on the screen simultaneously whenever you open the Stickies program.

The first time you launch Stickies, a few sample notes show up automatically, describing some of the program's features. You can dispose of each sample by clicking inside it, and then clicking the tiny close box in the upper-left corner of each note. Each time you do so, the Mac asks if you want to save the note. If you click Don't Save, the note disappears permanently.

To create a new note, choose New Note from the File menu and just start typing. (You can also paste stuff into a note, or even *drag* some highlighted text out of a word processor or an e-mail message.) Don't forget that you can make a note bigger just as you would any window: by dragging the small resize handle on the lower-right corner of each note.

For now, with Stickies open on your screen, click inside an empty note and then type this: *Dear Son, I've been a bit concerned with your spending habits lately. By my calculations, you currently owe me $*

And stop right there. (If you make a mistake as you type, press the big Delete key at the upper-right corner of your keyboard. This key means "Backspace.")

Now, by dragging your sticky note's title bar, move it so that you can see the Calculator window, too.

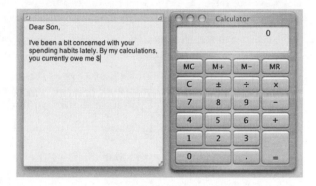

You're going to use two programs at once, making them cooperate with each other — one of the most remarkable features of the Mac.

Triangles in the Dock

Check your Dock. See how there are *two* tiny triangles under the icons there? The Stickies icon has a triangle, and so does the Calculator. That's the sign that both of these programs are *open* at the moment. You multitasking maniac, you.

Now see the menu name next to the menu? It says Stickies. That's the program you're in *right now.*

So how would you switch back to the Calculator? Right — you'd click the Calculator icon on the Dock.

The Calculator window moves to the front, and the name next to the menu changes to say Calculator.

Those of you still awake will, of course, object to using the Dock to bring the Calculator forward. You remember all too plainly from Chapter 1 that simply *clicking* in a window brings it to the front, which would have required less muscular effort.

Absolutely right! You may now advance to the semifinals. However, learning to use the Dock to switch programs was a good exercise. Many times in your upcoming life, the program in front will be covering up the *entire* screen. So *then* how will you bring another program forward, big shot? That's right. You can't *see* any other windows, so you can't click one to make it active. You'll have to use the Dock.

In any case, the Calculator should now be the active application. (*Active* just means it's in front.)

1. **Press the letter C key on your Mac keyboard, or click the C button on the Calculator.**

   You just cleared the display. We wouldn't want your previous diddlings to interfere with this tightly controlled experiment.

2. **Find the numbers in the block of keys at the far right side of your keyboard. (Or, if you have a laptop, use the row of number keys just above the letter keys.) Type in an equation like this:** *52+981*17+694=*

   In the computer world, the asterisk (*) means "times," or multiply.

With characteristic modesty, the Mac displays the answer to your math problem. (If you typed the numbers shown above, the answer is 17423. That's $17,423 your kid owes you.)

The cornerstone of human endeavor: Copy and Paste

Here's where the fun begins. Choose Copy from the Edit menu.

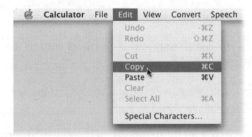

Thunder rolls, lightning flashes, the audience holds its breath . . . and absolutely nothing happens.

Behind the scenes, though, something awesomely useful occurred. The Mac looked at the number in the Calculator's little display window and memorized it, socking it away into an invisible storage window called the *Clipboard*. The Clipboard is how you transfer stuff from one window into another and from one program into another.

Now then. You can't *see* the Clipboard at this point, but in a powerful act of faith, you put your trust in me and believe that it contains the highlighted material (the equation).

Now switch back to Stickies. (Click any visible sticky note, or click the Stickies icon on the Dock.) Now, believe it or not, you can paste the copied number into the word processor, right after the dollar sign: Just click there and then choose Paste from the Edit menu.

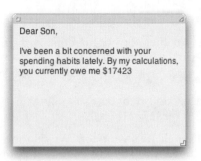

Incidentally, the Clipboard holds one thing at a time — whatever you copied *most recently*. If you copy something new right now, you'd wipe out the 17423 that's already on the Clipboard.

On the other hand, whatever's on the Clipboard stays there until you copy something new, or until you turn off the machine. In other words, you can paste it over and over again. Try it now — from the Edit menu, choose Paste again. Another 17423 pops into the window.

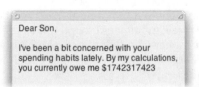

But you don't have to use the menu to issue a command. If you wish, you can use a keyboard shortcut to do the same thing. You may remember having used the ⌘ key in Chapter 2 to issue commands without using the mouse.

And how are you supposed to remember which letter key corresponds to which command? Well, usually it's mnemonic: ⌘-P means Print, ⌘-O means Open, and so on. But you can cheat; try it right now. Click the Edit menu to open it.

There's your crib sheet, carefully listed down the right side of the menu. Notice that the keyboard shortcuts for all four of these important commands (Undo, Cut, Copy, Paste) are adjacent on the keyboard: Z, X, C, V.

C is Copy. And V, right next to it, is Paste. (I know, I know: Why doesn't *P* stand for Paste? Answer: Because *P* stands for Print! And anyway, V is right next to C-for-Copy on your keyboard, so it *kind* of makes sense.)

Try it right now:

1. **While holding down the ⌘ key, type a V.**

   Bingo! Another copy of the Clipboard stuff (17423) appears in your Stickies note. (In the future, I'll just refer to a keyboard shortcut like this as "⌘-V.")

2. **Press ⌘-V again.**

   Yep, that kid's debt is really piling up. He now owes you $17423174231742317423!

   But after all, he's your son. Why not just let him make a down payment? In other words, why not *undo* that last pasting?

3. **From the Edit menu, choose Undo Paste.**

   The most recent thing you did — in this case, pasting the fourth 17423 — gets undone.

Rewriting history is addicting, ain't it?

Remember, though, that Undo only reverses your *most recent* action. Suppose you (1) copy something, (2) paste it somewhere else, and then (3) type some more. If you choose Undo, only the typing will be undone (Step 3), *not* the pasting (Step 2).

Did you get what just happened? You typed out a math problem in a word processor (well, in Stickies), copied it to the Clipboard, and pasted it into a number-cruncher (the Calculator). Much of the miracle of the Macintosh stems from its capability to mix and match information among multiple programs in this way.

Quitting a program

If you're finished fiddling with these program-ettes, quit each one. See the menu next to the , the one named after the program you're using? From the Stickies menu, choose Quit Stickies. Then switch to the Calculator, and choose Quit Calculator from the Calculator menu. That's how you get out of a program (and dismiss all its windows).

Hiding a program

But if you expect to use a certain program again later in your work session, don't bother quitting it. Instead, open the menu next to the menu and choose Hide Calculator (or whatever the program's name is). The program's windows disappear, but its icon remains on the Dock. Technically, the program is still open, ready for action when you click its Dock icon.

By hiding programs instead of quitting them, you save yourself the time it takes to quit and re-open them.

Exposé: Clearing the decks

On the other hand, sometimes you just want to get the current programs' windows out of your hair for a *moment*. Maybe you're working in Stickies, *and* the Calculator, *and* an e-mail program, and many others, and you just can't *find* anything. In short, maybe your screen looks like this:

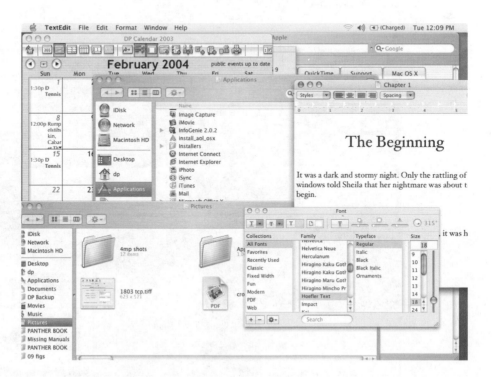

Memo to NASA scientists

Don't rely on the little Calculator program for calculating launch times or impact statistics, at least not without understanding how its math differs from yours.

The Calculator processes equations from left to right. It does *not* solve the multiplication and division components before the addition and subtraction, as is standard in math classes worldwide.

For example, consider this equation: 3+2*4=. (The * means "times" in computerland.) The scientific answer is 11, because you multiply before you add when solving such puzzles. But the Mac's answer is 20, because it processes the numbers from left to right.

The solution is a delicious feature called Exposé. When you tap the F9 key on the very top row of your keyboard, the Mac smoothly and visibly shrinks *all windows in all programs* to a size that fits on the screen, like index cards on a bulletin board, like this:

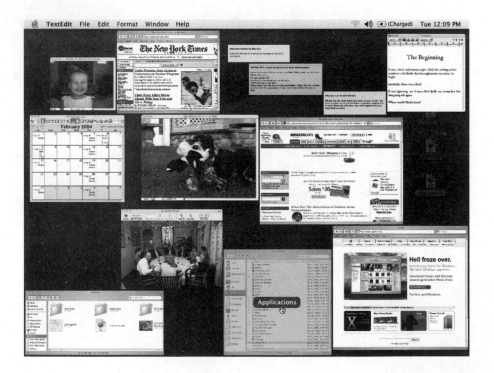

At this point, not a single window is hidden from you. As your cursor passes over each miniature frame, the window darkens and identifies itself, courtesy of the floating label that appears in its center.

When you find the window you're looking for, click inside it. It pops to the front, ready for work. It's fast, efficient, animated, and a lot of fun.

More Exposé

If you're not already swooning from the miracle of the F9 key, sit down and prepare yourself for the F10 and F11 keys.

The F10 key is designed to help you find a certain window only in the *program you're using* — a feature you'll probably find the most useful when you're Web browsing or word processing. When you tap F10, all of the windows *only in the frontmost program* spread out and shrink, if necessary, so that you can see all of them simultaneously, in full — and so that you can click the one you want. (All the windows of *other* programs just grow dim, as though someone has just shined a floodlight onto the windows of the program in question.)

The third keystroke, F11, sends *all* windows in *all* programs cowering to the edges of your screen, revealing the desktop beneath in all its uncluttered splendor. There they remain, out of your way, until you tap F11 again, click a visible window edge, double-click an icon, or take some other window-selection step.

This reveal-the-desktop trick is very useful when you need to duck back to the desktop for a quick second — to drag something to the Trash, for example.

And by the way: Pressing F9, F10, or F11 isn't the only way to trigger the Exposé feature, much to the relief of people who use those keys for other things. You can choose different keystrokes to trigger these functions, if you like, or even make Exposé kick in when you put your cursor in a certain *corner of the screen*.

How? By using System Preferences. Read on.

System Preferences

System Preferences is the master control panel for your Mac. The fact that its icon is on the Dock (it looks like a light switch) should suggest how important it is. Try clicking that icon — or, if you're not in the mood for Dock-clicking, open the menu and choose System Preferences.

System Preferences contains a bunch of icons, each of which controls some aspect of your Mac. It's a veritable playground for the control freak.

When you click one of the icons, the window fills with the corresponding controls. For example, if you click Date & Time, the window fills with the knobs and buttons you need to set your Mac's clock.

Never set your clock again

"They can send a man to the moon," many a computer fan mutters, "but they can't come up with a computer that sets its own clock!"

Actually, they can. If you set things up properly, your Mac can adjust its own clock by checking in, every now and then, with a highly accurate scientific clock — via the Internet. If you go online by dialing, this feature isn't very practical, since you probably won't be online at the particular moment when the Mac wants to check the time. But if you have a cable modem or DSL, you'd be crazy to miss this chance. Just turn on the "Set Date & Time automatically" checkbox.

From now on, your Mac will adjust its own clock each time it goes online. It will even adjust itself for Daylight Savings Time — something the clocks on your microwave and car dashboard can only dream about.

Then, once you're done adjusting the time (for example), you return to the menu of controls shown in the previous picture just by clicking the Show All button in the upper-left corner.

Your Mac would work perfectly well even if you never touched any of these controls. But taking ten minutes for a tour of these controls is easy, free, and better exercise than, say, lying on the couch. And besides, poking around in System Preferences will teach you about sliders, checkboxes, and other screen elements that you'll encounter over and over again in your upcoming computing career.

Here's a glance at a few of the most useful doodads in System Preferences.

Date & Time

The Mac's résumé features a long list under the Special Talents heading: DVD player, pocket calculator, Post-It Note simulator, and so on. But way, way down the list is another one: desk clock. As you may have noticed, the current time always appears in the upper-right corner of your screen. (And if you *click* the current time, a menu drops down showing the current *date.* The menu also lets you switch between digital and analog clock types, as befits your mood.)

Setting the date and time manually

Here, on the Date & Time panel (of the Date & Time module of System Preferences), is where you *set* this computer calendar and clock. Of course, you probably set the clock already, during the setup process described in Chapter 1. But if your Mac has accidentally drifted through a gap in the time-space continuum when you weren't looking, you can adjust the date by clicking the little arrow buttons next to the month and year labels. Then specify the *day* of the month by clicking a date on the mini-calendar. Click Save.

To set your clock, you can drag the actual hands on the clock face. (If you prefer, you can do it numerically: Click one of the numbers in the time boxes under the Current Time label, and then adjust the corresponding number by typing or by clicking the tiny up or down arrow buttons. To jump to the next number for setting, press the Tab key.) Finally, click Save.

Indicating your time zone

You probably told your Mac what time zone it's in during the startup process described at the beginning of Chapter 1, too.

But if you (a) discover your geography was a bit off or (b) move to another country, click the Time Zone button. Then click a section of the map to select a general region of the world. Finally, use the pop-up menu to specify your country within that region.

Desktop & Screen Saver

By clicking the Desktop icon in System Preferences, you open up this panel.

Here's where you choose a different background picture for your desktop — one that can replace the swooshy blue background that's probably been greeting you every morning since the day you first turned on the computer.

Interior decoration

To try a different piece of computer wallpaper, click one of the design categories on the left side — Nature, Solid Colors, and so on. With each click, the choice of color swatches changes. Just click one to try it on for size.

Of course, Apple's canned wallpaper options may be professional and shimmering, but they're not *yours*. It's much, much more fun to dress up your desktop with one of your *own* pictures. (This means you, scanner or digital camera owners.)

The trick is to find the actual graphics file that represents the photo you want to use. If your relationship with the Mac is only 30 minutes old, you may not have any photos yet. But eventually, thanks to the miracle of digital cameras, scanners, and grabbing pictures you find on the World Wide Web, your Pictures folder (whose icon shows up right here) may eventually contain a few pictures. Maybe you've even used iPhoto (Chapter 10); its icon, too, shows up in the Desktop & Screen Saver panel.

Either way, the process is the same: Click Pictures Folder or Photo Library, find the photo you want, and then click it to plaster that picture across your monitor.

You'll quickly discover that some pictures work better as screen backgrounds than others. For example, if it's too small to fill the whole screen, the Mac either repeats it over and over again like bathroom tiles — or just weirdly stretches it until it fills the screen. Photos of family, pets, or Britney Spears do just fine if you generally keep all of your files and folders in your Home folder, as Steve Jobs hopes you do. But if you tend to leave files and folders out on the desktop for quick access, complex photos may make it tough for you to find them. There's nothing worse than having to dig the latest draft of your speech out of Britney Spears's armpit.

Screen Saver

At the top of the window, you see *two* buttons. The one you've been playing with is Desktop. The other one is Screen Saver.

You're probably too young to remember *screen burn-in,* an upsetting phenomenon in which certain more or less permanent elements of the screen display — the menu bar, for example — would, over time, burn a ghostly, permanent image into the screen. But even you have probably seen the solution that programmers came up with: *screen savers.* These programs bounce around moving images on the screen when it's not in use, so that no image remains fixed long enough to do any damage.

Nobody's seen burn-in for years, thanks to advances in computer monitors. In fact, flat screens like the ones on most Macs *cannot* burn in, screen saver or no.

But screen savers are still with us, not as screen protection but as showoff-ware. To use the official terminology, they look really cool.

On the Screen Saver panel, you can choose from several different screen saver modules. Most of them look like nature shows in a planetarium, featuring jaw-dropping photographs (Beach, Cosmos, Forest) that grow, shrink, fade, and otherwise glide across the screen. If you've loaded up some digital-camera shots into iPhoto (Chapter 10, again), you can click Photo Library to use your *own* pictures as screen-saver fodder.

Either way, these photo shows are so brilliant and captivating that otherwise level-headed Mac fans have been known to bring the computer downstairs for dinner parties, just for dramatic effect.

When you click a name in the Screen Savers list (Cosmos or Forest, for example), a mini-version of it plays back in the Preview screen. Click Test to give the module a dry run on your full screen. (Moving the mouse or pressing any key kicks you out of test mode.)

Unless you tell it otherwise, the screen saver kicks in automatically about five minutes after the last time you actually used the Mac. (Use the "Start screen saver" slider to specify how long it waits.)

Tech note: All about resolution

The Resolution choices at the left side of the Displays panel are intriguing, especially for the technically inclined.

On a traditional, bulky computer screen, you can use these controls to magnify or shrink the screen image. The numbers here indicate how many tiny picture dots *(pixels)* fit onto the screen. When you click higher numbers, such as 1024 by 768, you're choosing higher *resolution*. At high resolutions, more fits onto your screen — two full side-by-side pages, for example — because those pixels are pretty tiny.

When you click lower numbers, like 800 by 600, you're switching to a *lower* resolution. Now fewer pixels — but bigger ones — fill the screen, in effect magnifying the image.

But on a screen like the flat-screen iMac's (or a laptop's), low resolutions don't just mean a bigger screen image — they also mean a *blurry* one. In fact, on those Macs, only one resolution setting looks really great: the maximum one (1024 by 768 on the 15-inch iMac, for example). That's because your screen is actually made up of 1024 by 768 tiny square shutters. At lower resolutions, the Mac does what it can to blur them together, but the effect is fuzzy and unsatisfying. (On a traditional, not-flat screen, by contrast, the electron gun can actually make the pixels larger or smaller, so there's no fuzziness at different resolutions.)

Displays

Most people, most of the time, won't find much here worth fiddling with. You could conceivably be curious about the Brightness slider — maybe you'd turn down the screen brightness when you're working in dim light — but there's a much easier way to adjust the screen brightness. Just press the Brightness *keys* on the top row of your keyboard (most Macs have these on keys F1 and F2, or F14 and F15) to make the screen dimmer or brighter, respectively.

Energy Saver

As noted in Chapter 1, your Mac nods off to sleep — its screen goes black and its appetite for electricity drops down to almost nothing — about 30 minutes after you stop using the machine.

Of course, if the whole point of your putting your Mac in a public area of the house or office is to show off its stunning screen saver, you certainly don't want its screen to go black in the name of saving a little power. Using the slider at the top of this dialog box, you can tell the Mac how long you want it to wait before nodding off — or *never* to do so.

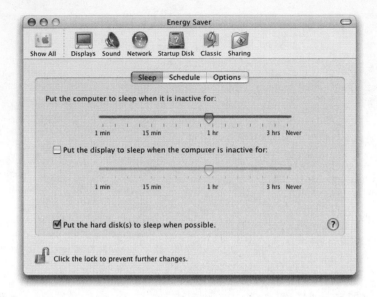

Energy Saver has another trick up its sleeve, too. By clicking the Schedule button, you can set up the Mac to shut itself down and turn itself back on automatically at certain times.

If you work 9 to 5, for example, set the Mac to turn itself on at 8:45 AM, and shut itself down at 5:30 PM — an arrangement that conserves electricity, saves money, and reduces pollution, but doesn't make you sit there while the machine gears itself up each morning (and winds itself down at night). In fact, you may come to forget that you've set up the Mac this way, since you'll never actually see it turned off.

(The Mac is nice enough *not* to shut itself off if you've left unsaved work on the screen.)

Exposé

Remember your old friend Exposé, the Mac's powerful screen-clutter elimina-tor? You press F9, F10, or F11 to find a window or reveal your desktop without actually closing any of your windows.

Exposé is wonderful and earth-shattering and all, but using the F-keys as trig-gers isn't necessarily the ideal setup. For one thing, those keystrokes may already be "taken" by other functions in your programs (like Microsoft Word) or even by your computer. For another thing, those keys are at the top of the keyboard where your typing fingers aren't used to going, and you may have to hunt to make sure you're pressing the right one.

Fortunately, you can reassign the Exposé functions to a huge range of other keys, using the controls on this panel.

For example, the four Active Screen Corners pop-up menus represent the four corners of your screen. You can assign an Exposé trigger to each corner; for example, if you choose Desktop from the first pop-up menu, when your pointer hits the upper-left corner of the screen, you'll hide all windows and expose the desktop. (To make the windows come back, twitch the cursor back into the same corner.)

Or, if you prefer, use the Keyboard section to assign a *different* keystroke to the three things that Exposé can expose. Just choose from the appropriate pop-up menu: "All windows," "Application windows," and "Desktop."

Keyboard & Mouse

On the obsolete invention known as *electric typewriters,* you could hold down the X key to cross out something you'd typed — XXXXXXX. On the very modern invention known as a Macintosh, *every* key behaves this way, making it a snap to type things like "Woo-HOOOOOOO!" or "GRRRRRRRRRRRR!"

The two sliders on the Keyboard panel govern this behavior. The right-side slider determines how long you must hold down the key before it starts repeating (to prevent triggering repetitions accidentally). The left-side slider controls how fast each key spits out letters once the spitting has begun.

Software Update

It's almost impossible to write completely bug-free software. Just ask any programmer. (Better yet, ask anyone who's ever used a computer.)

Fortunately, Mac OS X isn't frozen in time. Each time you go online to the Internet, the Software Update feature sends an invisible query to Apple: "Got anything for me?"

If Apple has indeed fixed a few bugs or added a few new features, the company's Web site automatically notifies you that a software update, or *patch,* is available.

One day you'll be merrily working away, and you'll see a dialog box like this:

That's your notice that the blessed event has occurred: Apple has sent you a morsel of software it believes will make your Mac better. You don't *have* to install it, of course, but these updates are usually worth accepting.

The purpose of this System Preferences pane is to specify *how often* the Mac checks for updates. Turn on the "Check for updates" option and use the pop-up menu to specify Daily, Weekly, or Monthly.

Sound

Whenever you do something that the Mac doesn't like — clicking somewhere it considers unseemly, for example — it beeps at you. But it doesn't have to *beep* at you; if you like, it can honk, bray, boop, or boing at you. Click each sound name in the Sound Effects list to find the one that seems the least intrusive (or the most intrusive, depending on your personality).

Quitting System Preferences

You quit System Preferences just as you would any other program: Choose the Quit command (Quit System Preferences, in this case) from the bottom of its application menu, the one next to the menu.

The Mac Keyboard

One look at the Mac's gleaming, clear-and-white or clear-and-black keyboard, and you'll realize that this is not your father's typewriter. If you've never used a computer before, you might be bewildered by the number of keyboard keys. After all, a typewriter has about 50 keys; your Mac has about 100.

Only some of the bizarro extra keys are particularly useful. Here's a list of the oddball extra keys and what they do.

✔ **F1, F2, F3 . . .** In most programs, including the Finder, the F1, F2, F3, and F4 correspond to the Undo, Cut, Copy, and Paste menu commands. On some Mac models, the F1 and F2 (or F14 and F15) keys also make your screen dimmer and brighter. And F9, F10, and F11, of course, are the Exposé keys.

A few of these F-keys (sometimes called function keys) act as menu-command shortcuts just in Microsoft programs.

Otherwise, though, these keys generally don't do anything. They're spares, sitting around for the benefit of add-on software.

✔ 🔉 🔊 🔇: These three buttons control your speaker volume. Tap the first one repeatedly to make the sound level ever lower, the middle one to make it louder. The symbol with no "sound waves" coming out represents the Mute button; tap it once to cut off the sound completely, and again to bring it back to its previous level. In any of these cases, you see a big white version of these same speaker logos on your screen as you tap — your Mac's little wink to let you know that it appreciates your efforts.

✔ ⏏: This is the Eject key. When there's a CD or DVD in your Mac, tap the key once to make the computer spit it out. If your Mac has a sliding CD/DVD *tray* (rather than just a slot that sucks in the discs), hold down this button for about a second to make the CD/DVD tray slide open, as though the Mac is sticking its big black tongue out.

✔ **Home, End:** "Home" and "End" are ways of saying "jump to the top or bottom of the window." If you're looking at a list of files, the Home and End keys jump you to the top or bottom of the list. In iPhoto, they jump to the first or last photo in your collection, respectively. In iMovie, the Home key rewinds your movie to the very beginning. You get the idea.

✔ **Pg Up, Pg Down:** These keys mean "Scroll up or down by one screenful." The idea is to let you scroll through word-processing documents, Web pages, and lists without having to use the mouse.

✔ **NumLock, Clear:** Clear means "get rid of this text I've highlighted, but don't put a copy on the invisible Clipboard, as the Cut command would do." The NumLock key doesn't do much of anything except in Microsoft Excel, and even then it's obscure and unimportant; I'll let you nuzzle up to the manual for that.

✔ **Esc:** *Esc* stands for *Escape*, and it actually means "Click the Cancel button," such as the one found in most dialog boxes.

Wanna try? Open a program like TextEdit. From the File menu, choose Page Setup. Then press Esc, and marvel as the box goes away.

✔ **Delete:** This is the backspace key.

✔ **Del:** Many a Mac fan goes for years without discovering the handiness of this delightful little key. First of all, force yourself to acknowledge that *Delete* and *Del* are two different keys.

The difference is that Delete, like Backspace, erases whatever letter is just *before* the insertion point. This key, the Del (also called Forward Delete) key, deletes whatever is just to the *right* of the insertion point, like this:

press Delete

a sudden f|light ⟶ a sudden light

press Del

a sudden f|light ⟶ a sudden fight

Anyway, the Del key really comes in handy when, for example, you've clicked into some text to make an edit — but wound up planting your cursor in just the wrong place.

✔ **Return and Enter:** In general, these keys do the same thing: wrap your typing to the next line. When a dialog box is on the screen, tapping the Return or Enter key is the same as clicking the OK button (or whatever button is blue and pulsing).

A few rare programs distinguish between the two. In AppleWorks, for example, Return begins a new paragraph, but Enter makes a *page break*, forcing the next typing to begin on a fresh page.

✔ **Command (⌘):** This key triggers keyboard shortcuts for menu items, as described in Chapter 2.

✔ **Control, Option:** The Control key *triggers contextual menus,* as described in Chapter 2.

The Option key lets you type special symbols. For example, press Option-G to make the © symbol, Option-4 for the ¢ sign, Option-R for ®, Option-Y for ¥, or Option-2 for ™.

Incidentally, the Option key is called the Option key in America; in the United Kingdom and other countries, it's labeled Alt. Don't let that throw you. Deep down, it's still the Option key.

↙ **Help:** In the Finder, Microsoft programs, and a few other places, this key opens up the electronic help screens. But you guessed that.

Top Ten Freebie Programs

Your Mac came with about 50 programs designed to charm and amaze you. Take a few minutes to savor your riches.

As you read, you might consider double-clicking each one in your Applications folder to get a feel for the process. When you're finished examining each one, close it up by choosing Quit, or hide it by choosing Hide, from the program's first menu, like this:

And, of course, if you fall in love with a program or two, by all means drag their icons onto the left side of your Dock so you'll be able to call them up again later when you need a software fix.

1. **Address Book.** It's the digital version of the little black book. To add somebody's information, click the + button beneath the Name column, type the name and address into the appropriate boxes (you can press the Tab key to jump from box to box), and then click Save. You'll get much more mileage out of the Address Book when you start doing e-mail (Chapter 8) and faxes (Chapter 18).

2. **Chess.** This little game is a lot like regular chess, with one big difference: It's on your screen. Your opponent, facing imminent devastation, can't knock over the chessboard in a hissy fit.

All right, there are a *few* other differences. One of them is that you can rotate the game board as though it's three-dimensional (just grab any corner and drag your mouse). Another is that by choosing Preferences from the Chess menu, you can actually specify what *materials* your chess pieces and board are made of: Fur, Marble, Metal, or *Grass.* (Every now and then, you have to wonder if the diets of the Apple programmers do not, perhaps, include items from all segments of the Food Pyramid.)

3. **iSync.** This simple program is designed to keep the calendars and phone lists on your various computers, Palm organizer, cell phone, and even your iPod in perfect synchronization, sparing you the headache of the modern age: inputting the same information over and over again.

4. **DVD Player.** Yes, your Mac can play DVDs from Blockbuster. See Chapter 11.

5. **iTunes.** Welcome to the digital jukebox. If you feed some music CDs into your Mac, iTunes can copy the songs to your hard drive, where they'll play any time you want them to — no hunting for the CD. Details in Chapter 9.

6. **Preview.** You'll rarely open this program yourself. Most of the time, it opens automatically when you double-click a graphics file — because Preview is a superb picture viewer. (Check out its View menu, whose commands let you rotate or flip the picture.)

7. **iChat AV.** Once you're on the Internet, you, like millions of preteens before you, can type little messages back and forth using this program. It gets better, though: As the letters AV imply, iChat is also an audio-visual communicator. If you and your distant pal each have Macs with microphones, you can actually make free long-distance calls over the Internet. And if you have a camcorder or an Apple iSight camera, you can even have face-to-face *video* chats. Details in Chapter 18.

8. **TextEdit.** TextEdit is a handy word processor that offers full-blown for-matting and graphics features. It's no Microsoft Word, although it *can* open and create Microsoft Word documents. (Details in Chapter 4.)

9. **System Profiler.** This program — which sits in the Utilities folder that's *in* the Applications folder — is like the printout that's taped to the inside of the window on a new car: It lists the features and options you've paid for. By clicking the various tabs and triangles, you can find out exactly what Mac version you have, how much memory and speed it offers, what kind of disk drives it has, and so on.

10. **GarageBand.** If you find a program called GarageBand in your Applications folder, you've got yourself a digital music recording studio right on your Mac. (It comes with every Mac sold since January 2004; it's also part of iLife, a suite of five programs — iMovie, iPhoto, and so on — for $50.)

The program comes with thousands of professionally recorded musical snippets — drums, guitar, bass, and dozens of other instruments. Even if you don't know a quarter note from a quarter pounder, you can drag these musical snippets as though they're building blocks, layering one track upon another until you have yourself a composition.

Just click the eyeball button, then click the name of the instrument you want (Drums, for example). Try listening to the *loops* (musical snippets) in the right-side list; when you find one you like, drag it up into an empty area like this:

Drag a loop's name into an empty area to place it into a new track.

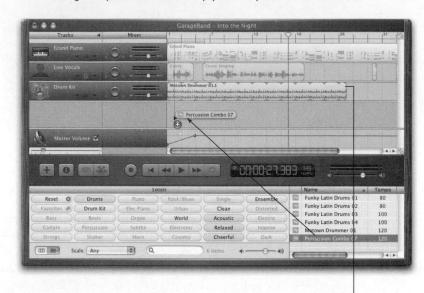

After that, drag the upper-right corner to make it repeat over and over.

By dragging the right end of a loop, you make it repeat over and over again for the number of measures indicated by the ruler. The most common use of this feature, of course, is to "lay down" the drum track for the entire song.

To add another instrument to your band, click Reset, and then click a different instrument button. When you drag *it* into the music area and then click the Play button shown here, you'll discover that all the loops sound great together.

Rewind   Fast Forward

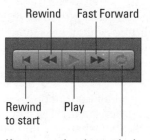

Rewind   Play
to start

Keep repeating the music denoted
by the yellow region on the ruler.

The Space bar also works to start and stop playback, by the way. Don't forget to drag the Playhead into position before you tap it, so that you don't have to start from the beginning each time.

If you do, in fact, have some musical talent, you can also hook up a synthesizer keyboard (or a *USB piano keyboard*) and record your performances. From the Track menu, choose New Track. A dialog box lists the software instruments available in GarageBand — the sounds that you can trigger with a USB or MIDI musical keyboard. Click an instrument family at left, and the individual instrument sound at right, and then play a few keys on your musical keyboard. When you've found the instrument you want, click OK.

Then, click the round, red Record button. GarageBand begins recording your performance, while simultaneously playing back any other tracks that you've laid down.

Actually, GarageBand has a third trick up its sleeve: It can also record your singing or playing a real-world instrument.

To get started, choose New Track from the Track menu. In the New Track dialog box, click the Real Instrument tab. Click the kind of instrument you're about to play — if you intend to speak or sing, click Vocals.

On the right side, specify what effects you want to apply to your recording. You're offered a long list of reverb and other processing effects; with a pair of headphones on, you can try them out one at a time by listening as you test your microphone. Then click OK and use the Record button to capture your performance.

When your piece is finished — your loops, keyboard performances, and vocal stylings sound good together — choose Export to iTunes from the File menu. After a moment, iTunes opens automatically (see Chapter 9), and your GarageBand piece appears in its list of music. From here, you can distribute your masterpiece online, transfer it to your iPod, burn it to a CD, export it as an MP3 (or AIFF or AAC) file, and begin your new life as a rock star.

Chapter 4

Typing, Saving, and Finding Again

*L*et's not kid ourselves. Yeah, I know, you're gonna use your Mac to retouch photos, create 3-D animations, and compose symphonies. But with the possible exception of e-mail and Web exploits, what you'll probably do the *most* of is good old *word processing*.

But just because everybody does it doesn't mean word processing isn't the single most magical, amazing, time-saving invention since microwaveable pasta. Master word processing, and you've essentially mastered your computer.

Your Very First Bestseller

Lucky for you, your Mac comes with a very nice word-processing program called TextEdit. As usual, it's in your Applications folder. (From the Go menu, choose Applications — or press Shift-⌘-A.) Once the Applications folder is open, type *TE* to jump to TextEdit. Drag TextEdit onto your Dock, if you like.

Top three rules of word processing

In the following steps, you'll do some actual typing. If you learned to type on typewriters, the first rules of *computer* typing may throw you — but learning them is crucial:

✔ **Don't press the Return key at the end of each line.** I'm dead serious here. When you type your way to the end of a line, the next word will automatically jump down to the next line. If you press Return in the middle of a sentence, you'll mess everything up.

➤ **Put only one space after a period.** From now on, everything you write will come out looking like it was professionally published instead of being cranked out on some noisy Selectric with a bad ribbon. A quick glance at any published book, magazine, or newspaper will make you realize that the two-spaces-after-a-period thing is strictly for typewriters.

➤ **Don't use the L key to make the number 1.** Your Mac, unlike the typewriter you may have grown up with, actually has a key dedicated to making the number 1. If you use a lowercase L instead, the 1 will look funny, and your spelling checker will think you've gone nuts.

There are a few other rules, too, but breaking them isn't serious enough to get you fired. So let's dig in.

The excitement begins

Double-click the TextEdit icon to open a new, blank sheet of "typing paper." You should see a short, blinking, vertical line at the beginning of the typing area. They call this the *insertion point*. It shows you where the letters will appear when you start to type.

Type the sentence below. If you make a typo, press the Delete key, just as you would Backspace on a typewriter. (For a rundown of the Mac's other unusual keys, see Chapter 3.) *Don't* press Return when you get to the edge of the window. Just keep typing, and the Mac will create a second line for you. Believe. *Believe.*

> *The screams of the lions burst Rod's eardrums as the motorboat, out of control, exploded through the froth.*

See how the words automatically wrapped around to the second line? They call this feature, with astonishing originality, *word wrap.*

But suppose, as your novel is going to press, you decide that this sleepy passage really needs some spicing up. You decide to insert the word *speeding* before the word *motorboat.*

Remember the blinking cursor — the insertion point? It's on the screen even now, blinking calmly away at the end of the sentence. If you want to insert text, you have to move the insertion point.

You can move the insertion point in two ways. First, try pressing the arrow keys in the lower-right cluster of your keyboard. You can see that the up- and down-arrow keys move the insertion point from line to line, and the right- and left-arrow keys move the insertion point across the line. Practice moving the insertion point by pressing the arrow keys.

If the passage you want to edit is far away, though (on another page, for example), using the arrow keys to move the cursor is inefficient. Your fingers would be bloody stumps by the time you finished. Instead, use this finger-saving technique:

1. **Using the mouse, move the cursor (which, when it's near text, looks like this: I) just before the word *motorboat*, and then click the mouse.**

   The I-beam changes to the insertion point.

   This is as confusing as word processing ever gets — there are *two* little cursors, right? There's the blinking insertion point, and there's this one I, which is called an *I-beam* cursor.

   In fact, the two little cursors are quite different. The blinking insertion point is only a *marker,* not a pointer. It always shows you where the next typing will appear. The I-beam, on the other hand, is how you *move* the insertion point; when you click with the I-beam, you set down the insertion point.

   In other words, editing stuff you've already typed, on the Macintosh, is a matter of *click and then type*.

2. **Type the word *speeding*.**

   The insertion point does its deed, and the Mac makes room on the line for the new word. A word or two probably got pushed onto the next line. Isn't word wrap wondrous?

Editing for the linguistically blessed

So much for *inserting* text: You click the mouse (to show the Mac *where*) and then type away. But what if you need to delete a bunch of text? What if you decide to *cut out* the first half of our sample text?

Well, unless you typed the challenging excerpt with no errors, you already know one way to erase text — by pressing the Delete key. Delete takes out one letter at a time, just to the left of the insertion point.

Deleting one letter at a time isn't much help in this situation, though. Suppose you decide to take out the *first part* of the sentence. It wouldn't be horribly efficient to backspace over the entire passage just so you could work on the beginning.

No, instead you need a way to edit any part of your work, at any time, without disturbing the stuff you want to leave. Once again, the Macintosh method, noun-then-verb, saves the day. Try this:

1. **Using the mouse, position the I-beam cursor at the beginning of the sentence.**

   This takes a steady hand; stay calm.

2. **Click *just* to the left of the first word and, keeping the mouse button pressed down, drag the I-beam cursor — *perfectly horizontally,* if possible — to the end of the word as.**

   As you drag, the text gets highlighted, or *selected*.

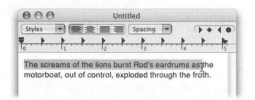

If you accidentally drag up or down into the next line of text, the high-lighting jumps to include a big chunk of that additional line. Don't panic; without releasing the mouse button, simply move the cursor back onto the original line you were selecting. This time, try to drag more horizontally.

If you're especially clever and forward-thinking, you'll also have selected the blank space *after* the word *as*. Take a look at the previous illustration.

All right, in typical Mac syntax, you've just specified *what* you want to edit by selecting it (and coloring in its background to show it's selected). Now for the verb:

1. **Press the Delete key.**

   Bam! The selected text is gone. The sentence looks pretty odd, though, since it doesn't begin with a capital letter.

2. **Using the mouse, position the cursor just before (or after) the letter *t* that begins the sentence. Drag the cursor sideways across the letter so that it's highlighted.**

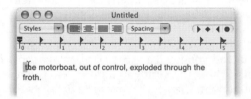

Here comes another ground rule of word processing. See how you've just selected, or highlighted, the letter *t?* The idea here is to capitalize it. Of course, using the methods for wiping out (and inserting) text that you learned earlier, you could simply remove the *t* and type a *T*. But since you've selected the *t* by dragging through it, replacing it is much easier.

3. **Type a capital** *T.*

The selected text gets replaced by the new stuff you type. That, in fact, is the fourth ground rule: *Selected text gets replaced by the new stuff you type.* As your Mac life proceeds, keep that handy fact in mind; it can save you a lot of backspacing. In fact, you can select 40 pages of text so that it's all highlighted and then type *one single letter* to replace all of it. Or you could *select* only one letter but replace it with 40 pages of typing.

Take a moment now for some unsupervised free play. Try clicking anywhere in the text (to plant the insertion point). Try dragging through some text: If you drag perfectly horizontally, you select text just on one line (shown below at top). If you drag diagonally, you get everything between your cursor and the original click (bottom).

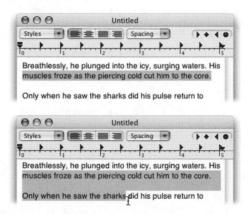

You *deselect* (or, equally poetically, unhighlight) text by clicking the mouse, anywhere at all (within the typing area).

Here's about the most fabulous word-processing shortcut ever devised: Try pointing to a word and then double-clicking the mouse! You've easily selected *exactly* that word without having to do any dragging.

As you experiment, do anything you want with any combination of drags, clicks, double-clicks, and menu selections. It's nice to know — and you might want to prepare a fine mahogany wall plaque to this effect — that *nothing you do using the mouse or keyboard can physically harm the computer.*

Puff, the Magic Drag-N-Drop

You kids today, with your long music and loud hair! You don't know how lucky you are! Why, when I was your age, if I wanted to rearrange a couple of words, I'd have to *copy and paste them!*

But not anymore. Nowadays, you can move text around on the screen just by *pointing* to it! This profoundly handy feature is known as *drag-and-drop.*

1. **In TextEdit, open the File menu and choose New.**

   If you've been following along with the chapter already in progress, TextEdit is still on the screen. Press the Return key a couple of times to move into an empty part of the page.

2. **Type up two phrases, as shown here:**

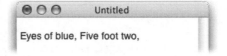

3. **Highlight *Eyes of blue.***

   You've done this before: Position the insertion-point cursor just to the left of the word *Eyes* and *carefully* slide directly to the right, highlighting the phrase (below, left).

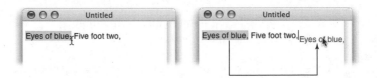

4. **Now position the arrow cursor right smack in the middle of the black-ened phrase. Hold down the mouse button for about one full second, motionless — and then *drag* the arrow to the end of the line (above, right).**

When your arrow is correctly positioned at the end of the line, you'll see the new insertion point appear there. (Troubleshooting note: If you don't see the actual words move along with your cursor, then you didn't wait long enough with your mouse button down before dragging.)

5. **Release the mouse!**

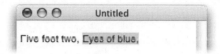

As you can see, you've just *dragged* the first phrase into position after the second phrase! Sam Lewis and Joe Young would be very grateful for your correcting their lyrics.

Now how much would you pay? But wait — there's more! Once you've mastered the art of dragging text around your screen, the sky's the limit! To wit:

✔ If you press the *Option* key while you drag some highlighted text, instead of *moving* that phrase, you actually make a *copy* of it, as shown here:

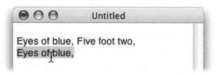

✔ You can actually drag text *clear out of the window* and into another program — for example, from TextEdit into Stickies.

✔ You can also drag text clear out of the window and *onto the desktop.* When you release the mouse button, you'll see that your little drag-and-dropped blurb has turned into a *text clipping,* as shown here:

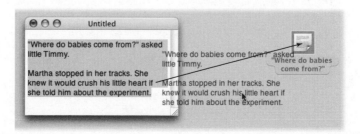

Next time you need that blob of text, you can point to the text clipping and drag it back into your word-processing program, and — presto! — the text appears there, exactly as though you'd typed it again.

Form and Format

When you use a typewriter, you set up all the formatting characteristics *before* you type: the margins, the tab stops, and (for typewriters with inter-changeable type heads) the type style.

But the whole point of a word processor is that you can change anything at any time. Many people type the text of an entire letter (or proposal, or memo) into the Mac and *then* format it. When you use a typewriter, you might discover, after typing the entire first page, that it's slightly too long to fit, and your signature will have to sit awkwardly on a page by itself. With a Mac, you'd see the problem and nudge the text a little bit higher on the page to compensate.

Word processing has other great advantages: no crossouts; easy corrections that involve no whiteout and no retyping; a permanent record of your correspondence that's electronic, not paper, so it's always easy to find; a selection of striking typefaces — at any size; paste-in graphics; and so on. It's safe to say that once you try processing words, you'll never look back.

For your next trick, you'll dress up your typing the way professional typesetters have for decades before you, although at much higher hourly rates. Open TextEdit, if you're not already in it. Choose New from the File menu, so you're looking at a clean, untitled page.

The return of Return

With all the subtlety of a Mack truck, I've taught you that you're forbidden to use the Return key *at the end of a line*. Still, that rectangular Return key on your keyboard *is* important. You press Return at the end of a *paragraph,* and only there.

To the computer, the Return key works just like a letter key — it inserts a *Return character* into the text. It's just like rolling the paper in a typewriter forward by one notch. Hit Return twice, and you leave a blank line.

The point of Return, then, is to move text higher or lower on the page. Check out this example, for instance:

¶
¶
¶

Dearest·Todd,¶
¶
I·have·never·loved·so·much·as·I·did·last·
night.·Imagine·my·joy·as·I·watched·you·
plunch·your·shining·scimitar·into·the·
greasy·flesh·of·that—that—hideous·thing·
from·the·deep.¶
¶
Unfortunately,·the·IRS·has·determined·
that·you·failed·to·file·returns·for·the·years·
1982–1986.·They·have·asked·that·I·notify·
you·of·¶

¶
Dearest·Todd,¶
¶
I·have·never·loved·so·much·as·I·did·last·
night.·Imagine·my·joy·as·I·watched·you·
plunch·your·shining·scimitar·into·the·
greasy·flesh·of·that—that—hideous·thing·
from·the·deep.¶
¶
Unfortunately,·the·IRS·has·determined·
that·you·failed·to·file·returns·for·the·years·
1982–1986.·They·have·asked·that·I·notify·
you·of·¶

Return characters move text down on the page. So, if you want to move text up on the page, drag through the blank space so that it's highlighted (above, left); of course, what you've really done is select the usually invisible Return characters. If you delete them, the text slides up the page (right).

Combine this knowledge with your advanced degree in Inserting Text (remember? you *click and then type*), and you can see how you'd make more space between paragraphs or push all the text of a letter down on the page.

Appealing characters

Another big-time difference between word processing and typing is all the great *character formatting* you can do. You can make any piece of text **bold**, *italic,* underlined, all of these, and more. You also get a selection of great-looking typefaces. By combining all these styles and fonts randomly, you can make any document look absolutely hideous.

Here's the scheme for changing some text to one of those character formats: noun-verb. Sound familiar? Go for it:

1. **Select some text by dragging through it.**

   Remember you can select a single word by double-clicking it; to select a bunch of text, drag the cursor through it so that it turns black. You've just identified *what* you want to change.

   Each word processor keeps its Bold, Italic, and Underline commands in its own specially named menu; in TextEdit, they're in the Format menu, in the pop-out submenu of the Font command.

2. **From the Font submenu of the Format menu, choose Bold.**

   You've just specified *how* you want to affect the selected text.

You can apply several of these formats to the same text, too, although you won't win any awards for typographical excellence.

You can make type bigger or smaller, too. Most word processors offer a Format menu or a Text menu that contains a Size submenu — AppleWorks works that way, for example.

In TextEdit and many other programs, the list of sizes hides on something called the Font Panel. Call it up by opening the Format menu, and then choosing Show Fonts from the Font submenu, as shown here at top. The font panel window opens, as shown at bottom:

Now select some text and then choose a type size from the list of sizes in the font panel. The font sizes are measured in points, of which there are 72 per inch. Works out nicely, too — a typical Mac monitor has 72 *screen* dots per inch, meaning that 12-point type on the screen really is 12-point.

Try changing the typeface also, using the same panel; the various fonts are called things like American Typewriter, Arial, Big Caslon, Times, and so on. Changing fonts works the same way: Select text and then choose the font.

Before you know it, you'll have whipped your document into handsome shape.

The efficiency zealot's guide to power typing

Because you *can* format text after you've typed it doesn't mean you *have* to. Most power-users get used to the keyboard shortcuts for the common style changes, like bold and italic. They're pretty easy to remember: In nearly every word-processing program, you get bold by pressing ⌘-B and italic with ⌘-I.

What's handy is that you can hit this key combo just *before* you type the word. For example, without ever taking your hands off the keyboard, you could type the following:

> He stared at the **Delinquent Birds** folder. No: it *was not* happening!
>   ↑   ↑   ↑   ↑
>   ⌘-B   ⌘-B   ⌘-I   ⌘-I

In other words, you hit ⌘-B once to turn bold *on* for the next burst of typing, and ⌘-B again to turn it off — all without ever having to use a menu. (You do the same with ⌘-I.)

Formatting paragraphs

Whereas type styles and sizes can be applied to any amount of text, even a single letter, *paragraph formatting* affects a whole paragraph at once. Usually these styles are easy to apply. To select a paragraph, you don't have to highlight all the text in it. Instead, you can just click *once,* anywhere within a paragraph, to plant the insertion point. Then, as before, choose the menu command that you want to apply to that entire paragraph.

This figure shows some of the different options every word processor provides for paragraph formatting — left-justified, right-justified, fully justified, and centered:

Her heart pounding, she looked toward the door. It swung open with a creak. The stench hit her first—an acrid, rotting swamp smell. She covered her mouth with the blood-soaked handkerchief and stepped backward, her naked back pressed hard against the fourposter.

Left-justified

Her heart pounding, she looked toward the door. It swung open with a creak. The stench hit her first—an acrid, rotting swamp smell. She covered her mouth with the blood-soaked handkerchief and stepped backward, her naked back pressed hard against the fourposter.

Right-justified

Her heart pounding, she looked toward the door. It swung open with a creak. The stench hit her first—an acrid, rotting swamp smell. She covered her mouth with the blood-soaked handkerchief and stepped backward, her naked back pressed hard against the fourposter.

Fully justified

Her heart pounding, she looked toward the door. It swung open with a creak. The stench hit her first—an acrid, rotting swamp smell. She covered her mouth with the blood-soaked handkerchief and stepped backward, her naked back pressed hard against the fourposter.

Centered

(In TextEdit, you get these effects by clicking a paragraph, and then clicking one of the four tiny icons in the ruler at the top of the window.)

You can control paragraphs in other ways, too. Remember in high school when you were supposed to turn in a 20-page paper, and you'd try to pad your much-too-short assignment by making it two-and-a-half spaced? Well, if you'd had a Mac, you could have been much more sneaky about it. You can make your word-processed document single-spaced, double-spaced, quadruple-spaced, or any itty-bitty fraction thereof. (Use the Spacing pop-up menu on the TextEdit ruler for this.) You can even control how tightly together the letters are placed, making it easy to stretch or compress your writing into more or fewer pages.

Take this opportunity to toy with your word processor. Go ahead, really muck things up. Make it look like a ransom note with a million different type styles and sizes. Then, when you've got a real masterpiece on the screen, read on.

Working with Documents

It might terrify you — and it should — to find out that you've been working on an imaginary document. Only a thin thread of streaming electrical current preserves it. Your typing doesn't exist yet, to be perfectly accurate, except in your Mac's *memory*.

Meet your memory

Whenever you open a program or a document that's sitting on your Mac's hard drive, the Mac quickly reads the hard drive as though it's a CD player and copies what it finds there into the computer's *memory*.

Memory, annoyingly called RAM by computer geeks, is really neat. After something's in memory, it's instantaneously available to the computer. The Mac no longer has to read the disk to learn something. Memory is also expensive (at least compared to disks), probably because it's a bunch of complicated circuits that people in dust-proof spacesuits etch onto a piece of silicon the size of a piece of Trident. That's why you have a lot more hard drive space than memory.

Put another way, the Mac uses the hard disk for *long-term, permanent* storage of *lots* of things, and it uses memory for *temporary* storage while you work on *one thing at a time*.

The Save command

The only problem with this scheme is that memory is fleeting. (Specifically, I mean *computer* memory, but if you find a more universal truth in my words, interpret away.) In fact, the memory is wiped away when you shut the Mac down — or when a system crash, a rare but inevitable event for any computer, turns it off *for* you. At that moment, anything that exists on the screen is gone forever.

Therefore, almost every program has a Save command. It's always in the File menu, and its keyboard shortcut is always ⌘-S.

When you save your work, the Mac transfers it from transient, fleeting, electronic memory onto the good, solid, permanent disk. There your work will remain, safely saved. It will still be there tomorrow. It will still be there next week. It will still be there ten years from now, when your computer is so obsolete that it's valuable again.

Therefore, let's try an experiment with your ransom note document on the screen. From the File menu, choose Save.

Uh-oh. Something weird just happened: A slithery, semi-transparent rectangle that Apple calls a *sheet* just dripped out from the top of your document window, like this:

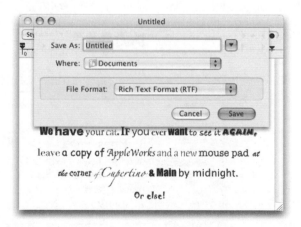

The Mac makes it pretty clear that it wants to know: "Under what name would you like me to file this precious document, Masssssster?"

And how do you know this? Because in the box where it says "Save as," a proposed title is highlighted (selected already). And what do you know about highlighted text? *Anything you start typing will instantly replace it.*

The Mac, in its cute, limited way, is trying to tell you that it needs you to type a title. Go ahead, do it: Type *Ransom Note*.

At this point, you could just click the Save button. The Mac would take everything in perilous, fleeting memory and transfer it to the staid, safe hard disk — in your Documents folder (which is in your Home folder), to be precise. There it would remain until you were ready to work on it some more.

However, a bunch of other stuff lurks in this sheet. A quick tour may be in order.

Navigating the Save File sheet

Before Mac OS X came along, some people *lost* files every day. They'd click Save, and wind up with some document filed somewhere in some folder of the hard drive where they never saw it again.

But on your Mac, it's almost impossible to lose a file you've created. Unless you've changed the setup of this Save sheet since you took the Mac out of its box, the Mac will always suggest that you store newly created files in your Documents folder, as you can see in the previous picture. When you want to work on something again, you can always find it in the Finder by clicking the Documents folder icon in the Sidebar, like this:

When you're feeling good about your mastery of the machine, though, you may one day want to explore the possibility of filing your documents into *other* folders.

For advanced thinkers like you, Apple has provided a small, down-pointing triangle button, shown in the picture below. When you click it, the sheet expands to reveal additional controls, like this:

The idea here is simple. You've already learned about the way your computer organizes files: with folders and with folders *in* folders. Remember the little exercise from Chapter 2, where you put state-named folders inside the USA Folder?

Well, all the stuff in the Save File box is a miniature version of that same folder-filing system. In fact, it looks just like column view, which was described in Chapter 2.

Here are some of the ways you might choose a filing folder for a document you're saving:

✔ Use the Sidebar at the left side of the window. It's exactly the same Sidebar as the one you saw in the Finder. In this case, you can use it to list the places you're most likely to want to stash a file you've just written: on the desktop, in your Home folder, and so on. (Some people like to save everything onto the desktop, where they'll find it sitting out on the colored backdrop of the screen when they're done working. At that point, they file it manually, by dragging it into a folder.)

✔ Using the column-view arrangement, navigate to the folder you want. When you've finally highlighted the name of the folder, click the Save button at the bottom of the box.

✔ Create a *new* folder in your Home folder or on the desktop. This is a great option when you've just finished writing Chapter 1 of something; after all, at this moment, you haven't yet created a folder to hold your new masterpiece.

So you'd click your Home folder (named after you) or Desktop in the Sidebar (to tell the Mac *where* you want the new folder to appear). Then you'd click the New Folder button, type a name for the new folder, and click Create. Then you'd click Save to file Chapter 1 into that newly created folder.

For the purposes of following along with this exercise, click Documents in the Sidebar. Then click the Save button at the lower-right corner of the box. The Save sheet slurps away upward, and behind the scenes, your file has been snugly tucked away into the Documents folder, which will be an increasingly important folder in your life.

Want proof, O Cynic? Try this cool trick: Press the F11 key. Suddenly all open word-processing windows disappear. You haven't lost your work windows — you've just temporarily hidden them, nudged them to the edges of the screen, so that you can see the desktop that they were covering up. (If it's been awhile since you read Chapter 3, what you've just done is triggered *Exposé.*)

Now you're back at the Finder, where your friends the folders, windows, and Dock pop up. If you want to make sure your file really exists, and it really got put where you wanted it, you could now go to your Home folder (choose Home from the Go menu). Inside, you'll find a Documents folder, which you can double-click to open. There, sure enough, is your ransom note, represented as an icon.

Why are we kicking this absolutely deceased horse? Because that same Sheet business (including the Sidebar) is used for *retrieving* files you've already created. You need to know how to work that sheet if you ever want to see your files again. More on this in a moment.

Closing a file, with a sigh

Return to TextEdit by pressing F11 again, which turns off Exposé. All of your word-processing windows pop back onto the screen, including your ransom note.

Worrywarts' corner

From the way I've described the terrifyingly delicate condition of a document that's on the screen (that you haven't saved to disk yet) — that is, precariously close to oblivion, kept alive only by electric current — you might think that closing a window is a dangerous act. After all, what if you forgot to save some work? Wouldn't closing the window mean losing that critical memo?

Not really — if you try to close a document, the Mac won't *let* you proceed until it asks you whether you're *sure* you want to lose all the work you've done. It will say something like:

Click Save if you do want to save your work. Click Don't Save if you were only goofing around and don't want to preserve your labors.

Click Cancel if you change your mind completely about closing the document and want to keep working on it.

Close all of your windows by clicking the close button on each one (the little red, leftmost dot in the upper-left corner). Once. If the Mac invites you to save the changes you've made to one of these windows, well, that's up to you. Clicking Don't Save is perfectly okay, especially because the work you've done in this chapter consists primarily of worthless noodlings.

In the Mac's universal language of love, clicking the small red round button up there means *close the window,* as you'll recall. If all went well, the window disappears.

How to find out what's going on

This gets sort of metaphysical. Hold onto your brain.

Just because you closed your *document* doesn't mean you've left the *program.* In fact, if you inspect the menu just to the right of the menu, you'll see that the TextEdit program is, in fact, still running. Its name still appears on your menu bar.

You could return to the desktop by clicking the first Dock icon (labeled Finder), or just by clicking anywhere on the desktop — without exiting the word processor. The Finder and TextEdit can both be running at the same time, but only one can be in front.

In fact, that's the amazing thing about a Macintosh. You can have a bunch of programs all open and running at once.

What gets confusing is that one program (say, TextEdit) may be active, but you'll *think* you're in the Finder. After all, you'll see your familiar icons, Trash, folders, and so on. But you'll be confused, because the menu commands you might be looking for, like Empty Trash or New Folder, won't be in the menus at all!

You need to understand that all this is simply *shining through* the emptiness left by TextEdit, which has no windows open at the moment. If a window *were* open, it would cover up the desktop behind it. The menus you're seeing now, in other words, are the menus of *TextEdit* (which, of course, has no Empty Trash or New Folder commands).

If that momentary disorientation strikes you — you're looking for a menu that doesn't seem to be there any more — your first thought should be to figure out what program you're actually in. Its name always appears next to the menu.

For the moment, stay in TextEdit.

Getting It All Back Again

Okay. You've typed a ransom note. Using the Save command, you turned that typing on your screen into an icon on your hard disk. Now it's time for a concept break.

Crazy relationships: Parents and kids

Two kinds of files are lying on your hard disk right now: *programs* (sometimes called applications) and *documents*. A program never changes; it's like a Cuisinart on your kitchen counter, sitting there day after day. Documents are what you *create* with a program — they're the coleslaw, crushed nuts, and guacamole dip that come out of the Cuisinart. You pay money to buy a program. After you own it, you can create as many documents as you want for free.

For example, you could use the Word Proc-S-R program (above, top) to create all the different word-processing documents below it and thousands more like them. If you love analogies as much as I do, you can think of the application as the mommy and the documents as the kiddies.

Here's what their family relationships are like:

- Double-click the *program* icon when you want to open a brand-new, untitled, clean-slate document.
- Double-click a *document* icon to open that document. Unbeknownst to you, double-clicking a document simultaneously opens the program you used to create the document.

When you double-click to open a document...

...the Mac automatically opens
the program that gave it birth, even
if it's buried in a folder somewhere.

File-name suffixes

How does a document know who its mommy is? That's an excellent question with a somewhat technical answer. It turns out that behind the scenes, almost every document you create has a secret three-letter suffix at the end of its name. A TextEdit document may look to you like it's called "Casey's Last Will and Testament," but its real name might be "Casey's Last Will and Testament.rtf." The Mac has an internal table that indicates which three-letter suffix "belongs" to which program.

So how come you've never seen these suffixes? Because the Mac normally *hides* them, in an effort to make the Mac look less intimidating and geeky.

If you'd like a peek at the secret suffix (also called a *file name extension*), highlight a document icon and, from the File menu, choose Get Info. From the pop-up menu at the top of the resulting dialog box, choose Name & Extension. You'll see something like this:

If this sort of thing gets your pulse racing, you'll find more about it in the troubleshooting chapter (Chapter 16), because you can generally ignore this entire topic until things go wrong.

Fetch: How to retrieve a document

Let's pretend it's tomorrow. Yawn, stretch, fluff your hair (if any). You find out that the person you've kidnapped actually comes from a wealthy Rhode Island family, and so you can demand much more ransom money. Fortunately, you created your ransom note on the Mac, so you don't have to retype anything; you can just change the amount you're demanding and print it out again.

But if you've been following the steps in this chapter, then there's *no* document on the screen. You're still *in* TextEdit, though. (Or you should be; check the name of the program next to the menu. If it doesn't say TextEdit, then click the TextEdit icon on your Dock.) So how do you get your ransom note file back?

Like this:

1. **From the File menu, choose Open.**

   A *dialog box* appears, so called because the Mac wants to have a little chat with you.

This one looks just like the Save dialog box, where you were asked to give your document a title. This one, navigationally speaking, works exactly the same way.

Unfortunately for my efforts to make this as instructional as possible, if you've been following these steps, your ransom note is staring you in the face right now. It's in whichever folder you saved it into. The Mac is nice that way — it remembers the most recent folder you stashed something in and shows you that location the next time you try to save or open something.

If you want to emerge from this experience a better person, though, pretend that you can't find your ransom note. On the Sidebar, click some other place icon— for example, Desktop. Now the display changes to show whatever's sitting on your desktop.

And from here, you know how to get back into your own stuff, don't you? Correct — click the Documents icon in the Sidebar. Sooner or later, you'll spot the icon for your Ransom Note file.

2. **Double-click the ransom note.**

This is what you've been working up to all this time. The ransom note appears on your screen in its entirety. Now, at last, you can edit it to your heart's content.

Save Me Again!

To continue this experiment, make some changes to your document. Once again, you have to worry about the fact that your precious work only exists in a fragile world of bouncing electrons. Once again, turning the Mac off right now means you'll lose the *new* work you've done. (The original ransom note, without changes, is still safe on your disk.)

Therefore, you have to use that trusty Save command each time you make changes that are worth keeping. (For you desk potatoes out there, remember that ⌘-S is the keyboard shortcut, which saves you an exhausting trip to the menu.) The Save dialog box will *not* appear on the screen each time you use the Save command (as it did the first time). Only the very first time you save a document does the Mac ask for a title (and a folder location).

You've probably heard horror stories about people who've lost hours of work when some glitch made their computers crash. Well, usually it's their own darned fault for ignoring the two most important rules of computing:

> **Rule 1. Save your work often.**

> **Rule 2. See Rule 1.**

"Often" may mean every five minutes. It may mean after every paragraph. The point is to do it a lot. Get to know that ⌘-S shortcut, and type it reflexively after every tiny burst of inspiration.

Now you know how to start a new document, edit it, save it onto the disk, reopen it later, and save your additional changes. You know how to launch a program (that is, open it) — by double-clicking its icon. But now you have to learn to get out of a program when you're finished for the day. It's not terribly difficult:

From the TextEdit menu, choose Quit TextEdit.

(Of course, substitute the name of whatever program you're using.)

If TextEdit was the only program you were running, then you return to the Finder. If you were running some other programs, then you just drop down into the next program. It's as though the programs are stacked on top of each other; take away the top one, and you drop into the next one down.

How to Back Up — and Burn CDs

Duty compels me to keep this chapter going just long enough to preach one other famous word of advice to you: Back up.

To *back up,* or to *make a backup,* means to make a safety copy of your work.

The importance of being backed up

When you're in the Finder, the documents you've worked on appear as icons on the hard disk. Like any of us, these disks occasionally have bad hair days, go through moody spells, or die. On days like those, you'll wish you had made a *copy* of the stuff on the hard disk so your life won't grind to a halt while the hard disk is being repaired.

You know the cruel gods that make it rain when you forget your umbrella? Those same deities have equal powers over your hard disk and an equal taste for irony. That is, if you don't back up, your hard disk will *certainly* croak. On the other hand, if you back up your work at the end of every day or every week, nothing will ever go wrong with your hard disk, and you'll mumble to yourself that you're wasting your time.

Life's just like that.

What to back up

The beauty of the Mac OS X system is that your whole world of files and settings lives in a single folder: your Home folder. That's the only folder you care about.

Even if a bolt of lightning, or a midnight thief, takes out your Mac, you're almost completely covered. You already have a backup of the operating system itself, and all programs that came with it, in the form of the backup CDs that came with your machine (more on this in Chapter 16). If you've bought more programs, you can back them up from the CDs they came on. The only thing you need to keep backed up, then, is your Home folder.

Method 1: Burn a CD or DVD

Among your Mac's many other skills, it can actually *record CDs,* a feat that once required a $25 million fabrication plant in Korea.

A couple of blank, all-silver CDs probably came in the box with your Mac. (They're stashed into the envelope of software CDs.) If the faint etched writing on them says *CD-R,* then they're just *recordable* blanks — you can fill them up only once. Which isn't so bad, really, since blanks cost less than 25 cents each.

But you can also buy slightly more expensive *CD-RW* blanks, which stands for *rewritable.* You can *re*-record these discs, using one CD as a backup disk that you erase and re-use over and over again. At discount-computer Web sites like *www.buy.com* (search for "CD-R spindle" or "CD-RW spindle"), you can buy a pack of 50 blank CD-R discs, or 25 blank CD-RW discs, for $20 or less. Prices have probably dropped even more since this book was published — in fact, they've probably dropped since you began reading this sentence.

Actually, it's even more fun than that. If your Mac is equipped with a so-called *SuperDrive* (you would remember having paid more for this feature), it can actually use blank *DVDs* as backup discs, too. These DVD-R discs are more expensive than blank CDs, but hold seven times as much. (In that case, mentally substitute "DVD" every time you read the word "CD" in the following steps.)

Either way, the process couldn't be simpler:

1. **Make sure there's nothing in your CD slot by holding down the Eject button on your keyboard.**

   It's the up-arrow key at the upper-right corner of the whole keyboard. Press for about two seconds. If there was another disc already in your machine, it spits out now, so you can file away. (If your older Mac lacks an Eject key, the F12 key generally does the same thing.)

   If your Mac uses a CD *tray* (rather than a slot that just inhales your CDs), its door snaps down and open like the entrance to the Bat Cave, and the tray shoots open with considerable power. (Oh, yeah: First remove any Styrofoam cups of coffee that you may have placed directly in front of the computer.)

2. **Put a blank CD (or a CD-RW disc) into the Mac.**

   Handle the CD by its hole and its edges; never touch the underside. The disc goes label side up.

   If your Mac uses a CD tray, put the disc into it and then tap the Eject key on your keyboard again.

   If your Mac has a CD slot, push the front edge of the CD gently into the slot until the Mac grabs it and slurps it in.

   If you've inserted a new, blank disc, you see this message:

   You inserted a blank CD. Choose what to do from the pop-up menu.

   Action: 🔲 Open Finder

   Name: Mary's Backup

   ☐ Make this action the default

   Eject   Ignore   OK

Type a name for your backup disk and then click OK. (Or press the Return key. Remember that any blue, pulsing button on your screen can also be "clicked" by pressing Return.)

In any case, a shiny CD icon appears on your desktop.

(Red-tape alert: If it's a CD-RW disc that you've used before, you have to erase it before you can re-use it. To do that, open the Disk Utility program, which is in the Applications folder, inside the Utilities folder. When the Disk Utility screen appears, click the Erase tab, click the listing in the left-side list that represents the disc — it probably says just, "641.04 MB" or something — click Erase, and then click Erase again. Wait a few minutes, and then quit Disk Utility. From now on, the disc will behave exactly as though it's a blank, which it is.)

4. **Open your Home folder window. Drag it, using the little "home" icon in the title bar as a handle (circled in the following picture), onto the CD icon.**

(Don't start dragging until the little house icon turns dark.)

That's it. The Mac begins copying your Home folder onto the blank CD.

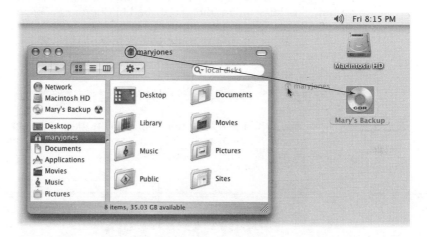

On a Macintosh, making a copy of something is as easy as dragging it to the disk you want it copied onto. You can also drag something into the disk's *window* (instead of onto its *icon*).

Nor should you feel limited to backing up your Home folder; you can drag folder icons from anywhere on your hard drive onto the CD icon.

By the way, if you have tons of digital photos and movies in your Home folder, the whole folder might not fit. In that case, open your Home folder and drag the individual folders to the backup disc's icon until you run out of room. Burn that CD, and then repeat with whatever folders you didn't copy the first time.

5. **From the File menu, choose Burn Disc. In the confirmation dialog box, click Burn.**

(Alternatively, eject the CD by choosing Eject from the File menu, or by dragging its icon onto the Trash icon on the Dock; the Mac will ask you if you want to burn it before ejecting it.)

Burning the CD takes a few minutes. When the progress bar indicates that the job is complete, you've got yourself a backup. You can open the CD to confirm that your files and folders are really there, or just take it out of the Mac (press the Eject key on your keyboard again). Remove the CD carefully, avoiding touching the bottom, and label the top with a permanent marker. Your data is safe — for now.

Burning CDs is also great for taking files and folders from one place to another, or for distributing files to other people. In fact, the CDs you make this way even work on Windows PCs.

You can make as many copies of a file as you want without ever experiencing a loss of quality. You're digital now, kids.

(P.S. — If you've signed up for a *.Mac account,* which costs $100 a year, you get a bunch of Internet goodies described in Chapter 6. One of them is a program called Backup that backs up your stuff *automatically,* which saves you the hassle of following all the steps you've just read.)

Method 2: Back up onto another Mac

If you have more than one Mac, here's a brilliant idea: Connect them with a network wire, a scheme described in Chapter 14. Then use your two Macs as backup disks for *each other.* Chapter 14 tells all.

Floppy? What floppy?

Many computer users back up their work by copying their important icons onto floppy disks. Unless your computer-store salesman was a fast-talking slimeball, however, it should be no surprise to you by now that your Mac *doesn't have* a built-in floppy-disk drive.

The truth is, floppy disks don't hold nearly enough to make good backup disks. If you have your heart set on one, though, you can buy an external floppy drive for about $80, as described on these pages.

Method 3: Buy a backup drive

The backup methods described so far are especially likeable because they're free, free, free!

But if your cheapskate gene isn't quite as dominant as mine, you may find comfort in *buying* a solution to the backup problem. You can, for example, buy a backup hard drive that plugs into the back of your Mac. (If you have an Apple iPod music player, you've got a *fantastic* backup hard drive. It works just like any other add-on hard drive.)

The advantage here is that you don't have to use up a CD, or completely erase a CD-RW, each time you want to back up; you can copy and erase files and folders to these disks selectively, as the mood suits you.

Once that hard drive is hooked up, turned on, and running, its icon shows up on the right side, just beneath your hard-disk icon. Drag your Home folder onto it, just as shown in Step 4 of the previous step-by-steps.

When What Was Found Is Now Lost

Okay. You've practiced saving and retrieving files. Yet still it happens: You can't find some file you were working on.

This is nothing to be ashamed of! Thousands of people lose files every day. But through the intervention of caring self-help groups, they often go on to lead productive, "normal" lives.

Here's what to do: Sit up straight, think positive thoughts, and open the folder that you think might contain the missing icon — even if that's your Home folder.

The Search bar

See the little Search box at the upper-right of the window? If you don't see the word *Selection* in light gray (meaning, "Search only inside the window I've opened"), click the magnifying glass and use it as a menu, like this:

Type a few letters of the missing file's name. (Capitals don't matter, but spaces do!)

As you type, the Mac turns into your personal electronic butler, which spends the next few seconds rummaging through the attics, garages, and basement of your Mac. Now the window lists only the icons whose names contain what you looked for. At this point, you can perform any of the following stunts.

Click here to make the Search box empty again and return to the regular list of all files in this folder.

Double-click an icon to open it.

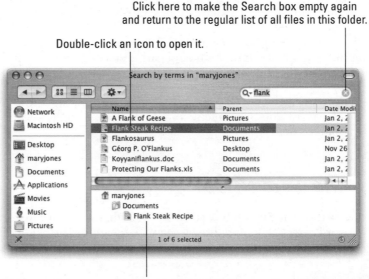

This area shows you where the highlighted file is, no matter how many folders deep it's buried. You can double-click any file or folder in this list, too, to open it.

The Find command

The trouble with that little Search box is that it searches only the *names* of your files. What if you can't *remember* what you called it — you just know you wrote it last Sunday? Or what if you want to find and throw away only *very big* files, regardless of their names, to make more free space on your hard drive?

Now you know why the File menu has a Find command. It brings up a dialog box that lets you hunt down icons using extremely specific criteria. If you spent enough time setting up the search, you could use this program to find a document whose name begins with the letters *Psy,* is over one megabyte in size, was created after 3/1/04 but before the end of the year, was changed within the last week, has the file name suffix *.doc,* and contains the phrase "aversion therapy."

To use the Find window, you need to feed it two pieces of information: *where* you want it to search, and *what* to look for.

Where to look

The pop-up menu at the top of the window lets you specify where you want Find to do its searching. Your choices are Everywhere; Local Disks (that is, your hard drive but *not* any other computers on the office network, if you're on one); Home (your Home folder); and Specific Places, which lets you limit your search to certain disks or folders, just by dragging them into the list like this —

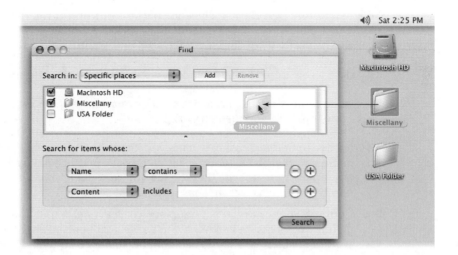

— and making sure that their checkboxes are turned on.

What to look for

The first time you ever open the Find window, two boxes appear that need filling in: Name and Content (that is, words *inside* the files).

But those are only starting points. Using the pop-up menus that appear here, you can define a search using up to 11 different criteria, like this:

To add a criterion to the list, click one of the + buttons at the right end of the dialog box. A new row appears in the Find window, whose pop-up menus you can use to specify *what* date, *what* file size, and so on.

To delete a row from the Find window, click the – button at its right end.

Here are a few examples of the kinds of information you can search for, as they appear in first pop-up menu of a row.

- ✔ **Name.** To find a file whose name you know, just type a few letters of its name into the blank. (Capitalization doesn't matter.) Use the second pop-up menu to specify that the file you're seeking *contains* the phrase you typed, *begins* with it, *ends* with it, and so on.

- ✔ **Content.** Sooner or later, it happens to everyone: A file's name doesn't match what's inside it. Maybe you wrote a 253-page thesis on Wombat Worship Societies, but you accidentally *named* that file "Gift Ideas for Marge."

   Fortunately, the Mac is smart enough to search for words *inside* your documents. Choose Content from the first pop-up menu. Then, in the empty text box, type *wombat,* or whatever words you're looking for.

(They don't have to be together. If you type in *French fries,* the Find program will also find a file containing a sentence like, "The French electrical
committee found that voltage over 14,000 watts often fries the very
wires that conduct it.")

✔ **Date created, date modified.** These options let you search for files
according to when you first created them or when you last saved them.

You don't have to be especially precise. For example, you can set up the
pop-up menus so that they say, "is within" and "1 month" may be just
what you need when you only vaguely remember when you last worked
with the file.

If you hit the + button again, in fact, you can create a *second* Date row —
a great trick that lets you round up files that you created or edited
between two dates. Set up the first Date row to say "is after," and the
second one to say "is before."

✔ **Kind.** These two pop-up menus let you search for everything that is, or
isn't, a certain kind of file — a folder, a picture (image), and so on.

✔ **Label.** As noted at the end of Chapter 2, Mac OS X lets you tag certain
icons with text-and-color labels. Even better, it lets you round them up
later, for backing up, deleting, or burning to a CD en masse, for example.
This pop-up menu lets you specify which label you want to use for finding them all, wherever they may be hiding.

✔ **Size.** Using this control, and its "is less than"/ "is greater than" pop-up
menu, you can restrict your search to files of a certain size.

You have to type in the file's size in KB, or kilobytes. In time, you'll get a
good feeling for these, but a one-page text document might occupy
about 10 KB on your hard drive; a 4 x 6 digital photo might fill up 900 KB;
and digital movies take you into the realm of *megabytes* (MB) and *gigabytes* (GB). (There are 1,024 kilobytes in a megabyte, and 1,024
megabytes in a gigabyte. Yes, those are strange numbers, but computers
don't have ten fingers like you do; they think in multiples of 8 or 16.)

Once you've set up the search, click the Search button (or press your Return
key). After a moment, the window changes to show you a list of the files it
found that match your criteria. From this list, you can double-click a file to
open it, drag it out of the window to move it or copy it, and so on.

Top Ten Word-Processing Tips

1. Select a word by double-clicking — and then, if you keep the mouse
button on the second click and drag sideways, you select additional text
in complete one-word increments.

2. Never, never, never line up text using the space bar. It may have worked in the typewriter days, but not any more. For example, you may get things lined up like this on the screen:

1963   1992   2001
Born   Elected President   Graduated college

Yet, sure as death or taxes, you'll get this when you print:

1963   1992   2001
Born   Elected President   Graduated college

So instead of using spaces to line up columns, use *tab stops* instead.

3. You can select all the text in your document at once by using the Select All command (to change the font for the whole thing, for example). Its keyboard equivalent is almost always ⌘-A.

4. Don't use more than two fonts within a document. (Bold, italic, and normal versions of a font only count as one.) Talk about ransom notes!

5. Don't use underlining for emphasis. You're a typesetter now, babe. You've got *italics!* Underlining is a cop-out for typewriter people.

6. The box in the scroll bar at the right side of the window tells you, at a glance, where you are in your document.

   By dragging that box, you can jump anywhere in the document.

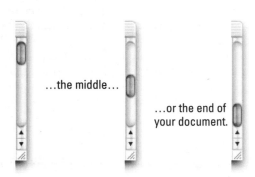

A scroll bar is like a map. The position of the blue handle tells you whether you're at the beginning...

...the middle...

...or the end of your document.

You can move around in two other ways, too:

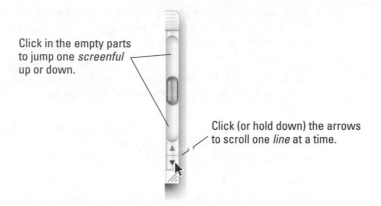

Click in the empty parts to jump one *screenful* up or down.

Click (or hold down) the arrows to scroll one *line* at a time.

7. You've already learned how to *copy* some text to the Clipboard, ready to paste into another place. Another useful technique is to *cut* text to the Clipboard. Cut (another command in the Edit menu) works just like Copy, except it snips the selected text out of the original document. (Cut-and-paste is how you *move* text from one place to another.)

8. It's considered uncouth to use "straight quotes" and 'straight apostrophes.' They hearken back to the days of yore — your typewriter, that is. Instead, use "curly double quotes" and 'curly single quotes' like these.

   You can produce curly double quotes by pressing Option-[(left bracket) and Shift-Option-[for the left and right ones, respectively. The single quotes (or apostrophes) are Option-] (right bracket) and Shift-Option-], for the left and right single quotes, respectively.

   But who can remember all that? Fortunately, all word processors (TextEdit, AppleWorks, Microsoft Word, and so on) all offer an *automatic* curly quote feature, which is a much better solution.

   (On the other hand, don't type or even paste curly quotes into an e-mail message; they come out as bizarre little boxes and random letters at the other end.)

9. In the business world, the word processor almost everyone uses is Microsoft Word. If you have it, great; you'll be treated as one of the gang.

   If you don't, you can use TextEdit to create Word files for sending to other people, no matter whether they use the Macintosh or a Windows PC. (It can also open Word files that *they* send *you).*

   First, make sure that there's a command in the Format menu called Make Plain Text. (Don't *choose* this command, just *look* for it. If it says Make Rich Text instead, you can't create a Microsoft Word file. Unless you *choose* Make Rich Text first. If that makes any sense.)

Then, after typing up and formatting your document, open the File menu and choose Save As. When the Save dialog box appears, you'll note a pop-up menu at the bottom that says File Format — and one of the choices here is Word Format. That's what you want.

When you send the resulting document to other people, they'll have no idea that you did not, in fact, spend $300 on a copy of the real Microsoft Word.

10. You know how to select one word (double-click it). You know how to select a line (drag horizontally). You know how to select a block of text (drag diagonally through it). By now, you're probably about to reach Selection-Method Overload.

But none of those techniques will help when you want to select a *lot* of text. What if you want to change the font size for *ten pages'* worth?

Instead, try this two-part tip: First, click at the *beginning* of the stuff you want to highlight so that the insertion point is blinking there.

Now scroll to the *end* of what you want to highlight. Hold down the *Shift key* with one hand and click the mouse button with the other. Magically, everything between your original click and your Shift-click gets highlighted!

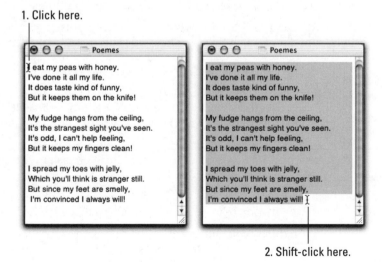

1. Click here.

2. Shift-click here.

Chapter 5

A Quiet Talk about Printers, Printing, and Fonts

• •

In This Chapter

▶ Printers and how much they cost

▶ How to hook up and start printing

▶ The truth about fonts — and Font Book

• •

*Y*ou, gentle reader, are fortunate that you waited until now to get into the Mac. You completely missed the era of *dot-matrix* printers, whose print-outs were so jagged that they looked like Dante's *Inferno* written in Braille.

If you bought a printer, it probably falls into one of two categories: *laser printers* and *inkjet printers*.

Inkjet Printers

The least expensive kind of printer is called an *inkjet*. Hewlett-Packard (HP), Epson, and Canon all make excellent color models. A typical inkjet looks like this:

Tales of dpi

Why have America's scientific geniuses invented all these different kinds of printers?

In a word, they're on a quest for higher *dpi*. That stands for "dots per inch," and it measures the quality of a printout. We're talking about *tiny* dots, mind you — there are about 100 of them clumped together to form the period at the end of this sentence. Clearly, the more of these dots there are per inch, the sharper quality your printouts will have.

Old laser printers manage 300 dpi, and today's generally do 600 dpi. A typical inkjet printer, such as a DeskJet, sprays 720 or even 1,440 dpi onto your paper. Photos printed by a 1,440 dpi printer *look* like photos, let me tell you.

Pretty good, you say? Yeah, well, so's yer ol' man — this book was printed on a *2,400* dpi professional printer!

When you buy one, a critical point is this: *Make sure it's compatible with Mac OS X.* Ask the catalog or computer-store representative specifically.

Inkjet printouts generally look terrific, whether it's text or photos (especially when you print the photos on expensive, fancy shiny photo paper). The printers are also small, lightweight, and almost silent. You can feed all kinds of nonliving things through them: tagboard, envelopes, sheet metal, whatever. And they can be had for less than $100.

So what's the catch? Well, they're inkjet printers. They work by spraying a mist of ink. Therefore, the printing isn't laser-crisp if your stationery is even slightly absorbent. You have to replace the ink cartridges fairly often, too, and they're not cheap; if you print photos, you can easily burn through several times the price of the printer just to buy ink. Note, too, that plain-paper printouts smear if they get the least bit damp, making them poor candidates for use during yacht races.

Still, inkjet printers are so compact, quiet, and inexpensive that they're hard to resist, especially if you want to print in color.

Laser Printers

If you can afford to pay something like $300 for a printer, and you don't care about printing photos, some real magic awaits you: *laser printers.*

The printouts are much like photocopies: They're crisp and black, heat-fused to white paper. These laser printers can also print phenomenal-looking black-and-white graphics, like all the diagrams in Macintosh magazines and the weather maps in *USA Today*. They're quick, quiet, and hassle-free; most can print envelopes, mailing labels, and paper up to legal-size (but not tagboard). They're generally much bigger and bulkier than inkjets, as you can see by this example.

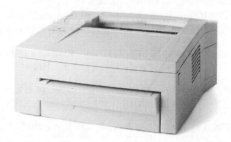

Just remember that laser printers, while superior to inkjets for *black-and-white* quality, aren't what to buy if you want color. Sure, you can *buy* a color laser printer — for several thousand dollars — but the printouts aren't even as realistic as color *inkjet* printers' printouts.

Hooking Up the Printer

Most modern inkjet printers connect to the Mac with a *USB* cable — and USB means U Should B thrilled. Anything you plug into your Mac's USB jack works the first time, every time, with no hassle, no figuring out, and no turning the computer on or off. (And if that sounds perfectly normal to you, then you obviously weren't using computers in the 1980s.)

Note, however, that inkjet printers don't *come with* the USB cable you need to hook them up. You can get one at a computer store, or at a Web site like *www.buy.com*.

If you have a laser printer, you connect it to your Mac either via a USB cable, just like inkjets, or by adding it to your office network as described in Chapter 14 (in which case you use an *Ethernet* cable).

The beauty of Mac OS X is that setting up a printer for the first time is incredibly easy. The first time you want to print something, follow this guide:

1. **Connect the printer to the Mac, and then turn the printer on.**

   Incidentally, if you have a network-connected laser printer, take a moment to perform step 1.5 at this point: From the menu, choose System Preferences. (You read about System Preferences in Chapter 3.)

   Click Network. Double-click your network connection (like Ethernet or AirPort; details in Chapter 14). Click the AppleTalk tab; turn on Make AppleTalk Active, and then click Apply Now.

2. **Open up something that you want to print — a memo you've written in TextEdit, or whatever. Choose Print from the File menu.**

   The Print dialog box appears. This is where you'd specify how many copies of the printout, what pages, and so on.

3. **In the Print dialog box, open the Printer pop-up menu and choose Edit Printer List.**

   A program called Printer Setup Utility opens automatically. You could also have opened it manually from your Utilities folder (which is inside the Applications folder).

   If you've never before hooked up a printer to your Mac, Printer Setup Utility shows you this message:

4. **Click Add.**

   Now a strange little window appears. If the name of your printer shows up automatically at this stage, skip to Step 6.

   But if you find the Directory Services window empty, you need to tell Printer Setup Utility where to look to find its new printer:

5. **From the *upper* pop-up menu, choose the kind of printer you intend to use: USB, AppleTalk, or whatever.**

In other words, tell Printer Setup Utility how the printer is connected to the Mac. For example, choose USB if you've connected an inkjet printer to your USB jack. (You may see a brand-named version here, like Epson USB or HP USB; choose that, if it matches your printer brand.) Choose AppleTalk if you're connected to a laser printer via an Ethernet network cable or AirPort wireless network.

After a moment, the names of any printers that are turned on and connected appear in the printer list. For most people, that means just one printer — but one's enough.

6. Click the name of the printer you want to use, like this:

As an optional step, you can open the Printer Model pop-up menu at the bottom of the dialog box. Choose your printer's manufacturer (like HP or Canon), and then, in the list that appears, choose your particular printer's model name, if you can find it. That's how your Mac knows what printing features to offer you when the time comes: double-sided, legal size, second paper tray, whatever.

7. Click Add.

After a moment, you return to the main printer list window, where your printer now appears. You're ready to print.

After All That: How You Actually Print

The moment has arrived: You'd actually like to *print* something.

Make sure whatever you want to print is on the screen: the ransom note you prepared in TextEdit, perhaps. From the File menu, choose Print. A dialog box appears; it looks different depending on your printer, but this one is typical.

Tab!   Tab!   Return Key!

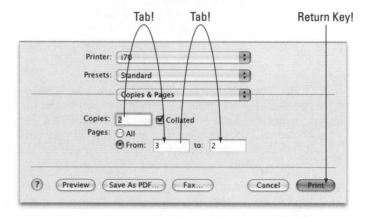

For 95 percent of your life's printouts, you'll completely ignore the choices in this box and simply click the Print button.

For the other 5 percent of the time, the main thing you do in this dialog box is tell the Mac which pages of your document you want it to print. If you just want page 1, type a *1* into *both* the From and To boxes. If you want page 2 to the end, type *2* into the From box and leave the To box empty.

Specify how many copies you want, if you want more than one, by clicking and typing a number in the Copies box.

And if you're some kind of lottery winner, and you own *more than one* printer, this is also where you can choose which one you want to use (by choosing its name from the top pop-up menu).

Using the Tab key in dialog boxes

Now would be a good time to mention what the Tab key does in dialog boxes. Suppose you want to print *two* copies of page 3. Instead of using the mouse to click in each number box on the screen, you can just press Tab to jump from box to box.

Therefore, you'd just type **2** (in the Copies box); press Tab and type **3** (in the From box) and press Tab and type **3** again (in the To box), as shown in the previous illustration. And the mouse just sits there gathering dust.

Anyway, after you're done filling out the options in this box, you can either click the Print button *or* press the Return key. (Remember, pressing Return is always the same as clicking the blue, pulsing button.) The Mac should whir for a moment, and pretty soon the printout will come slithering out of your printer.

This handy shortcut — using the Tab key to move around the blanks and pressing the Return key to "click" the OK or Print button — works in *any* dialog box. In fact, any time you ever see a blue, pulsing button, as shown in the preceding illustration, you can press the Return or Enter key instead of using the mouse.

Other options

See the Copies & Pages pop-up menu in the previous illustration? Hidden inside is a long list of other commands. Each changes the controls in the Print dialog box itself. The precise options are different for every printer model, but here are a few favorites:

✔ **Layout.** You can save paper and ink or toner cartridges by printing several miniature "pages" on a single sheet of paper, as illustrated here:

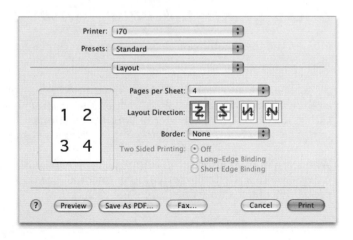

By asking the Mac to print several pages per sheet, you can compare various designs, look over an overall newsletter layout, and so on. Using the Border pop-up menu, you can also request a fine border around each miniature page.

✔ **Scheduler.** This option lets you specify *when* you want your document to print. If you're a freelancer, sitting at home with an inkjet on your desk, you'd probably just as soon get your printouts *right now*. But if you're printing 500 copies of your résumé in a big office where other people on the network are waiting for *their* printouts, you might see the value of this option.

✔ **Paper Handling.** Here, you can opt to print out your pages in reverse order so that they stack correctly, or you can print just odd or even pages so that you can run them through again for double-sided printing.

✔ **Quality & Media.** Here's where you tell the printer what kind of paper you've put into it: glossy photo paper, plain paper, whatever.

✔ **Save As PDF.** If you click this button, you won't get a paper printout at all. Instead, you'll get a file on your hard drive — a *PDF file,* or *Acrobat file,* as it's known.

If you're a novice at this kind of thing, you may not care about PDF files. But in the real world, you encounter them fairly often. Each PDF file contains a complete, self-contained image of your printout, suitable for sending to a print shop, or, indeed, anyone with a computer. They'll be able to open and print your document without requiring the program you used to create it, the fonts you used — or even the document itself.

Once everything looks good, click Print to set your printer into motion.

Micro-managing your printouts

Most of the time, you'll simply want to print a document and get on with your life.

It's worth noticing, though, that you have a lot of control over the printouts as they're being born. The key is to open the program called Printer Setup Utility. It's in the Utilities folder of your Applications folder (you might want to drag Printer Setup Utility onto your Dock so it's easier to get to).

When you open Printer Setup Utility, you'll see a list of printers (which, unless you're a particularly wealthy individual, or you work in a corporation, probably contains only one printer).

If you double-click a printer's name *after* you've started printing some things but *before* they're finished being printed, you see them listed here, like this:

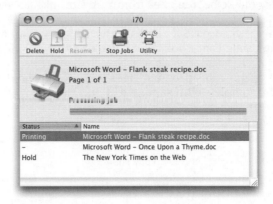

Here are some of the ways in which you can control these waiting printouts, which Apple collectively calls the *print queue:*

- **Delete them.** By clicking an icon and then clicking the Delete button at the bottom of the window, you remove items from the list of waiting printouts. Now they won't print.

- **Put them on pause.** By highlighting a printout and then clicking the Hold button, you pause that printout. It won't print out until you highlight it again and click the Resume button. This pausing business could be useful when, for example, you need time to check or refill the printer.

- **Halt them all.** You can stop all printouts from a specific printer by clicking the Stop Jobs button. (They resume when you click the button again, which now says Start Jobs.)

Font Book: Just Your Type

The various *fonts* (typefaces) listed in the Font menus of your programs (like Microsoft Word) or in the Font Panel (of programs like TextEdit) are amazing. They look terrific on the screen and even better when printed, and they're never jagged-looking like the computer fonts of the early days.

But the paltry 100-plus typefaces that come with Mac OS X may be more than you need — so many that you have to hunt through the menus for your favorites — or not nearly enough, in which case you might want to buy more or try out some free ones from Web sites like *www.macfonts.com.*

Either way, Mac OS X comes with a simple way to add or remove fonts: a program called Font Book, which you can find in your Applications folder.

Just opening this program gives you one special treat: a handy list of all your fonts, complete with sample text, like this:

Fonts in the Mac OS 9 System Folder

Fonts everyone shares

Your personal fonts

Click a triangle to see the font variations in a font family.

The Font Book list also makes it clear that your Mac actually maintains *three different* sets of fonts, for three different purposes. If you feel up to peeking into something that's perhaps a tad more technical than you're used to, click the All Fonts triangle to expose the names of these three font sources, which are indicated in the picture above:

✔ **User fonts.** When you read Chapter 13, you'll discover that in school, family, and business situations, different people may use the Mac at different times. To keep all their stuff separate, Mac OS X offers something called *user accounts.* You've been using one since the day you turned on the machine, whether you realized it or not.

Each account has its own Home folder, its own e-mail collection, its own desktop picture, and so on — and its own private font collection. That's what's meant by "User fonts": typefaces that *only you* get to use when you've signed in to your account. (Behind the scenes, these fonts are in your Home folder, in the Library folder, in a Fonts folder.)

If you don't share your Mac with anyone, then you may as well ignore this folder.

✔ **Computer.** This set represents fonts that *all* account holders can use. (If you open the Macintosh HD icon on your desktop, then open Library, you'll find this Fonts folder.)

✔ **Classic Mac OS.** Here, you'll find the fonts that are available when you use your Mac in *Classic mode* (see Chapter 12). But as a handy bonus, you also get to use these fonts when you're using Mac OS X.

Inspecting your fonts

To inspect your fonts, click Computer, for example, click the first font name, and then press the down-arrow key. As you walk down the list, the rightmost panel shows you a sample of each font.

Blurry vision, even with glasses

Text on your Mac's screen generally looks extra smooth, as though everything you type has been professionally typeset. That's because Mac OS X slightly blurs the edges of every letter, as shown here at top.

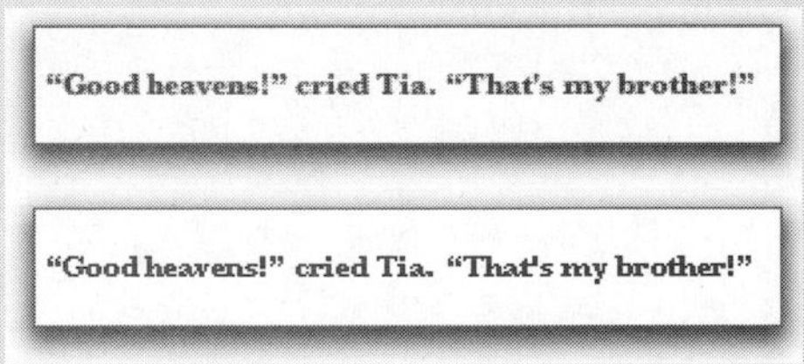

"Good heavens!" cried Tia. "That's my brother!"

"Good heavens!" cried Tia. "That's my brother!"

But at smaller type sizes, some people feel that this text-smoothing business actually makes text *less* readable.

If the smoothing bugs you, you can turn it off, which will make text appear as it does here at bottom.

To do so, open System Preferences (choose its name from the menu, for example). In the System Preferences window, click the Appearance icon. At the bottom of the window, you'll see an option called, "Turn off text smoothing for font sizes __ and smaller."

Use the Size pop-up menu to designate a different cutoff point. Choose 12 from this pop-up menu, for example, to turn off smoothing for 12-point (and smaller) type. (These settings have no effect on your printouts, by the way — only on screen display.)

You can also open any font family's flippy triangle (or highlight its name and then press the right arrow) to see the font *variations* it includes: Italic, Bold, and so on.

Adding, removing, and hiding fonts

Here's what you can do with Font Book:

- ✔ **Install a font.** When you double-click a font file's icon in the Finder, Font Book opens and presents the typeface for your inspection pleasure. If you like it, click Install Font. You've just installed it into *your account's* Fonts folder, so that it appears in the Font menus of all your programs. (It also shows up in the User font category within Font Book. If you'd rather make it available to *all* account holders, drag the font's name out of the User fonts list and onto the Computer category name.)

- ✔ **Remove a font.** If you don't think you'll have much use for a certain font — one of the foreign-language fonts that come with Mac OS X, for example — click its name in the Font Book list and then press the Delete key. (You'll be asked to confirm the decision.)

- ✔ **Hide a font.** Instead of *deleting* a font, you may prefer to simply *disable* it, thereby making it disappear from the Font menus of the programs you use. (You can always turn a disabled font back on if you ever need it again.)

  To disable a font, just click it and then click the Disable button beneath the list. Its name now appears gray, and the word Off appears next to it. (To turn the font on again, highlight its name and then click the Enable button.)

Most of the time, any changes you make in Font Book have an immediate effect on programs that are already open. In some cases, though, you may have to quit and re-open a program to make the changes "take."

Part II
The Internet Defanged

The 5th Wave   By Rich Tennant

"Well, right off, the response time seems
a bit slow."

In this part . . .

1 know, I know: If you hear one more person start droning on about the Internet, the Web, or the Information Superhighway, you'll tie them to a chair and make them watch 18 hours of the Home Shopping Network.

Actually, though, despite the overwhelming abundance of ridiculous, time-wasting chaff in cyberspace, there's also a lot of useful stuff, plus Dilbert cartoons for free. The next few chapters tell you how to get it.

Chapter 6

Faking Your Way onto AOL and the Internet

*1*f you haven't heard of America Online or the Internet by now, you must've spent the last ten years in some Antarctic ice cave. These days, you can't make a move without seeing an e-mail address on someone's business card, a World Wide Web address (like *www.moneygrub.com*) on a magazine ad, or the glazed raccoon look of the all-night Internetter on a friend's face.

Going online gains you endless acres of features: the ability to send e-mail, instantly and for free; incredible savings when you buy stuff (no middleman!); vast amounts of reading and research material (*Time* magazine, *The New York Times*, and so on, *free*); discussion bulletin boards on 60,000 topics (left-handed banjo-playing nuns, unite!); live, typed "chat rooms" that bring you together with similarly bored people from all over the world; literally millions of files and programs that you can *download* (transfer) to your Mac, including games, pictures, and so on; and much more.

Before you begin this adventure, though, a grave warning: Going online is every bit as addictive as heroin, crack, or reality shows, but even more dangerous. As you explore this endless, yawning new world, filled with surprises at every turn, you're likely to lose track of things — such as time, sleep, and your family. Take it slow, take it in small chunks, and use these services always in moderation.

Above all, remember that Apple didn't design the Internet. It existed long before the Macintosh. It was invented by a bunch of military scientists in the '60s whose idea of a good conversation was debating things like *TCP/IP, FTP,* and *ftp.ucs.ubc.ca*. As a result, going online is all quite a bit more complicated and awkward than everyday Mac activities.

In other words, if you can't figure out what's going on, *it's not your fault.*

Or in *other* other words, *using* the Internet is pretty easy; *setting it up* has intimidated more than one first-timer. The following pages guide you through the task — but if you'd feel more comfortable asking your neighbor, kid, or neighbor's kid to come over and help you with the first-time setup, you'll be forgiven.

Two Ways to Go Online

Your TV can't show you *The Bachelor* unless it has some way of receiving the broadcast signal (antenna or cable, for example). In the same way, your Mac can't show you your e-mail or a Web page unless *it* has a way to receive the Internet signal.

Most people connect to the Internet using a little circuit board called a *modem,* which dials the Internet over ordinary phone lines.

But a rapidly growing minority connects over higher-speed wires, using *broadband* connections (translation: *much faster* ones) called cable modems or DSL. You pay twice as much for these services (about $40 a month instead of $20), but they have a lot to offer. See the following sidebar for details.

Cable modems and DSL

If you're willing to pay a little extra money each month, you can contact your local cable TV or phone company about installing a high-speed, ultra-rewarding avenue to the Internet known as a *cable modem* or *DSL* (digital subscriber line). These services cost $35 to $50 per month, and require a visit (and a bill) from a service technician to install. (If you already get cable TV, you might be able to get a good deal on cable-modem service.)

But the results are worth slobbering over: Your Mac is online *constantly,* without even using its built-in modem, and without tying up your phone line. Your Mac gets its own direct umbilical to the Net, at speeds several times faster than even the fastest standard phone-line modem. Web pages appear faster, and files that you download arrive *much* faster. Without a doubt, cable modems, DSL, and similar *broadband* (that is, high-speed) connections are the wave of the future.

If there's only one computer in your house, the service guy will connect the DSL box or cable modem directly to it. If you'd like to *share* your high-speed Internet connection, so that two or more machines can all enjoy it, see Chapter 14.

If you've signed up for one of these broadband connections, you can skip all of the following pages, which describe getting online by dialing up over phone lines. You don't need America Online or EarthLink to connect you.

(On the other hand, both AOL and EarthLink would *love* for you to subscribe to their services *in addition* to your broadband service. They're willing to cut their monthly fee by more than half, and provide bonus goodies like video clips and Internet radio stations, if you connect to them via your own broadband connection.)

Connecting via Modem

Your Mac contains a built-in *modem,* the little glob of circuitry that connects your computer to the phone jack on the wall.

When the Mac makes a call, it dials the phone many times faster than, say, a teenager, but ties up the phone line just as effectively. Therefore, you need to figure out how you're going to plug in your modem:

 ✔ **Share a single line with the modem.** You can visit your local Radio Shack to buy a *splitter,* a Y-jack, a little plastic thing that makes your wall phone jack split into two identical phone jacks — one for your phone and the other for your Mac. This arrangement lets you talk on the telephone whenever you aren't using the modem, and vice versa.

 ✔ **Install a second phone line.** This is clearly the power user's method: Give the modem a phone line unto itself.

 Pros: (1) Your main family phone number is no longer tied up every time your modem dials up the latest sports scores. (2) You can talk to a human on one line while you're modeming on the other. (3) If you're in an office with one of those PBX or Merlin-type multiline telephone systems, you have to install a new, separate jack for the modem *anyway.*

 Cons: (1) This option is expensive. (2) It involves calling up the phone company, which is about as much fun as eating sand. (3) It's only a little bit less expensive than getting a cable modem or DSL installed instead.

If you opt for the dial-up method, plug a telephone wire into the Mac's modem jack. (The modem jack is on the back or side of the computer, marked by a little telephone icon.) Plug the other end into a telephone wall jack.

(If you've equipped your Mac with an AirPort Card — you'd remember having paid extra for it — the setup is slightly different; see Chapter 14.)

America Online or Direct to the Internet?

Seems as though almost every scrap of high-tech fun these days requires paying another monthly fee, and Internet access is no exception.

When it comes to visiting the vast, seething world of cyberspace, you can sign up with one of two sorts of companies: America Online, which kind of pre-packages the Internet to make it cleaner, easier to navigate, and more self-contained; or a company like EarthLink, which ushers you to the front door to the Internet, and then leaves you to fend for yourself. The geeks call Internet-access companies (like EarthLink) *ISPs*, short for *Internet Service Providers*.

I find the term Internet Service Provider — let alone *ISP* — overly nerdy, like calling a writer a "Literature Service Provider." Unfortunately, you can't crack open a magazine or visit a computer club without hearing people talk about ISPs. ("My ISP only charges $15 a month!" "Really? Maybe I'll change ISPs then.") So, with your permission, I'll refer to the companies who rent you time on the Internet as *ISPs,* just like everyone else does.

This chapter describes both methods of getting online: America Online or a traditional ISP. Each route has significant pros and cons, however, which you'll find in the following table. Photocopy, distribute to your family members, and discuss over dinner.

America Online (AOL)	*Internet Service Provider (ISP)*
$24 per month, unlimited access.	$20 to $23 per month, unlimited access.
Occasional busy signals between 6 p.m. and midnight.	Busy signals are rare.
Hangs up on you after several minutes of your not doing anything.	Doesn't hang up on you.
The one program on your hard drive — the America Online program — does everything: e-mail, World Wide Web surfing, chat rooms, and so on.	You generally use a separate program for each function.
Ideal for kids; no pornography on AOL itself.	Adult supervision required.
Very simple, sometimes frustrating; the geeks look down on people with AOL accounts.	More complex, less limiting; nerds admire you for having a "real" Internet account.

America Online (often called AOL) is an *online service*. That is, its offerings are hand-selected by the company's steering committee and sanitized for your protection. Contrast that with the Internet itself, where the offerings constantly change, nobody's in charge, and it's every Mac for itself.

Going onto AOL is like going to a grocery store, where every product is neatly organized, packaged, and labeled. Going onto the Internet, by contrast, is like going to a huge farmer's market that fills a football stadium, packed with whichever vendors happened to show up with their pickup trucks. At the farmer's market, wonderful bargains may await — but it's hard to find anything particular, the turnips may be rancid, and there's no clerk to ask for help.

On the other hand, don't forget that America Online *also* gives you the actual Internet, in addition to its own hand-picked goodies. That is, the AOL grocery store has a back door into the farmer's market.

America Online (AOL), the Cyber-Grocery

If you've decided that AOL is the way to go, your first task should be to install the America Online software for Mac OS X. Lucky for you, Apple stashed it away on your hard drive, in anticipation of exactly this moment.

To find it, open your Applications folder, and then open the Installers folder inside *it*. There you'll see something called Install AOL for Mac OS X. (If you don't see it there, then call America Online at 800-827-6364 and request the starter CD for Mac OS X.)

Click it, click Continue, click Install, and otherwise slog through the series of screens that puts the America Online software on your hard drive. (You can install AOL only if you have an *Administrator* account, as described in Chapter 13.)

When the installation is over, you'll find, inside your Applications folder, a soon-to-be-familiar America Online icon. This is the icon you double-click to get started. (You might want to drag this triangular icon onto your Dock, so you'll be able to find it faster the next time.)

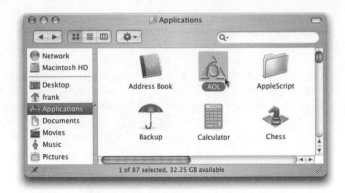

Your first online session

The first time you double-click this icon, you'll be guided through a series of setup steps. You'll be asked:

- ✔ For your name, address, and credit-card number. Remember, though, that you get some ridiculous number of free hours during the first month. Cancel within the first month, and your card is never charged.

- ✔ To choose a local *access number* from a list (and a backup number). Fortunately, AOL has worked out a clever scheme that lets you, as one of 90 percent of Americans living near metropolitan centers, make a *local* call to America Online. Somehow, this system carries your call all the way to Virginia for free. (That's where the actual gigantic AOL computers live.)

- ✔ To make up a "screen name" and a password.

The *screen name* can't contain punctuation. You can use a variation of your name (A Lincoln, MTMoore, Mr Rourke) or some clever CB radio-type handle (FoxyBabe, Ski Jock, NoLifeGuy). Do understand, however, that America Online has about *25 million* members, and *each* of them (including you) can choose up to seven different names, one for each family member. In other words, you can pretty much bet that names like Bob, Hotshot, and Mac Guy were claimed some time in the Mesozoic Era.

If you pick a name that someone has already claimed, the program will make you keep trying — assisted by its own suggestions — until you come up with a name that hasn't been used before.

When all this setup information is complete, your modem begins screaming and making a hideous racket, and you see an AOL logo screen that says things like "Checking Password." Finally, if everything goes well, you're brought to an advertisement screen. Find and click the button that says No Thanks, Cancel, or whatever comes closest to expressing the disgust you must feel at having come so far only to have a slab of crass commercialism thrust into your face. At last you arrive here:

You also get to hear a recording of the famous Mr. Cheerful, the man who says "Welcome!" as though you're *just* the person he's been waiting for all day. If you've got e-mail waiting, he also says "You've got mail!" which he's *really* happy about. (To read the mail, click the "You've Got Mail" icon.)

Exploring by icon

AOL, you'll quickly discover, is a collection of hundreds of individual screens, each of which represents a different service or company. Each day, several of them are advertised on the welcome screen. To jump directly to the advertised feature, click the corresponding icon.

The broader America Online table of contents, however, appears in the floating list at the left side of your screen. Each of *these* buttons takes you to yet another screen, where you can visit related services — for example:

> ✔ The *Research & Learn* button lets you consult a dictionary, a national phone book, or a choice of encyclopedias.
>
> ✔ The *Personal Finance* page is stock-market city: You can check quotes, actually buy and sell, get mutual-fund stats, read tax and investing advice, and so on.
>
> ✔ If you click the *Travel* button, you can actually look up plane fares and even make reservations.

Navigating by keyword

If you poked around enough, clicking icons and opening screen after screen, you'd eventually uncover everything America Online has to offer. In the meantime, however, you'd run up your phone bill, develop mouse elbow, and watch four Presidential administrations pass.

A much faster navigational trick is the *keyword* feature. A keyword is like an elevator button that takes you directly to any of the hundreds of features on AOL, making no stops along the way. Just click inside the strip at the top of the screen (you don't have to delete "Type Keyword/Web address" first) — and then type the keyword of your choice. When you press Return, you're teleported directly to that service.

Here are a few typical AOL services, along with their keywords. Arm yourself with this list so that you make the most of your free month-long trial.

Keyword	Where It Takes You
Access	A list of local phone numbers for America Online. Use this before a trip to another city.
Banking	Check your accounts, pay bills, and so on (certain banks only).
Beginners	A collection of help topics for Mac newcomers.
Billing	Current billing info, disputes, and so on.
Encyclopedia	Your choice of several different published encyclopedias. You just saved $900!
Help	Assistance about America Online itself.
Homework	A place for students to get live, interactive help with homework and research.
Macgame	Files, messages, and discussions of Mac games.
Star Trek	*Star Trek.*
Stocks	Check the current price of any stock. You can even see your current portfolio value.

And how, you may well ask, do you find out what the keyword *is* for something you're looking for? Easy — just type in keyword: *keyword!* You'll get a screen that offers a complete list of keywords.

How to find your way back to the good stuff

With several hundred places worth visiting on AOL — and several *million* places worth visiting on the Internet — it'd be nice if there were a way to mark your place. Suppose you stumble onto this *great* English Cocker Spaniel Owners' area, for example, but you've already forgotten which buttons you clicked to get there.

Simple solution: When you're looking at a screen (or Web page) you might someday like to return to, open the Favorites menu and choose Add Window To Favorite Places (or, while holding down the ⌘ key, tap the + key).

Actually, there's another way: Click the red heart, wherever you see it, as shown here at left:

When the dialog box shown here at right appears, click OK.

Anyway, whenever you want to revisit a Favorite that you've designated in any of these ways, choose its name from the Favorites menu.

To delete something from this list, choose the very first command (Edit Favorite Places) from the Favorites menu. In the resulting window, just click a place's name once and then click the Delete button.

The e-mail connection

One of the best things about AOL is the e-mail — mainly the sheer, ego-boosting joy of *getting* some.

If, in fact, anybody has bothered to write to you (which you'll hear announced by Mr. "You've got mail!"), click the YOU HAVE MAIL button on the welcome screen to see your messages.

After you've read the message, you can (a) reply to it (by clicking the Reply button); (b) send it on to somebody else (by clicking the Forward button); (c) print it (by choosing Print from the File menu); or (d) close its window without saving it. If you do that, the message hangs around in your Old Mail folder for about a week and then disappears forever.

If you'd like to preserve a piece of mail, click the Save To pop-up menu below the list of mail, and choose Incoming/Saved Mail. You've just copied the mail to your Mac, where it's safe and sound. (To find it again later, open the File menu and choose Filing Cabinet.)

As you'll soon discover, a certain percentage of the e-mail you receive is *spam* — junk mail, better known as sleazy advertisements. There's not much you can do with it except (a) click Notify AOL, which is like telling the teacher when some bully is picking on you, and (b) read the discussion at the end of Chapter 8, which tells you how to avoid getting on the spam-senders' lists to begin with.

To *send* a message to somebody, click Write on the toolbar. Type your lucky recipient's e-mail address, a subject, and your message in the appropriate blanks. (Don't forget to press the Tab key to move from blank to blank.) When you're done typing, just press Enter (or click the Send Now button).

If you need to look up somebody's screen name, use this keyword: *members*.

The party line

By far the most mind-blowing aspect of AOL is the *chat rooms*. In a chat room, you'll find up to 23 people chatting away (by typing). The nutty thing is that everybody's talking at once, so the conversation threads overlap, and hilarious results sometimes ensue.

Things to know before entering the Party Zone

If it's your first time in a chat room, you may be nonplused by the gross excesses of punctuation that seem to go on there. Every five minutes, it seems that somebody types {{{{{{{{ Jennifer!!!}}}}}}}} or ****BabyBones!****

Actually, there's nothing wrong with these people's keyboards (or their brains). The braces are the cyberspace equivalent of hugging the enclosed person; the asterisks are kisses. That's how you greet friends who enter the room — online, anyway.

Nonetheless, the chat rooms are an unusual social opportunity: For the first time, you can be the total belle of the ball (or stud of the studio) — the wittiest, charmingest, best-liked person — without so much as combing your hair.

To get to the chat rooms, click the People & Chat button on the main welcome screen. If you click the button called Chat Room Listings, you'll discover that dozens of parties are transpiring simultaneously, each founded on a different topic. Double-click a room's name to go there.

Talking behind their backs

What makes the live chats even more fun is that you can whisper directly into the ear of anybody there — and nobody else can hear you. This kind of behind-the-scenes direct communication is called an Instant Message. To send one, choose Send Instant Message from the People menu (or press ⌘-I). You get a box like this:

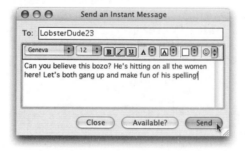

As soon as you type your whispered message and click Send (or press Enter), the window disappears from your screen — and reappears on the recipient's screen! That person can then whisper back to you.

Meanwhile, somebody *else* in the room may have been Instant-Messaging *you*.

If you try to maintain your presence in the main window *and* keep your end of all these whispered conversations in *their* little windows, the hilarity builds. *Nothing* makes a better typist out of you than the AOL chat rooms.

P.S. You can also carry on Instant-Message chats with people who aren't America Online members — that is, people who have standard Internet (ISP) accounts instead, as described later in this chapter. They, however, must first download and install a free program called AOL Instant Messenger onto their computers. For details, use keyword: *aim.*

How to find — and get — free software

For many people, the best part of AOL is the free software. Heck, for many people, that's the *only* part of AOL. Just use keyword: *filesearch;* click Shareware; in the Find What? blank, type the name of the file, or kind of file, you're looking for; and click Search.

In a moment, you're shown a complete listing of all files in the AOL data banks that match your search criteria. Keep in mind that roughly 500,000 files hang out on those computers in Virginia, so choose your search words with care.

If you think a file sounds good, double-click its name to read a description. If it *still* sounds good, click Download Now. The Mac asks where you want the downloaded item stashed. If you choose Desktop from the "Where:" pop-up menu before clicking Save, you'll avoid the crisis of "Where did my downloaded goodies go?" syndrome suffered by 1 in 6 American adults. When you finish using America Online, you'll see the file you received sitting right on the colored backdrop of your Mac (or, as we say in the biz, *on the desktop*).

Your modem then begins the task of *downloading* (transferring) the file to your hard drive. (Make sure that you read the section "How to Open Downloaded Goodies," later in this chapter, for a follow-up discussion on downloading stuff.)

Signing Up with EarthLink

If you've decided to sign up for a direct Internet connection (instead of going the AOL route), send a thank-you note to Apple; signing up for such an account on a Mac is as easy as signing up for AOL. In fact, you may have set up your Internet account the very first time you turned the machine on, as described in Chapter 1.

The EarthLink sign-up program

If not, open your Applications folder, open the Utilities folder inside it, and double-click the program called EarthLink Total Access.

Now the EarthLink sign-up program takes over, showing you a series of screens, asking for your administrator's name and password (see Chapter 13), address, credit-card number, and so on.

Your modem dials an 800 number a couple of times. Along the way, you'll be asked to make up a cybername for yourself (such as *BionicMan83*) and a password that protects your account.

When it's all over, you'll be an official, card-carrying member of the Internet. Now you, too, can have an e-mail address with an @ sign on your business card. Now you, too, can banter at cocktail parties about the ghastly new color scheme on the Microsoft Web site. Now you, too, can slowly drift away from family, job, and reality as you recede into cyberhermitdom.

A little ISP housekeeping

Before you dive headlong into the Internet via EarthLink, you'll thank me later if you take a few minutes to adjust some settings first. The following advice applies *only* to people who dial into the Internet over phone lines — not to the lucky ducks who have cable modems or DSL.

Start by opening System Preferences (click the light-switch icon on the Dock). Click the Network icon. Double-click the line that says Internal Modem. On the PPP screen, you see something like this:

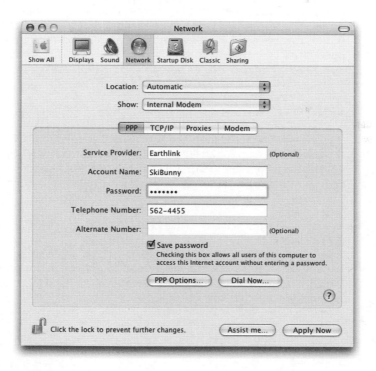

Here you should see, among other things, the EarthLink name and number you'll be using to go online. But at the bottom is a very handy button called PPP Options. It opens a special box that offers an option called "Connect automatically when needed." Turn this on, if it's not already checked. (It makes sure that your Mac dials automatically each time you try to check your e-mail or go onto the Web.)

You might also want to inspect the "Disconnect if idle for __ minutes" option, which prevents your Mac from tying up the phone line all day, even after you've wandered away from the machine to do some yard work. You can change the number of minutes, if you like, or turn off the option altogether.

When you're finished inspecting these options, click OK. Now click the Modem tab (shown in the previous picture), turn on "Show modem status in menu bar," and then click Apply Now. (You've just installed a tiny telephone icon on your menu bar, which you can use as a shortcut to go online and offline; more about this in a moment.) Finally, quit System Preferences.

What's on the Internet

In the following pages, you'll read about the various things that you can do on the Internet. As you read, keep in mind that all these features are available to you regardless of whether you have an AOL account or a real Internet (ISP) account.

E-mail

If you have America Online, see "The e-mail connection" earlier in this chapter. If you've signed up for an ISP like EarthLink instead, see Chapter 8. Either way, get psyched for a feature that'll change your life; as a technology, e-mail ranks right up there with cable TV, frequent-flyer miles, and microwave popcorn.

The Web

Except for e-mail, by far the most popular and useful Internet feature is the World Wide Web. In fact, it gets a chapter all to itself (the next chapter). For now, all you need to know is this:

✔ **On America Online:** A Web browser is built right into your AOL software. In many cases, you wind up on the Web just by innocently clicking some button within AOL — that's how tightly the Web is integrated with America Online these days. (You can tell when you're visiting a Web page, not an AOL page, when the address in the white strip at the top of the window begins with the letters *http.*)

✔ **With an ISP account:** You use a program called Microsoft Internet Explorer (its icon is already on your Dock). It's described in the next chapter.

Newsgroups

The next important Internet feature is called *newsgroups*. Don't be fooled: They have nothing to do with news, and they're not groups. (That's the Internet for ya.)

Instead, newsgroups are electronic bulletin boards. You post a message; anyone else on the Internet can read it and post a response for all to see. Then somebody else responds to *that* message, and so on.

There are about 30,000 different newsgroups, ongoing discussions on every topic — chemists who like bowling, left-handed oboists, Mickey Mouse fans who live in Bali — anything. Here's how you reach these discussion areas:

✔ **On America Online:** Use keyword *newsgroups*. If you then click Search All Newsgroups, you're offered the chance to search the list of 30,000 bulletin boards for one-word topics that interest you: *Seinfeld* or *sailing* or *dogs* or *realestate* or whatever. After you've typed the word you want, click the List Articles button.

Look over the list of results. To try one out, double-click the bulletin board name you want (like *alt.tv.seinfeld*); in the resulting dialog box, click the underlined *Subscribe to newsgroup* link.

A Preferences dialog box appears, where you can specify how many days' worth of messages you want to see. Finally, click Save.

From now on, whenever you feel like doing a little bulletin-board reading and writing, go to keyword: *newsgroups*. Then just double-click your way into a board, as shown here.

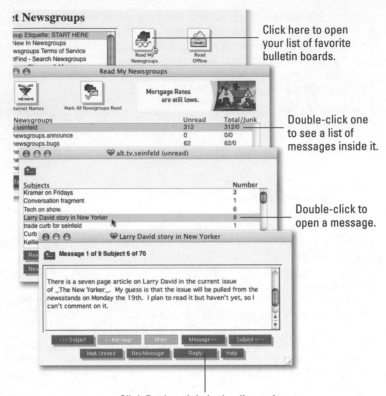

Click here to open your list of favorite bulletin boards.

Double-click one to see a list of messages inside it.

Double-click to open a message.

Click Reply to join in the discussion.

After you've read a message, you can either respond to it (click the Reply button) or just keep reading (click the Next>> button).

✓ **With an ISP:** Mac OS X doesn't come with any software for reading newsgroup messages. But if you've bought Microsoft Office, you can use Entourage, one of its programs, to do so. And if Microsoft Office isn't in your immediate future, go online to a Web site like *www.versiontracker.com* — a massive storehouse of Mac software to download — and download a Mac OS X-compatible newsgroup reader like Thoth, MT-Newswatcher, Hogwasher, or MacSoup.

Newsgroup-reading programs are hairy to set up properly; the assistance of your ISP's cheerful help-line rep is often an important element to your success.

In any case, once you've got the program running, you'll eventually want to pursue a several-prong attack on the newsgroups of the Internet. First, you'll want to download the *list* of those thousands of newsgroups. Then you'll want to search those discussions for something that interests you.

In Entourage, for example, you'll see an icon called *Newsgroup List* (or whatever you called it) at the left side of the screen; double-click it. Entourage asks you if you want to download a list of newsgroups available on that server. Click Yes.

Entourage goes to work downloading the list, which can be quite long and takes several minutes. Once that's done, though, you won't have to do it again. You *should* occasionally update the list, however, by opening the View menu and choosing Get New Newsgroups.

If you're looking for a particular topic — Macs, say — you can view a list of only those discussions containing *Mac* in the titles by typing in a phrase into the "Display newsgroups containing" field at the top of the window. Entourage hides any newsgroups that *don't* match that text.

To read the actual messages in a newsgroup, double-click its name. Another window opens, listing all the messages inside; double-click the one you want to read. (This business of burrowing deeper and deeper looks much like the America Online illustration above.)

Working with newsgroup messages is very similar to working with e-mail messages. You reply to them, forward them, or compose them exactly as described in Chapter 8.

I realize that all of this is about as simple as human genome sequencing, but as I said, nobody ever called the Internet easy.

How to Hang Up

When you're finished with an AOL session, hanging up is no big deal; from the AOL menu, just choose Quit AOL. Your phone line is available once again to the other members of your family.

Getting off the Internet if you have a direct Internet account (ISP), however, is trickier. Imagine that you call another branch of your family tree on New Year's Day. You yourself place the call, but then you hand the phone off to various other family members. "And now here's little Timmy! Timmy, talk to Grandma. . . ."

Using the Internet works the same way. Your Mac places the call. But aside from tying up the phone line, your Mac doesn't actually *do* anything until you open one of the programs you read about in this chapter: an e-mail program or a Web browser, for example. Each of these Internet programs is like one of your family members, chatting with the Big Internet Grandma for a few minutes apiece.

The point here: When you quit your e-mail or Web program, *the phone line is still tied up,* just as though Timmy, when finished talking to Grandma, put the phone on the couch and wandered out to play. When you're finished Internetting, therefore, end the phone call by doing one of the following:

🖝 Wait. After 15 minutes of your not doing anything online (or whatever time you've specified in the Network panel of System Preferences, as described earlier), your Mac hangs up automatically.

🖝 Of course, if other people in your household are screaming for you to get off the line so that they can make a call, you can also hang up manually by choosing Disconnect from the little black telephone icon on your menu bar, like this:

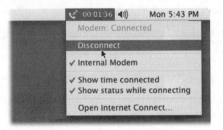

🖝 If, for some reason, you don't see the phone icon on your menu bar, you can also hang up by opening the Internet Connect program (in your Applications folder). Its big fat Disconnect button stares you in the face.

How to Open Downloaded Goodies

It's easy to download software — either from AOL or the Internet. Sometimes people send you files by e-mail (see Chapter 8). Sometimes you'll find something worth downloading on a Web page (see the next chapter).

Either way, learning to *find* and *open* the newly arrived file is something of an art.

In the olden days, the first problem was just *finding* whatever-it-was that you'd downloaded. Fortunately, the Mac makes this a problem of the past. Web browsers like Safari, Internet Explorer, and America Online all plop downloaded files right on your desktop. (And files that arrive by e-mail appear right there in your e-mail program; details in Chapter 8.)

But that's not the end of the problems. The first thing many people discover when they examine a file they've just downloaded is that it's not what they expected. It has some strange file name suffix like *.dmg* or *.sit* or *.zip,* and definitely doesn't look like the photo/program/document they *thought* they'd downloaded.

Two questions, then: How are you supposed to expand your downloaded file back into usable form? And how are you supposed to make sense of things when you download *one* file and windup with *three* on your desktop?

Problem 1: It's encoded

Almost everything on America Online and the Internet has been especially encoded into in a compact format that takes less time to transfer. You'll eventually appreciate this feature. You can think of the downloading time you save as free minutes tacked onto your life.

You can tell that you've downloaded a compressed file by the final letters of its name, which may be *.dmg, .sit, .zip, .tar,* or *.gz.*

Here's the great news: As an added convenience, Web browsers like Safari (Chapter 7), America Online, and Internet Explorer unstuff these files *automatically* when you log off the service.

But here's the bad news: They often *leave behind* the original compressed file on your desktop.

For example, suppose you've just downloaded a file whose name ends in *.dmg.* That is, you've got yourself a *disk image* — a file that, when double-clicked, turns into a simulated CD or floppy disk on your desktop, containing the software you downloaded.

Here's a step-by-step example of how you might work with this disk image.

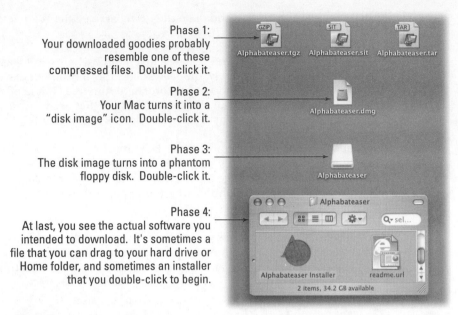

Phase 1:
Your downloaded goodies probably resemble one of these compressed files. Double-click it.

Phase 2:
Your Mac turns it into a "disk image" icon. Double-click it.

Phase 3:
The disk image turns into a phantom floppy disk. Double-click it.

Phase 4:
At last, you see the actual software you intended to download. It's sometimes a file that you can drag to your hard drive or Home folder, and sometimes an installer that you double-click to begin.

Phase 5:
After the installation, you can discard the files from Phases 1 and 3. You may want to hang onto the Phase 2 (.dmg) file, though, in case you ever want to install the software again.

When you're finished working with the simulated floppy drive, you can remove it from your desktop by dragging it to the Trash (whose icon turns into a big silver Eject key as you drag), clicking the Eject button next to its name in the Sidebar, or highlighting it and choosing Eject from the File menu. (You've still got the original .dmg file you downloaded, so you're not really saying goodbye to the disk image forever.)

Problem 2: Wrong format

Bill Gates, as you may have heard, is the wealthiest human on earth. He got that way by foisting something called Windows onto all the office computers of the world.

Fortunately, you've got something that works better: a Mac. Unfortunately, sooner or later, you'll encounter files on the Internet intended for Windows people — or files that are meant to be used by *both* Macintosh and Windows. In both cases, you may be befuddled.

The giveaway is the three-letter suffix at the end of a downloaded file's name. As described in the previous section, suffixes like *.sit, .hqx, .zip, .uu,* and others mean that the file is compressed. But sometimes, even *after* being decompressed, a three-letter suffix remains, such as the common ones revealed in this table:

Suffix	How to Open It
.doc	You've got yourself a Microsoft Word file, the most common word-processing format in the world.
	If you *have* Microsoft Word (you'd probably remember having spent $300 for it), double-clicking a .doc file opens it automatically. If not, double-clicking this kind of document opens into TextEdit, which you encountered in Chapter 4.
.exe	An *executable* file — in other words, a Windows program. By itself, your Mac can't run Windows programs, just as Windows computers can't run Macintosh programs. If your life (or your work life) absolutely depends on your being able to run that Windows program, you can buy and install a program like VirtualPC (*www.microsoft.com/mac*), which is a Windows simulator for the Macintosh.
.jpg or .gif	You've downloaded yourself a photograph! When you double-click it, it will open up into the Mac's picture-viewer program, called Preview.
	If you want to make changes to the photo, you need a photo-*editing* program like Photoshop or AppleWorks.
.pdf	This downloaded item is probably a manual or brochure. It came to you as a *portable document format* (PDF) file, better known as an Adobe Acrobat file. When you double-click it, the PDF file probably opens up into either Preview (the Mac's own PDF reader) or something called Acrobat Reader.
	PDF files are nice because they look like finished documents, complete with pictures, text, fonts, and an attractive layout. You always know that you're looking at precisely what the document's creator intended (which isn't always true of, say, word processing documents).
	You can search a PDF document, and you can usually copy text out of it. But you can't make changes to a PDF document; they're "look, don't touch" files.
.html	A file whose name ends in *.html* or *.htm* is a Web page. In general, Web pages hang out only on the Internet. Every now and then, however, you may find that you've downloaded one to your Mac's hard drive. When you double-click it, Safari, the Mac's Web browser, opens automatically and shows it to you.

The Internet as Giant Backup Disk

As described in Chapter 4, *backing up* means making a safety copy of your work. Some Mac fans buy disk drives for this purpose. Others burn CDs or send files to themselves as e-mail attachments (see Chapter 8). But one of the most convenient ways to back up your Mac is to use the *iDisk.* It's a simulated backup disk that Apple maintains for you, thousands of miles away, somewhere on the Internet — safe from fire, theft, or spilled cans of soda.

The iDisk is one of several features that you get by signing up for a *.Mac account* (say "dot Mac"), which costs $100 per year. The other features include:

- **Backup** is a program that copies your important files to the iDisk automatically.

- **HomePage** lets you create your own Web page *incredibly* easily. You can create a handsome photo gallery of your latest digital camera pictures, for example, or even some of your home movies. You'll find tutorials for this feature in Chapters 10 and 11.

- **iSync** is a clever little program that can keep two Macs up to date with each other's calendar, address book, and Web bookmarks. If you add a phone number at work, for example, you'll find that the same number has magically appeared on your home Mac. (It can actually keep your PalmPilot, iPod, and certain cellphone models up to date, too.)

For details on the .Mac service, and to sign up for a two-month free trial, visit *www.mac.com* and click the Free Trial button. As always, have your credit card handy.

Once you have an account, you can bring your iDisk's icon onto the screen just by choosing its name from the Go menu, like this:

After a while — sometimes a *long* while — you'll see a special disk icon appear at the right side of your screen, and a window showing its folder contents, like this:

The folders include a set of folders whose names match what's in your own Home folder — Documents, Music, Pictures, and so on. You'll also find a Software folder, which is filled with great Mac OS X-compatible programs for you to try.

Copying files to your iDisk

As noted above, the Backup program can copy files to your iDisk automatically. You can sleep well, secure in the knowledge that even if your Mac blows up, your house gets razed to the ground, and your entire neighborhood gets swallowed up by a sinkhole, your files are safe, thousands of miles away on one of Apple's computers. (See the following sidebar for instructions.)

But if you want to copy files to or from your off-site iDisk by hand, just drag them into one of the folders on the iDisk icon. You can't drag stuff onto the iDisk icon itself, nor loose in its window — only into one of the *folders* on it. Remember, too, that the iDisk holds only 100 megabytes of your stuff. That's plenty for word-processing files, graphics, and so on, but probably not enough for movies.

Auto-backup

When you sign up for a .Mac membership, you also get (from the *www.mac.com* Web page) a program called Backup. It gives you an effortless, even automatic backup system for your most important files.

After you've downloaded and installed Backup, you'll find the Backup icon in your Applications folder. When you double-click it, you see the screen shown here.

Start by telling Backup which files and folders you want to have copied onto your iDisk. As you can see, Backup offers a list of *Quick Picks* — checkboxes for stuff Apple thinks you might want to back up. You can turn on these checkboxes; you can also drag important folders and files *right off your desktop* into the Backup list. (To remove something from the list, click it and then press the Delete key.)

As you build your list, Backup shows you how much space (or how many discs) you'll need. Remember that the iDisk holds only 100 megabytes, unless you pay for more space.

Next, specify where you want Backup to put your safety copies, using the top pop-up menu.

The iDisk is only one possibility; you can also save your backed-up files onto a blank CD or DVD, onto another hard drive, onto an iPod, or whatever. (If you have too much stuff to fit on a CD or DVD, on the other hand, Backup can split the job across multiple discs.)

Finally, click Backup Now.

If you've opted to back up onto blank CDs or DVDs, Backup asks you to name the backup set (like *Essentials, 8/2/04*), then tells you when to insert new discs.

In any case, Backup now whirls into action, making the safety copies (and replacing any earlier copies of them).

And by the way: If you're backing up onto your iDisk or a hard drive, you can set up Backup to make *automatic* backups according to a schedule, just by clicking the Schedule Backups button. Backup will kick in at the scheduled time, assuming your Mac is on and the Backup program *isn't* already running. (To find out if your scheduled backup took place, choose Show Log from the File menu.)

If disaster should ever befall your files — dead hard drive, clueless spouse, overtired self — you'll be glad you went through this exercise. Insert the CD or DVD (or connect the hard drive or iDisk) and then use the appropriate Restore command from Backup's top pop-up menu. Turn on the Restore checkboxes next to the stuff you want, and then click Restore Now.

Copying files to the iDisk can take a long time; it's times like these that make you glad you keep a stack of magazines next to the computer. Sooner or later, though, the job is done.

When you're finished performing your backup, drag the iDisk crystal-ball icon to the Trash, or click the Eject button next to its name in your Sidebar.

The Public folder

On your iDisk, you'll even find something called a Public folder. It's a handy convenience: Anything you put in here can be downloaded by other people without your having to tell them your password. Just tell them to proceed like this:

✔ **From a Mac running Mac OS X 10.3 (Panther).** From the Go menu, choose iDisk, then Other User's iDisk. Type in the person's member name and hit Return.

✔ **From a Mac running Mac OS X 10.1 or 10.2.** From the Go menu, choose Connect to Server. At the bottom of the dialog box, type *http://idisk.mac. com/skibunny/Public*. (Replace *skibunny* with the actual .Mac account name.) Click Connect. If a password is required, use *public* as the user name and, well, the password as the password.

✔ **From a computer running Windows XP.** The easiest method is to download a program called iDisk Utility for Windows XP. (It's free from the Web page at *www.mac.com/1/idiskutility_download.html*.) Just double-click it and then type in the .Mac member name whose Public folder you want to open.

Top Ten Best/Worst Aspects of the Net

No question: The Internet is changing everything. As it continues to grow and touch every life, here's what to look forward to:

1. Best: Everyone is anonymous, so everyone is equal. It doesn't matter what you look, sound, or smell like — you're judged purely by your words.

2. Worst: Everyone is anonymous, so everyone is equal. You can pretend to be someone you're not — or a *gender* you're not — for the purposes of misleading other Internet surfers.

3. Best: The cost — $23 a month for unlimited access, or about twice as much for a high-speed connection like a cable modem or DSL.

4. Worst: That's a lot of money.

5. Best: The Internet connects you to everyone. You're only an e-mail or a Web page away from anyone else on the planet.

6. Worst: The Internet *disconnects* you from everyone. You become a hermit holed up in your room, as family, friends, and relationships pack up and leave.

7. Best: The Internet is drawing people away from TV. Statistics show that as more people discover the Web, they spend less time in front of the boob tube.

8. Worst: The Internet is drawing people away from TV. The TV industry is going crazy wondering what to do.

9. Best: The Internet is complete freedom of speech for everyone. No government agency looks over your shoulder; the Net is unsupervised and uncontrolled.

10. Worst: The Internet is complete freedom of speech for everyone. Including pornographers, neo-Nazi groups, and others you may not want your 10-year-old getting chummy with.

Chapter 7

The Weird Wide Web

*T*he most popular part of the Internet is the World Wide Web — you can't help hearing about this thing. Fourth graders run around urging schoolmates to "check out their Web pages." Web addresses show up everywhere — on business cards, in newspaper ads, on TV. (Have you noticed *www.sony.com* or *www.nytimes.com* flashing by at the end of TV commercials? Those are Web addresses.)

The Web has become incredibly popular for one simple reason: It *isn't* geeky and user-hostile, like the rest of the Internet. It looks friendly and familiar to actual humans. When you connect to the Web, you don't encounter streams of computer codes. Instead, information is displayed attractively, with nice typesetting, color pictures, and interactive buttons.

Getting to the Web

The Mac is many things at different times. When you want to jot down a note to yourself, you open Stickies. When you want to check your math, you open Calculator.

And when you want to visit the World Wide Web, you use a program called, with astounding originality, a *Web browser*.

If you use America Online, you're already familiar with your Web browser; it's the same AOL program you've been using since Day One. Click in the keyword strip at the top — where it says, "Type Search words, Keywords or Web addresses here" — and type the Web address you want (such as *www.hamsters.com*).

If you're getting to the Internet in any other way — via EarthLink, a cable modem, or a DSL box — you have your choice of several Web browsers. In your Applications folder, for example, you'll find Microsoft's Internet Explorer. Out on the Internet, you can try browsers called Netscape Navigator, Mozilla, iCab, and Opera.

But the one whose icon came installed on your Dock, and the one that Apple wrote just for the Mac, is called *Safari.* Its icon looks like a compass.

To go a-browsing, fire up your Web browser. If you've set up your Mac to go online, as described in Chapter 6, then your Mac now connects to the Internet, hisses and shrieks (if you connect via modem), and finally shows you a Web page.

Internet Made Idiotproof: Link-Clicking

Navigating the Web requires little more than clicking buttons and those underlined blue phrases, which you can sort of see in the following figure.

When you click an underlined phrase, called a *link,* you're automatically transported from one Web page (screen) to another, without having to type in the usual bunch of Internet codes. One page may be a glorified advertisement; another may contain critical information about a bill in Congress; another might have been created by a nine-year-old in Dallas, to document what her dog had for lunch.

Unfortunately, all of this amazing online multimedia stuff stresses your modem nearly to the breaking point. If you're connected via dial-up modem, you may have to wait a few seconds for each Web page to float onto your screen. (Now you start to understand why some people consider it worth paying $40 a month for cable modem or DSL service, which reduces the wait to almost nothing.)

Where to Go, What to Do on the Web

Once you're staring at your first Web page, getting around is easy. Just *look* at all the fun things to see and do on the Web!

(If you don't see all of these handy buttons, choose
their names from the View menu to make them appear.)

A B C D E F G H

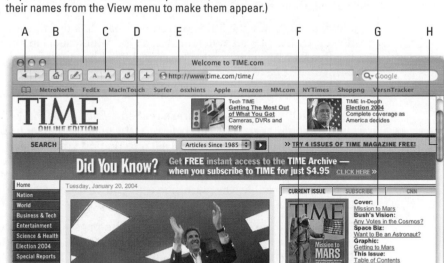

A. Click the Back button to revisit the page you were just on — or the
Forward button to return to the page you were on *before* you clicked the
Back button. (Does that make sense?)

B. The little house icon means, "Take me to my home page" — that is, the
Web page where you start your explorations each day. More on choosing
a home page later in this chapter.

C. Very often, you'll encounter text that's too small to read. This is true in
the real world, of course, but even more so on the Internet.

But Safari can do something *Newsweek* and your typical Dosage
Instructions sticker can't: It can enlarge the type. Just click the larger A
button here. (Click the smaller one to shrink the text.)

D. Web pages often have little text boxes to fill out, like this Search box.
Similar blanks appear when, for example, you're asked to fill out a
survey, type in your mailing address, and so on.

E. Type a new Web page address into the thin horizontal strip at the top of
the browser window and press Return to go to the site. A Web address,
just so you know, is known by the nerds as a *URL* — pronounced "U. R. L."

And where do you find good Web addresses? From friends, from articles, on television, and so on. Every Web address begins with *http://* or *www*.

Incidentally, enjoy the little colored bar that "fills up" this address strip. It's a progress bar, an indicator that says, "Wait a sec, I'm not done painting this Web page picture for you. Until I've filled in the whole address bar, you just have to wait."

F. Clicking a picture or a button often takes you to a new Web page.

G. Clicking a blue underlined phrase (called a *link*) usually takes you to a different Web page. As a handy bonus, these links change to some other color when you see them next. That's to remind you that you've been that way before. (On the other hand, trendy Web designers don't always use blue underlined type for links, which makes it hard for you to figure out what's clickable. One sure sign that you've found a link: Your cursor changes from an arrow into a white-gloved, pointing hand.)

H. Use the scroll bar to move up and down the page — or to save mousing, just press the space bar each time you want to see more. (If that space bar trick doesn't work, first click any blank area of the Web page.)

Ways to search for a particular topic

Suppose you're looking at the Kickboxing Haiku Web page. But now you want to check the weather in Detroit. Because the World Wide Web is indeed a big interconnected web, you could theoretically work your way from one Web page to another to another, clicking just the proper blue underlined links, until you finally arrived at the Detroit Weather page.

Unfortunately, there are several *billion* Web pages. By the time you actually arrived at the Detroit Weather page, the weather would certainly have changed (not to mention Detroit). Clearly, you need to be able to *look something up* — to jump directly to another Web page whose address you don't currently know.

For this purpose, the denizens of the Web have seen fit to create a few very special Web pages whose sole function is to search all the *other* Web pages. If you're on the Web, and don't know where to look for, say, information about Venezuelan Beaver Cheese, you can use the Find commands at sites like Google and Yahoo!.

Searching Google from Google.com

All of these search pages work alike, but Google is the fastest and most accurate. Here, for example, is what Google looks like as you type in a search request for information about dolphins.

After clicking the Google Search button, you're shown a brand-new Web page listing *hits* — that is, Web pages containing the word "dolphin."

See how useful a search page is? This handy Google thing narrowed down our search to a mere *2,900,000 Web pages!* You're as good as home!

Not. You can see here, in a nutshell, the problem with the Web: There's so much darned stuff out there, you spend an *awful* lot of your time trying to find exactly what you want. In this case, most of the matches you've found have to do with the *Miami* Dolphins football team — probably not exactly what your Marine Mammals 101 instructor had in mind.

In this case, you could have clicked the little Help link on the main Google screen. It would have told you that to find a page containing the word "dolphins" *without* "Miami," you can put a minus sign just before the word Miami, like this: *dolphins -Miami.* That would have ruled out all the "hits" containing "Miami."

Who ever said these things were user-friendly?

Searching Google using Safari

Most of the world's Internet addicts use Google by typing *www.google.com* into the address bar, pressing Enter to go there, and then typing *platypus mating habits* into the Google search box. (All right, they don't *always* search for "platypus mating habits," but you get the idea.)

But because you have Safari, the super-browser, you have a much easier way to search Google — a way that doesn't even involve *going* to Google. Just type what you're looking for right into the Search bar, like this —

— and then press the Enter or Return key. Safari automatically sends your request to Google, and then takes you to its screen full of matches.

Searching using Sherlock

When trying to locate a certain piece of information on the Web, most of the world's citizens use a searching Web page like Google. As a Mac owner, however, you are more fortunate. You have Sherlock, a handy program that's specifically fine-tuned to bring you certain popular kinds of up-to-date info from the Internet — minus the waiting, the searching, and the ads.

To try it out, click the the detective-hat-and-magnifying-glass icon on your Dock. (If it's not on the Dock, open your Applications folder and double-click the Sherlock icon there.)

The Sherlock *channels* (icons on its toolbar) bring Web information directly to your Sherlock window, formatted for maximum impact: graphs when you search for stock prices, maps when you search for flights, and so on.

All of the channels are pretty useful — but in particular, don't miss these:

- **Phone Book** offers you a Yellow Pages of every business and organization in the entire United States — an electronic set of books that, in real form, would otherwise fill up your entire bedroom. Remember this feature the next time you're in a strange city and suddenly become desperate for an all-night movie theater, Chinese restaurant, or pharmacy.

- **Flights** shows you a list of flights that match your itinerary, or if you already know a flight number, tells you whether or not it's going to be on time and which airport terminal to go to.

✔ **Translation** translates a phrase you type into any of 17 languages. No, it doesn't have quite the precision of, say, a native speaker of those languages. But it's a lot quicker than a six-month Berlitz language course.

If you live in the United States, though, you'll probably have the most fun with Movies. It's an instantaneously updated database of movies and show times for your neighborhood.

Type your city and state — or just your zip code — into the text box at the top, and then press Enter. After a moment, you'll see a list of movies playing near you — in the first column. Click one to see the theaters where it's playing (in the second column); click one of those to see today's show times (in the last column). Meanwhile, you even see the address of the theater, the movie poster, the movie's rating and length, a description, and — if you wait long enough — even the QuickTime trailer for the movie, if any. Life is sweet.

Useful Web pages: The tip of the iceberg

But there's more to the Web than getting meaningful work done, as millions of American office workers can attest. Here are some good starting places for your leisure hours.

Note, by the way, that their addresses generally begin with *http://www* and end with *.com*. But anyone who actually takes the time to type all that is a sucker. Whenever you spot an address that takes that form, all you have to type into your browser is the *middle* section, omitting the *http://www* and *.com* portions. Safari supplies those letters automatically when you press Enter.

(**Disclaimer:** Web pages come and go like New York City restaurants. I guarantee only that these pages existed the day I typed them up.)

- ✔ *www.louvre.fr* — The Louvre museum home page, where you can actually view and read about hundreds of paintings hanging there.

- ✔ *amazon.com* — An enormous online bookstore, with five million books available, most at a 30 percent discount. Reviews, sample chapters, the works. (All right, also clothes, garden supplies, CDs, appliances, and just about everything else ever manufactured. But books are the best part.) Don't freak out about typing in your credit-card number online; you're far more likely to be ripped off by handing your Visa card to the gas-station attendant or restaurant waiter.

- ✔ *www.dilbert.com* — Today's Dilbert cartoon. And a month of past issues.

- ✔ *www.zap2it.com* — Free TV listings for your exact area or cable company. You can customize it to show only comedies, only prime-time shows, and so on.

- ✔ *www.shopper.com, www.shopping.com, www.mysimon.com* — Comparison-shopping sites that produce a list of Web sites that sell the particular book, computer gadget, iPod, or other consumer good you're looking for. This quick, simple research can save you a *lot* of money.

- ✔ *http://terraserver.microsoft.com* — Satellite photographs of everywhere (your tax dollars at work). Find your house!

- ✔ *www.dictionary.com* — An online dictionary, of course. (Then again, you can also use Sherlock to look up a word.)

- ✔ *www.homefair.com/homefair/cmr/salcalc.html* — The International Salary Calculator.

- ✔ *www.imdb.com* — The Internet Movie Database: An astoundingly complete database of almost every movie ever made, including cast lists, awards, and reviews by the citizens of the Internet.

- ✔ *www.____.com* — Fill in the blank with your favorite major company: Microsoft, Apple, Honda, Sony, CBS, Palm, Symantec, NYTimes, Disney, DavidPogue, and so on. If it's a big company, you can probably guess its Internet address.

Safari Tip-O-Rama

If that tip about leaving off the *http://www* and *.com* business left you patting moist towelettes onto your forehead, you'll really love these other browser tips.

More address shortcuts

When you begin to type into the Address bar, Safari compares what you're typing against a list of Web sites you've recently visited, and displays a list of Web addresses that seem to match what you're typing, like this:

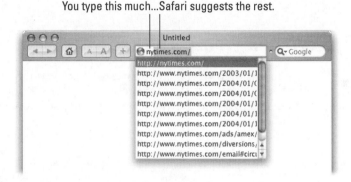

You type this much...Safari suggests the rest.

To spare yourself the tedium of typing out the whole thing, just click the correct complete address with your mouse, or use the down arrow key to reach the desired listing and then press Enter. The complete address you selected then pops into the Address bar.

Even less typing

Safari can also remember user names, passwords, and other information you have to type into Web page text boxes *(forms)* over and over again.

This feature will make itself known, in fact, the first time you type a name and password *into* a Web page. A dialog box like this one pops right up into your face:

(If this doesn't seem to be happening for you, open the Safari menu, choose Preferences, click the AutoFill button, and make sure all three checkboxes are turned on.)

Next time you visit this Web site, you'll find your name and password already filled in. The time you save could be your own.

Saving a good picture

When you see a picture you'd like to keep, hold down the Control key in the corner of your keyboard. When you click the photo, a pop-up menu appears at your cursor tip. From this pop-up menu, choose "Download Image to Disk," as shown here.

After you click the Save button, the result is a new icon on your hard drive — a graphics file containing the picture you saved. (Control-clicking objects on the screen, as you've just done, often produces what's called a *shortcut menu* or *contextual menu*. It's a very common tactic on the Mac, and the equivalent of "right-clicking" on a Windows PC.)

Where's home for you?

Every time you sign onto the Web, your browser starts by showing you the same darned starting page — let me guess: a very complex and daunting-looking Apple page. Wouldn't it be great if you could change the startup page?

You can! From the Safari menu, choose Preferences. Click the General icon, as shown here.

Now just change the Web address in the "Home page" blank to a more desir-able starting point. For example, you might prefer *www.dilbert.com*, which is a daily comic strip . . . or *www.macintouch.com*, which is daily news about the Mac . . . or even your own home page, if you've made one.

Faster — please, make it faster!

If the slug-like speed of the Web, as it trickles into your house over a puny piece of phone wire, is making you sob quietly into your late-night coffee, despair no more. You can quadruple the speed of your Web surfing activities — *by turning off the pictures.*

Yes, graphics are what make the Web look so compelling. But all those pictures are 90 percent of what takes Web pages so darned long to arrive on the screen! You owe it to yourself to try, just for a session or two, turning graphics *off*. You still get fully laid-out Web pages; you still see all the text and headlines. But wherever a picture would normally be — wherever you would have had to wait for eight seconds — you'll see an empty rectangle containing a generic "graphic goes here" logo, often with a label that tells you what picture belongs there. Here, for example, is the CNN page (*www.cnn.com*, of course) with all its graphics gone. See? It's really not so bad — and you feel especially good that you haven't sat there waiting for the *ad* graphics to appear.

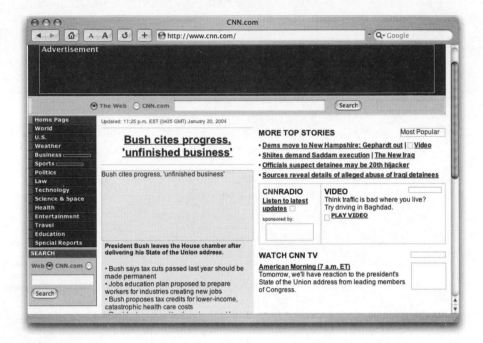

If you like the sound of this arrangement, here's how to make it so. From the Safari menu, choose Preferences. Click the Appearance button, and turn off "Display images when the page opens."

The speed you gain is incredible. And if you wind up on a Web page that seems naked and shivering without its pictures, you can always return to the Preferences box and turn that checkbox on again.

Bookmark it

When you find a Web page you might like to visit again, you're not condemned to writing the address on the edges of your monitor, like some kind of geeky bathroom graffiti. Instead, just choose Add Bookmark from the Favorites menu (or press its keyboard shortcut, ⌘-D).

You're rewarded by the appearance of a little dialog box like this:

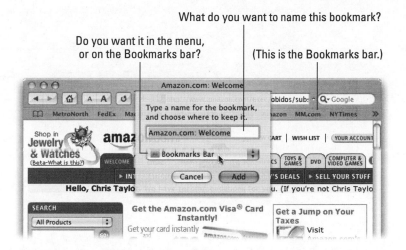

What do you want to name this bookmark?

Do you want it in the menu,
or on the Bookmarks bar?

(This is the Bookmarks bar.)

It's asking you two questions:

🖝 Where would you like me to list this Web page for quick access later? I can either add it to the list in the Bookmarks menu, or I can list it on the Bookmarks *bar* (shown above).

If you opt to list it in the Bookmarks *menu,* you can, if you wish, humor your fastidious inner child by clicking one of the *folders* inside the Bookmarks menu — handy little sub-groupings that keep the menu tidy.

🖝 What would you like to call this bookmark? *Oprah and Me: The Inside Story of the World's Most Powerful Entertainment Figure as Told by Her Superstar's Wardrobe Consultant's Son* may make a dazzling bookmark, but it makes a lousy bookmark *title.* It would fill up your entire Bookmarks bar all by itself, and possibly even protrude beyond the edges of your screen, littering your desk with broken glass.

So Safari is offering you the chance to *rename* this bookmark, perhaps calling it something simpler or shorter *(Dad's Oprah Book).*

Thereafter, the *next* time you want to visit that page, you're spared having to remember *http://www.madonnahairstyles.com* or whatever; you can just choose the page's name from your Bookmarks menu, or click its button on your Bookmarks bar.

To get *rid* of something in your Bookmarks menu, or to rearrange what's in it, click the little book icon at the left end of the Bookmarks bar. You see a window like this:

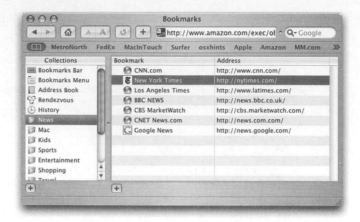

Click the little bullseye next to a page's name (*not* the name itself), and then press the Delete key to get rid of it.

While this bookmark-organization window is open, you can also rearrange your various favorites (by dragging them up or down) or rename them (by clicking *on* the name itself to type a new bookmark name).

When you're finished fiddling with your bookmarks, click the little book icon again to return to the Web already in progress.

Stop the pop-ups!

The citizens of the Internet quietly endure the advertising that fills the top inch of almost every Web page. We understand these ads pay for our free TV listings, free *New York Times,* free Dilbert cartoons, and so on.

But there's a big difference between a calm banner across the top of the screen and a seizure-inducing, blinking, flashing, *pop-up* advertisement that sprouts in a little window right in front of the Web page you're trying to read. Or, even sneakier, a *pop-under* ad that lurks *behind* the page you're reading; you don't see it until you close the main window.

If pop-up and pop-under ads make you, too, itch for a sledgehammer, open the Safari menu and choose Block Pop-Up Windows, so that a check mark appears.

(Occasionally, you'll encounter a Web site that tries to present a *legitimate* pop-up window: one that contains instructions, an important form to fill out, an e-mail message, or whatever. In these cases, just choose the Block Pop-Up Windows again to turn the check mark off.)

Impersonating Internet Explorer

Sooner or later, you'll run into a Web site that doesn't work in Safari. Maybe it doesn't look right, maybe the buttons on it don't respond to your clicks, or maybe you just get a message that says, more or less: "You appear not to be using a browser we recognize. Go buy a different computer and try again."

The reason: When you arrive at a Web site, your browser identifies itself. Many Web sites are programmed to welcome big-name Web browsers like Microsoft Internet Explorer, and to deliberately lock out up-and-comers like Safari.

In such times of trouble, you have two options. First, you can use Internet Explorer instead. (It's in your Applications folder. Although it's slower and can't block pop-up ads, it's otherwise a lot like Safari.)

Second, if you're willing to dip your big toe into slightly more techie territory, you can make Safari *impersonate* Internet Explorer, which is often good enough to fool the picky Web site into letting you in.

The key to this trick is Safari's Debug menu, which is generally hidden. You can make it

appear by downloading Safari Enhancer, a free program available at *www.versiontracker.com*. It offers a simple checkbox that turns on the Debug menu.

When you next open Safari, the new Debug menu appears right next to Help. Most of its commands are designed to appeal to programmers, but the one you want — User Agent — is useful indeed. It lets Safari masquerade as a different browser. Choose Mac MSIE 5.22, for example, to assume the identity of Internet Explorer for Macintosh.

While this tactic often works to gain Safari entrance to those uppity Web sites, there's a dark side to using this trick. If enough people pretend that they're using Internet Explorer, whoever created the Web site will never know how many people are actually using Safari — and will never get around to fixing the Web site in the first place.

Whenever you encounter a Web site that gives Safari trouble, therefore, you should also take a moment to notify the creators of the site that you want Safari compatibility.

Open a new window

Usually, clicking a link is like changing the TV channel: A new image fills the same window you've been watching.

If you click a link while pressing the ⌘ key, however, you open up a *second* browser window in front of the first. That's an especially useful tactic when you're browsing a list of Web sites — the results of a search, for example — that you want to investigate one by one. Just ⌘-click the first one to open it into a new window; check it out; then close that window to return to the one containing your list. ⌘-click the second one in the list, and so on.

Open a new tab

Actually, ⌘-clicking a link to open it into a new window is only the beginning of the window fun you can have in Safari. True aficionados go one step further by turning new links not into *windows,* but *tabs* of the *same* window. This arrangement makes the top of your window look like this —

— and keeps things extra tidy, because all of your Web pages are actually in a single window. You can freely click from tab to tab, essentially keeping a whole passel of Web pages open simultaneously.

To turn on *tabbed browsing,* as this delicious experience is known, open the Safari menu and choose Preferences. Click the Tabs button. Turn on the first two checkboxes, like this:

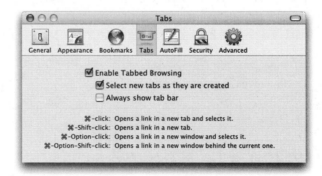

Close the Preferences window.

Now, whenever you ⌘-click a link, or type an address and press ⌘-Return or ⌘-Enter, you open a new *tab,* not a new window as you ordinarily would. You can now pop from one open page to another by clicking the tabs just under your Bookmarks bar, or close one by clicking its X button (or pressing ⌘-W).

You'll thank me in the morning.

The Complete Cookie Cookbook

Spend enough time in the 21st century, and you're bound to hear people talk about their fear of *cookies*. Unless they're avid dieters, they're probably talking about *Web* cookies.

Cookies are something like Web page preference files. Commercial Web sites (Amazon.com, for example) deposit these tiny, mostly invisible preferences onto your hard drive, so that they'll remember your name, address, and other information the next time you visit. If Amazon.com greets you, "Welcome, Casey!" (or whatever your name is), you have a cookie to thank.

Most cookies are perfectly innocuous — and, in fact, are extremely helpful, because they spare you the effort of having to type in your name, address, credit card number, and so on, every single time you visit these Web sites.

But in this age of privacy paranoia, plenty of people worry that sinister cookies may be tracking your movement on the Web. If you're worried, Safari is ready to protect you.

In Safari, choose Preferences from the Safari menu, and then click the Security button. The Accept Cookies buttons let you control just how careful you want to be: You can choose "Never," "Always," or "Only from sites you navigate to" (that is, don't accept cookies sneakily shoved onto your Mac by evil Web sites you don't even know about).

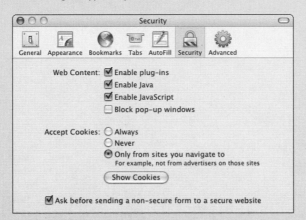

If you choose "Never," you create an acrylic shield around your Mac. No cookies can come in, and no cookie information can go out. You'll have absolute privacy, but you'll also find that the Web is a very inconvenient place, because you'll have to re-enter your information upon every visit, and some Web sites may not work properly. "Only from sites you navigate to" is the best choice.

Learn to love history

The History menu lists the Web sites you've visited in the last week or so, neatly organized into subfolders like "Earlier Today" and "Yesterday." (A similar menu appears when you click *and hold* on the Back or Forward button.) These are great features if you can't remember the Web address for a Web site that you remember having visited, say, yesterday.

And if you find it creepy that Safari maintains a complete list of every Web site they've seen recently, right there in plain view of any family member or coworker who wanders by, choose the Clear History command at the very bottom of the menu. (After all, you might be nominated to the Supreme Court some day.)

Chapter 8

E-mail for He-males and Females

*I*f you have any intention of getting the most from your expensive high-tech appliance, you *gotta* get into e-mail. E-mail has all the advantages of the telephone (instantaneous, personal) with none of the disadvantages (interrupts dinner, wakes you up). It also has all the advantages of postal mail (cheap, written, preservable) with none of its drawbacks (slow speed, paper cuts).

Chapter 6 covers the glorious world of e-mail on America Online. If you're on the Internet courtesy of EarthLink, a cable modem or DSL company, or some other Internet service provider (ISP), however, read on.

Getting into E-Mail

To read and write electronic mail, you need an e-mail *program*. A free Apple program called Mail, for example, is sitting right there on your Mac's hard drive (in the Applications folder), and its icon comes pre-installed on your Dock.

The grisliest part of joining the e-mail revolution is setting up your account for the first time. The good news is that if you signed up for an EarthLink account using the automatic set up program described in Chapter 6, or a .Mac account (also described in Chapter 6), all the blanks should be filled in for you. You're all ready to go a-mailing.

Otherwise, Mail asks you to fill in a bunch of evil-looking blanks — things like SMTP Server, POP3 Server, and so on — the first time you open it. Don't say I didn't warn you. Call up your ISP company and ask for help filling them in.

After asking you to fill in the blanks, Mail offers to import your e-mail collection from whatever e-mail program you *used* to use. In your case, that may be a courteous but irrelevant request; you probably *have* no previous e-mail collection on this Mac. Click the No button.

At last you arrive at the main Mail screen, which looks something like this:

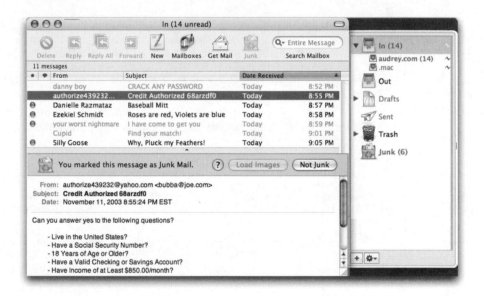

Sending e-mail

To write an e-mail, click the New icon on the toolbar. An empty e-mail message appears, filled with blanks to fill out. Here's how to fill them out, keeping in mind that, as anywhere else on the Mac, you can press the Tab key to jump from box to box:

Click here to save this, without sending it yet, into your Drafts "mailbox.

This person gets the message. (The colored capsule means that this person is in your Address Book.)

Click here when you're finished.   These people get copies.

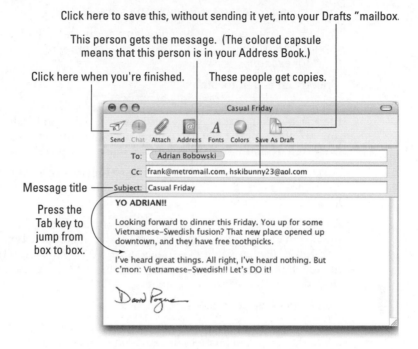

Message title

Press the Tab key to jump from box to box.

1. **Type the e-mail address of the recipient into the To field.**

   If you want to send this message to more than one person, separate their addresses with commas: *sarah@earthlink.net, billg@microsoft.com, george@bush.com.* As you'll quickly discover, e-mail addresses can't include any spaces, always have an @ symbol in them, and must be typed *exactly* right, even if they look like *cc293fil@univ_amx.intermp.com.* Capitals don't matter.

   You don't have to remember and type those addresses, either. If somebody is in your address book (click the Address book icon on the toolbar), just type the first couple letters of his name; Mail automatically completes the address. (If the first guess is wrong, just keeping typing until Mail revises its proposal or until you've typed out the whole address, whichever comes first.)

2. **To send a copy of the message to other recipients, enter the e-mail address(es) in the Cc field.**

   Cc stands for *carbon copy.* Getting an e-mail message where your name is in the Cc line implies: "I sent you a copy because I thought you'd want to know about this correspondence, but I'm not expecting you to reply."

3. **Type the topic of the message in the Subject field.**

   To demonstrate your fine breeding and etiquette, put 1.5 seconds of thought into the Subject line. Use "You left your gloves here" instead of "Yo," for example.

4. **Specify an e-mail format.**

   There are two kinds of e-mail: *plain text* and *formatted* (which Mail calls Rich Text). Plain text messages are faster to send and faster to open, are universally compatible with the world's e-mail programs, and are greatly preferred by many veteran computer fans.

   Formatted messages, for their part, take longer to download, take longer to open, and introduce the risk that you might design something tacky looking.

   To control which kind of mail you're about to send, open the Format menu and choose either Make Plain Text or Make Rich Text. (You can also tell Mail what you'd like to use *most* of the time. From the Mail menu, choose Preferences. Click the Composing icon, and make a selection from the Format pop-up menu.)

5. **Enter the message in the message box.**

   You can use all the standard editing techniques, including text drag-and-drop, the Copy and Paste commands, and so on. If you selected the Rich Text style of e-mail, you can even use the Fonts and Colors button to dress up the message, like this — well, *not* like this:

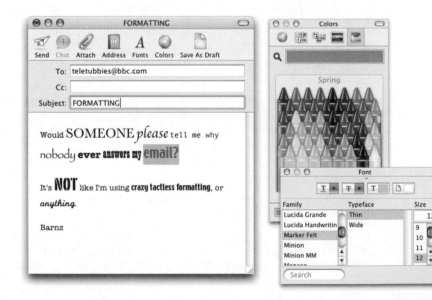

As you type, Mail checks your spelling, using a dotted underline to mark questionable words. Fortunately, you're not expected to know the correct spelling — the computer is perfectly happy to supply that for you. While pressing the Control key, click the underlined word; a list of suggestions appears in the resulting pop-up menu. Click the word you really intended, like this:

6. **Attach any files that you want to send along for the ride.**

   Fortunately, there's more to e-mail than just sending typed messages back and forth. You can also send files from your hard drive — in the form of *attachments* to your e-mail messages. Companies use this method to exchange design sketches, movie clips, and spreadsheets. Authors turn in chapters (written in Microsoft Word or AppleWorks) to publishers this way. And new parents send baby pictures this way.

   To pull this off, make sure that your message refers to the attachment, so that your recipient doesn't miss it (for example: "By the way, I've attached an AppleWorks file. It's a drawing little Cindy did of a tobacco-company executive in a paroxysm of self-loathing and doubt.")

   Then locate the icon of the file you want to send — in your Home folder, for example. This may entail adjusting the windows on your screen so that you can see *both* your e-mail message *and* the icon of the file you want to send, like this:

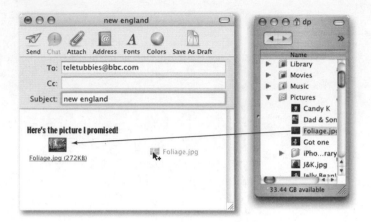

Drag the file directly into the message window.

Alternatively, click the Attach icon on the toolbar. The usual Open File dialog box appears, so that you can navigate your hard drive and find the files you want to include. As in the preceding figure, the icons show up at the bottom of the window to indicate that your dragging was successful.

(Caution: Don't attach big files like movies or photos that you haven't scaled down to a smaller size, as described in Chapter 10. Files like these are too big to send, and too big to receive — you'll probably spend half an hour waiting for them to upload, only to find that your recipient never even got them. Instead, you'll receive an error message by e-mail telling you that you overwhelmed the size limitations of that person's e-mail box.)

(Oh, and one other thing. If you intend to send a bunch of files at once, you can add them as a group — *or* you can "zip" them into a single, more compact file that your recipients can "unzip" at the other end. To do that, switch to the desktop. Highlight the files all at once, or just click the folder they're in, and then from the File menu, choose Create Archive of 2 items, or whatever. The Mac automatically copies the selected files or folder into a single, compressed icon whose name ends with .zip.)

7. **Click Send (the paper-airplane icon on the toolbar).**

   If everything's set up right, your Mac now connects to the Internet and sends your e-message.

Sending files to Windows people

As you may have heard, Windows is a more technical computer system than Macintosh. Therefore, the following discussion is by far the most technical one in this book. Fear not, however: This page has been reinforced with invisible microfilaments for added strength.

When you're sending files to Windows PCs, you have to worry about three conditions. First, *you must send a file Windows can open.* Just as Betamax VCRs can't play VHS tapes, so Windows programs can't always open files from your Mac. Here are some kinds of files that Windows *can* open: documents created by TextEdit, Microsoft Word, Excel, or PowerPoint; graphics in JPEG or GIF formats; Web pages (.html or .htm to files) you've created or downloaded; FileMaker and Photoshop files; and other files where the same application is sold in both Macintosh and Windows formats.

The second consideration is that *every file on every Windows computer has a three-letter suffix* that tells the computer what sort of file it is. Without this code, your poor suffering Windows friends won't be able to open what you send them. A Microsoft Word file might be named Thesis.doc, a photo might be called Mama.jpg, and so on.

Fortunately, every Mac OS X program automatically adds the proper three-letter suffix to the files named even though you can't see it. (Apple hides these suffixes when they're on the Mac, to avoid making the computer look too computery.) You do, however, have to worry about adding these filename suffixes when you've switched your Mac into Mac OS 9, as described in Chapter 12.

The third consideration: *You must send your file in a format Windows e-mail programs can understand.* The Internet, technically speaking, can't transmit files at all — only pure typed text. Behind the scenes, anything else that you transmit, such as photos or AppleWorks documents, must first be converted into a stream of text gibberish that's reconstructed at the other end.

Fortunately, the Mac's Mail program automatically uses an encoding scheme that both Macs and Windows PCs can understand. (Your normal attachment may show up on the PC accompanied by a useless, second attachment whose name starts with "._," but your recipients can just ignore it.)

If your attachments seem not to be going through, though, open the Edit menu, choose Attachments, and choose Send Windows Friendly Attachments from the submenu. The files you send this way are guaranteed to be readable by Windows e-mail programs — but they may not open on Macs.

America Online, unfortunately, is a different story. If you try to attach more than one file to a single outgoing message, America Online compresses them using the StuffIt format, which Windows users can't read. Your only option is to send files one at a time, making sure that the "compress Attachments" checkbox *isn't* selected after you click the Attach File icon.

Four tips for sending mail

Just sending feeble little ordinary messages is a great start, but six weeks from now, you'll surely begin to feel pangs of desire for a little further personal growth. Mastering these tips is just the ticket:

✔ If you're interrupted halfway through composing some masterful message, click the Save As Draft button on the toolbar. (The icon — a partially folded paper airplane — makes a lot more sense when you compare it with the Send icon.)

You've just saved the message in your Drafts folder. (The Drafts folder is in a special, side-of-the-window, slide-out panel called the mailbox drawer. To see it, click the Mailboxes icon on the toolbar.) To reopen a saved draft later, click the Drafts icon in the mailbox drawer, and then click the draft that you want to work on.

✔ If it's taking you 20 minutes to write each piece of e-mail, you'll drive yourself crazy waiting for the modem to connect to the Internet over and over again, once per message. Fortunately, there's a way to write a bunch of messages without ever going online — and then send them all at once when you're good and ready.

The trick is to open up the Mailbox menu and choose Go Off line. Now, whenever you write a message and then click Send, Mail won't actually attempt to connect to the Internet. When you're finally ready to send the batch of messages you've written, choose Go Online from the Mailbox menu.

✔ A *blind carbon copy* is a secret copy, sent to a secret recipient. None of the main addressees will even be aware that your message was surreptitiously copied to a third party.

Suppose, for example, that you've addressed a message to your coworker that says, "Frank, you seem to have fallen into the habit of pouring your unfinished soda into the vents of the computers, and I'm concerned that it may not be the best thing for the electronics." You might send a blind carbon copy to your boss, so that Frank won't think you're squealing on him.

To open up a box where you can type in a Bcc address, open the View menu and choose Bcc Header. Type a secret address into the new address box that appears in your outgoing message.

✔ *Signatures* are bits of text that get stamped at the bottom of your outgoing e-mail messages. A signature may contain a name, postal address, or some cute quote from *Friends*.

To compose your signature, open the Mail menu and choose Preferences. In the resulting dialog box, click the Signatures icon. Now click the Add Signature button, which opens an editing window where you can type your new signature (and define a name for it). Click OK when you're done.

Back in the Mail Preferences dialog box, use the Automatically Select Signature pop-up menu to choose the signature you just made. Then close the dialog box.

From now on, Mail automatically stamps that signature at the bottom of every message you write. (You can always delete the signature on a message-by-message basis — a handy feature when, for example, you're sending a message to your grandmother, and your signature is "Party hearty, dudes!")

Four ways not to be loathed online

Like any country, the Internet has its own weird culture, including rules of e-mail etiquette that, if broken, will make nasty comments and snideness rain down upon the offender. If you want to be loved online, read up:

- ✔ Don't type in ALL CAPITALS. It's just hard to read (imagine a screen full of it). They'll *murder* you for that.

- ✔ Don't ask what LOL means. It stands for "laughing out loud." And while we're at it: IMHO is "in my humble opinion," ROTFL is "rolling on the floor laughing," and RTFM is "read the freakin' manual."

✔ Quote what you're responding to. If someone e-mails you with a question, don't just write back, "No, I don't think so." The question-asker may have long since forgotten his/her own query!

Instead, begin your reply with the question itself. (In Mail, the easy way to do that is to highlight the relevant portion of the *incoming* message, like this —

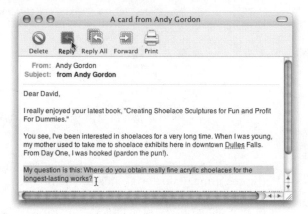

— so that when you click the Reply button, that "quoted back" portion appears at the top of your reply, denoted with a vertical bar like this:

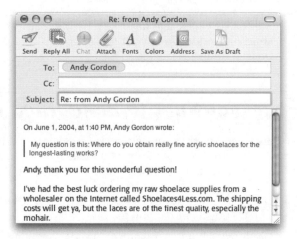

Then type your actual answer.)

✔ One more thing: You'll see these little guys all over the place:

:-)

Bend your head 90 degrees to the left, and you'll see how it makes a little smiley face. That's to indicate, of course, the writer's facial expression (which you can't otherwise see). A thousand variants of that punctuation-face are available — and an equally large number of people who absolutely can't stand those little smileys.

Checking Your Mail

If the messages you send out to your friends are witty and charming enough, you may actually get a few responses.

To check your e-mail, click the Get Mail icon on the toolbar. Your Mac connects to cyberspace and fetches any waiting mail. You'll see it in a list, as shown here.

The blue dot means you haven't read it yet.

Click a column heading to sort the list by that criterion.

Drag this divider to adjust the column width.

Drag this bar up or down to adjust the
relative sizes of the two window panes.

As a bonus, you'll see a bright red starburst on the Mail icon on your Dock, showing the number of unread messages that await your inspection. These new messages are also indicated by what looks like colorful globs of hair gel in the main list.

To read one of your messages, just click its name once (to view the incoming memo in the lower pane of the main window) or twice (to open it into its own, larger window).

Processing a message you've read

When you're finished reading an e-mail, you have number of choices:

- ✓ **Write a reply.** To do so, click the Reply button on the toolbar. (Or, if this message was sent to a group of people, click Reply All if you want everyone to see your response.)

  Now you're back into I'm-Writing-An-E-mail-Message mode, as described earlier in the chapter. (Mail thoughtfully pretypes the e-mail address of the person you're answering — along with the date, time, and subject of the message. If I had a machine that did that for my *U.S.* mail, I'd be a much better paper correspondent.)

  If you don't first highlight a portion of the incoming message as described earlier, then in your reply, Mail automatically pastes the *entire* original message — the one you're answering — at the bottom of the window, denoted by a vertical line and in color (or > brackets). This common Internet technique helps your correspondent grasp what the heck you're talking about, especially since some time may have passed since he or she wrote the original note.

- ✓ **Forward it.** If you think somebody else in your cyber-world might be interested in reading the same message, click the Forward button at the top of the window. A new message window opens up, ready for you to address, that contains the forwarded message below the notation, "Begin forwarded message." If you like, you can type in a short note of your own above that line ("Casey — thought this might annoy you") before clicking the Send button.

- ✓ **Mark it as spam.** If you click the Junk button on the toolbar, you teach Mail that the message you're reading (or the one you've highlighted) is junk mail. Over time, Mail gets better and better at identifying what you consider to be spam, and flagging it with a brownish highlighting color.

  Unfortunately, you're still left with the task of trashing these unwanted messages yourself. Once Mail has gotten pretty good at identifying spam, though, you can open the Mail menu, choose Preferences, click

Junk Mail, and turn on "Move it to the Junk mailbox (Automatic)." From now on, Mail automatically files what it deems junk into a Junk Mail box, where it's much easier to scan and delete the messages en masse.

✔ **File it.** If you don't see the mailbox *drawer* at the side of your main window, as shown in the following picture, click the Mailbox icon.

But once the drawer is visible, you can make new mailbox folders to hold your messages. You might create one for important messages, another for unimportant ones, and another for jokes. You can even create mailboxes *inside* these mailboxes, a feature that's beloved by Type A personalities worldwide.

To create a new mailbox folder, begin by clicking the mailbox in the drawer that will *contain* it. For example, click Personal Mailboxes if you want to create a new mailbox within it, or click Inbox if you want to create folders inside *it*. Now open the Mailbox menu and choose New. The Mac asks you to title the new mailbox; once you've done so, a new icon appears in the mailbox drawer, ready for use.

Then, to move a message (or group of messages) into your newly created folder, just drag its name, like this:

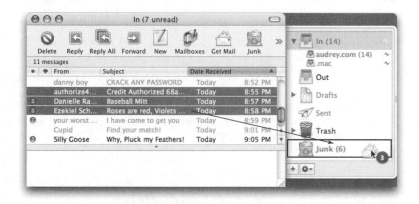

Later, whenever you want to see the contents of one of these folders, just click it.

✔ **Print it.** From the File menu, choose Print.

✔ **Add the sender to your Address Book.** If you choose, from the Message menu, the Add Sender To Address Book command, Mail memorizes the e-mail address of the person whose message is on the screen. In fact, you can highlight a huge number of messages and add them all simultaneously using this technique.

Thereafter, you'll be able to write new messages to this person just by typing the first couple letters of the name. Your computer, ever humble, attempts to complete the rest of the address, saving you that much effort.

✔ **Open an attachment.** Just as you can attach files to a message, so people often send files to *you*. Only the presence of the file's icon in the message body tells you that there's something attached.

The easiest way to rescue an attached file from the message that's holding it hostage is to drag the file's icon directly out of the message window and onto any visible portion of your desktop.

You can also double-click the attachment's icon in the message. If you were sent a document (such as a photo, Word file, Excel file, and so on), it now opens in the corresponding program (Preview, Word, Excel, or whatever). *Important:* At this point, you should *use the Save As command* in the File menu to save the file into a folder of your choice. Otherwise, your Mac won't preserve any changes you make to the document.

✔ **Trash it.** Highlight a message in the list. Press the Delete key, or click the Delete button on the toolbar, to send the message to the great cyber-shredder in the sky.

Well, sort of. Actually, you've just moved the message to the Deleted Items folder, which works like the Mac's Trash. If you like, you can click this icon to view a list of the messages you've deleted. You can even rescue some by dragging them into any other mailbox (such as right back into the Inbox).

Mail doesn't truly nuke the messages in the Deleted Items folder until you "empty the trash." To do that, open the Mailbox menu and choose Erase Deleted Messages (and choose In All Accounts from the submenu). Alternatively, wait about a week — Mail will vaporize those messages automatically.

The Anti-Spam Handbook

No doubt about it: Unsolicited junk e-mail, better known as *spam,* is the ugly underbelly of e-mail paradise. You'll know it if you've got it — wave after wave of daily messages like "MAKE EZ MONEY AT HOME CARVING TOOTH-PICKS!", "HERBAL V.I.A.G.R.A.," and "SEXXXY APPLIANCE REPAIRMEN WAITING FOR YOUR CALL!"

Unfortunately, we can't hunt down the lowlife scum that send out these billions of junk e-mails, even though there's a Federal anti-spam law. Meanwhile, our e-mail boxes fill up with useless crud that makes it harder to find the *real* messages among them. (Mail's built-in Junk Mail feature can help a great deal, as described earlier in this chapter. But even it's not perfect.)

You may have wondered: How did you wind up on these junk lists to begin with? Sometimes, spammers use automated name-guessing software that tries sending junk to *skibunny 23@aol.com, skibunny 24@aol.com,* and so on. (That's how so many Hotmail and America Online members wind up on spam lists.)

In most other cases, they get your e-mail address from *you*. Every time you post a message on an online bulletin board, fill in a form on the Web, or do a chat in a chat room, you've just made yourself vulnerable to the spammers' software robots. These little programs scour America Online, newsgroups, and the Web, looking for e-mail addresses to collect.

"But if I can never post messages online," I can hear you protesting, "I'm losing half the advantages of being online!"

Not necessarily. Consider setting up a second mailbox — that is, a second e-mail address for your same America Online or Internet account. (That's easy to do on AOL; go to keyword *names* to set up a new one. If you have an Internet account, call your ISP's help line to arrange an additional mailbox. Or sign up for a .Mac account, as described in Chapter 6, and use the e-mail address Apple issued you — *yourname@mac.com,* for example.)

Thereafter, the game is easy to play: Use *one* e-mail address for public postings, chats, and so on. Its Inbox will be inundated with junk mail — but you'll never waste time reading it.

Use your second, private address *for e-mail only*. Spam robots can't read private e-mail, so your secret e-mail address will, for the most part, remain virginal and spam-free.

Part III
Software
Competence

The 5th Wave   By Rich Tennant

"Well, the first day wasn't bad—I lost the 'Finder', copied a file into the 'Trash' and sat on my mouse."

In this part . . .

The next few chapters introduce you to the software that came with (or can be added to) your Mac. These remarkable programs include iPhoto (for mastery of digital camera photos), iTunes (for mastery of digital music files), and iMovie (for mastery of camcorder video editing), among others.

Without software, your Mac is little more than an art object — cool-looking and futuristic, to be sure, but not much help when it's time to print some photos.

Chapter 9

iTunes, iPod, iConquered

For decades, life as a Mac user was fraught with social hazards. You'd be at a party, and somebody would say, "Oh, I got this cool new program — but it only works on Windows." You'd have no choice but to avert your gaze in embarrassment, often by burying your face in the onion dip.

These days, Apple's fighting back. Your Mac came with an assortment of amazing software programs that run only on the Mac. These programs, called things like iPhoto, iDVD, and iMovie, are designed to make you the ringmaster in control of pictures, music, and movies.

Nobody has ever seen anything quite like the "i-programs," as some people call them: They're beautiful to look at, extremely easy to use, and capable of feats that simply can't be duplicated on other computers. It's time to see a little onion dip on the cheeks of Windows fans for a change.

Chapter 10 describes iPhoto; Chapter 11 goes into digital moviemaking with iMovie and iDVD. This one describes iTunes.

Meet iTunes

iTunes, a program that came with your Mac, is the ultimate digital jukebox. It plays music CDs, brings you Internet radio stations, creates and plays *MP3 files* (remarkably compact sound files that store CD-quality music), and even lets you burn new music CDs of your own, composed of your favorite tracks from *other* CDs. This, ladies and gentlemen, is power: You can actually create modified versions of your favorite CDs, in which all of the songs you can't stand have been eliminated.

As a bonus, iTunes is the front door for the famous Apple music store on the Internet, where over 500,000 songs are yours for the buying at $1 apiece. It's the consumer's revenge for years of having to buy $15 CDs just to get the two good songs on each one.

And as a *bonus* bonus, iTunes can also load up your entire music collection to the iPod, the world's best-selling (and best designed) pocket music player.

Opening iTunes

You'll find iTunes in your Applications folder. The first time you run it, you encounter something called the iTunes Setup Assistant: a series of interview screens that let you specify (a) whether or not you want iTunes to be the program your Mac uses for playing MP3 files from the Internet (and similar electronic music files — AIFF, AAC, and so on), (b) whether or not you want it to ask your permission every time it connects to the Internet, and (c) if you want the program to scan your hard drive for all MP3 files already on it. In general, you want to accept all of these proposals.

At last you arrive at the main iTunes screen, thoughtfully pre-stocked with a few songs. To play one, double-click its name. Or click its name and then click the big Play triangle at the upper-left corner of the screen (or press the space bar). Click the same button (or press the space bar again) to stop the music.

Here's some of the other fun you can have with your little database of music:

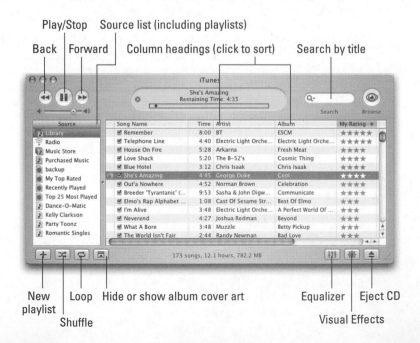

- **Back, Forward:** Hold down these buttons with your mouse to fast-forward or rewind through a particular song. Click *without* holding down the button to jump to the next or previous song. (The little speaker icon to the left of the song names lets you know which song is playing.)

- **Volume:** Drag the slider to make the music louder or softer. (Pressing ⌘-up arrow or ⌘-down arrow does the same thing.)

- **Shuffle, Loop:** These buttons work just as they do on a CD player. The Shuffle button plays the songs in a random order, so that you don't have to listen to them in the same sequence every time. When you've clicked the Loop button, your songs will play to the end and then repeat. If you see a tiny digit 1 superimposed on this button, your playlist will loop only once.

- **Visual Effects:** When you click this button, iTunes presents an onscreen laser-light show that pulses, beats, and dances in perfect sync to the music. The effect is hypnotic and wild. (For real party fun, invite some people who grew up in the '60s to watch.)

  Once the show begins, by the way, don't miss the Full Screen command in the Visuals menu. It makes the laser-light show fill your entire screen. No, you won't get a lot of work done, but staring at this psychedelic display may well expand your mind by several sizes.

- **Equalizer:** If you click this button, iTunes displays a handsome, brushed-aluminum control console that lets you adjust the strength of each musical frequency independently. Drag the sliders (bass on the left, treble on the right) to accommodate the strengths and weaknesses of your speakers or headphones. Or just use the pop-up menu above the sliders to choose a canned set of slider positions for Classical, Dance, Jazz, Latin, and so on.

Window Fun

The iTunes window may look like it's made of brushed metal. But in fact, you can push and pull the various parts of the window like taffy. For example:

- **Resize the various panels of the iTunes window.** Look for a shallow dot between panes; it denotes strips that you can drag to resize adjacent panes.

- **Sort the song list any way you like.** The main song list is separated into several columns. Click a column title (like Artist or Album) to sort the song list alphabetically by that criterion. Click the heading a second time to reverse the sorting order.

✔ **Change the order of the columns by dragging.** For example, if you want to have Album right next to the Song Name, drag the word Album horizontally until it's next to Song Name.

✔ **Change the column widths.** To adjust the width of a column, drag the vertical divider line on its right side.

✔ **Add or remove columns.** To add more kinds of information to your list of columns (or less), Control-click any column title, as shown here at left. (That is, press the Control key, and while it's down, click the column title.)

Then, from the pop-up list of column categories (Bit Rate, Date Added, and so on), choose the name of the column you want to add or remove, as shown at right.

By the way, once you're listening to your iTunes music while you do other work on your Mac — one of the *key* uses for this program — you don't have to look at its window *at all.* The program keeps right on playing even when you start working in a different program.

In fact, you can even control the playback without having to return to iTunes. See its little icon on your Dock? It's a pop-up menu remote control!

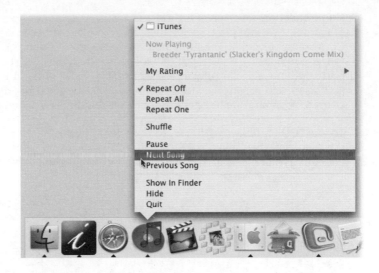

Audio CDs

If you're a college student or a teenager, the main thing you may hope to accomplish with iTunes (or, indeed, the Mac itself) is to collect MP3 files of your favorite pop music. (More on this topic in a moment.)

But if that's not your particular passion, you may want to fill up the main list in iTunes just by inserting a music CD into your Mac. The songs on it immediately show up in the list.

At first, they may show up with the exciting names "Track 01," "Track 02," and so on. Fortunately, without even being asked, iTunes thoughtfully goes online and consults cddb.com, a global database of music CDs and their contents. If it finds a match among the thousands of CDs there, it copies the album and song names right into iTunes, where they reappear every time you use this particular music CD.

Copying CD songs to your hard drive

You're entitled to be puzzled by the heading above this paragraph. You already have your music on CDs — what possible good does it do you to copy their songs to your hard drive?

Good question, and here's a good answer: Once you copy your songs onto the Mac itself, you can play them whenever you like, without requiring the original CD. Once you've collected the music from *several* CDs in this way, furthermore, you can mix and match the songs on them in ways you'd never be able to do with a single CD player. You can search, sort, and study all of your music en masse, and record *new* CDs with a song sequence that you dictate. And, of course, you can transfer all of this to an iPod player, if you have one.

To *rip* a CD in this way (that is, to copy its songs onto your hard drive), insert the disc, and then make sure that only the songs you want to capture have checkmarks in the main list, like this:

Then click the Import button at the upper-right corner of the window. Watch the display at the top of the window to see how long the conversion is going to take, and which song iTunes is working on; iTunes plays the music as it works. (You can click the tiny X in this display window to cancel the importing.) As iTunes finishes processing each song, you see a small, circled checkmark next to its name in the main list to help you remember that you've got it on board and no longer need the CD in your machine.

When it's all over, you'll find the imported songs listed in your Library (click the Library icon in the left-side Source list). From there, you can drag them into any other *playlist,* as described next.

Playlists

When you click Library in the left-side Source list, you see, in the main part of the screen, every song file iTunes knows about. Here's the best part: To find a particular song, just type a few letters into the Search box above the list. iTunes hides all but the ones that match, instantly, even if there are thousands of songs there. (Click the little circled X button, at the right end of the Search bar, to see your full list again.)

But you may not want to listen to *all* your songs every time you need a little musical diversion. That's why iTunes lets you create *playlists* — folders in the Source list that contain only certain songs, like albums of your own devising. You might create one called Party Tunes, another called Blind Date Music, and so on.

To create a new playlist, click the + button in the lower-left corner of the window. A new playlist shows up in the list above it. You can rename a playlist by clicking its name. Then all you have left to do is to add songs to it, just by dragging them out of the main Library list and onto the new playlist icon.

Now, you're not actually copying songs; you're simply putting imaginary duplicates of them — pointers, really — in the playlist folders. It's perfectly okay to put the same songs into as many different playlists as you like.

Smart Playlists

Actually, you don't have to build your playlists manually, dragging songs into folders as described above. You've got a *computer,* for goodness' sake — and isn't it supposed to be a labor-saving device?

Thanks to *Smart Playlists,* your Mac can examine your music library and come up with its own mix for you, based on criteria that you specify. You might tell one Smart Playlist to assemble an hours' worth of songs that you've rated higher than four stars but rarely listen to, and another to play your most-often-played songs from the Seventies.

To start a Smart Playlist, choose New Smart Playlist from the File menu. A dialog box appears that, by the time you're finished, will look something like this:

Give the program detailed instructions about what you want to hear. You can select the bands you want to hear, choose only songs that fall within a certain genre or year, songs that don't last longer than two minutes, and so on.

Click the little + sign at the end of each line to keep adding criteria, or click the - sign to remove one.

And if you turn on the "Live updating" checkbox, iTunes will always keep this playlist updated as your collection changes, as you change your ratings, as your Play Count changes, and so on.

The Smart Playlist illustrated above would seek out Billy Joel songs in your collection that have a fast tempo (that is, greater than 120 BPM, or beats per minute), on albums released before 1990, and that you haven't listened to more than nine times.

When you click OK, iTunes pours through the current contents of your music library and generates the playlist.

Burning music CDs

This is a great time to be alive, isn't it? Only a few years ago, creating your own music CDs required a $50 million fabrication plant, an airtight "clean suit," and a knack for working with lasers. Now here you are with your little Mac, all set to become your own private record label — with little more talent than the ability to click a button.

Internet radio

Audio CDs and MP3 files aren't the only sources of sound you can listen to as you work. iTunes also lets you tune in to any of hundreds of Internet-based radio stations, which may turn out to be the most convenient music source of all. They're free, they play 24 hours a day, and their music collections make yours look like a drop in the bucket.

When you click Radio in the left-side Source list, you'll see, in the main list, categories like Blues, Classic Rock, Classical, and so on. Click the little triangle beside a name to see a list of radio stations in that category.

When you see one that looks interesting, double-click its name. Wait a moment for your Mac to connect to the appropriate Internet site, and then let the music begin!

There's no easy way to capture Internet broadcasts or save them onto your hard drive. You can, however, drag the name of one into another "folder" in the Source List to make it easier to get to later on.

When it's all over, you'll be able to play the resulting CDs on almost any standard CD player, just like the CDs from Tower Records — but containing only the songs you like, in the order you like, with the annoying ones subtracted away.

Start by creating a playlist, as described in the previous section, filled with the songs you want, and dragged into the order you want. Keep an eye on the readout at the bottom of the list, which tells you how much time the songs will take; 74 minutes is about the limit for a CD.

When everything is set up, click the Burn Disc button at the upper-right corner of the screen. Insert a blank CD into the Mac and then click Burn CD again. (Use CD-R discs, the kind that you can record only once. CD-RW discs — the ones that you can erase and re-record — are not only more expensive, but may not work in standard CD players.)

The burning process takes some time, but you can switch into other programs to get some work done while iTunes chugs away. When the process is over, the freshly burned CD pops out of the Mac. Label the top of it with a magic marker, and enjoy the head rush that comes from being a master of your own music.

The iTunes Music Store

If you've read this far in the chapter, you now understand that the music from a CD can be turned into a great-sounding digital file on your computer. And what do we know about files on the computer? Anyone? Anyone?

That's right. You can make infinite numbers of *copies* of them, each a pristine duplicate of the first.

If you've seen a newspaper, opened a magazine, or turned on the TV news at all during the last couple of years (admittedly a risky business these days), you might have heard about *music swapping*. It didn't take long for people to figure out that they could turn their pop songs into MP3 files and then swap them on the Internet, essentially making every song ever recorded available for free.

It's a wildly popular activity with just about everybody under 25, except perhaps those who work for the record companies.

Record-company executives came up with a brilliant plan for fighting back: file lawsuits against people it believed were swapping music files.

Apple has a better idea: Give people a simple, quick, well-designed, *legal* alternative. Create a Web site where you can find and buy almost any song for $1, or buy a whole CD for $10.

That's the idea behind the iTunes Music Store, which you get to by clicking the Music Store icon at the left side of the iTunes window.

Welcome to the Music Store

The iTunes Music Store offers almost the entire catalogs of the five major record companies, plus an increasing number of independent ones. Its inventory contains over 500,000 songs from the famous (Bob Dylan, U2, Missy Elliott, Jewel, Sting, and so on) and not-so-famous, in a range of popular styles like Rock, Pop, R & B, Jazz, Folk, Rap, Latin, Classical, and more — and the collection grows by thousands of songs a week. You can also browse, sample, or buy any of 5,000 electronic "books on tape."

To visit the Store, make sure your Mac is online. Then click the Music Store icon in the iTunes Source list on the left pane of the program's window, if you haven't already.

Finding music

The iTunes Music Store looks and works like a Web page. Song names, performer names, and album covers are *links* — that is, you can click them to see what tracks are included. If you see a small, gray, circular icon bearing a white arrow, click it to view details about the subject, like a discography page next to a singer's name in the Artist column.

Click the Back button in the Store window to go back to the page you were just on, or click the button with the small house on it to return to the Music Store home page.

The main iTunes Music Store page also displays links to new releases, exclusive songs that can be purchased only from the Music Store, Apple staff favorites, songs scheduled to become available in the near future, sneak peeks at unreleased tunes, and so on.

Click to open Music Store

Genre pop-up menu

Billboard "Top 100" Charts

Click to see more

You can wander through the entire collection just like you surf your own collection of songs in iTunes. For example, if you type part of a song or performer's name into the Search box — *billy joel, lucy in the sky, fifth symphony,* or whatever — and then press the Return or Enter key, the iTunes store shows you a list of matches from its collection, like this:

Once you've found a list of candidates, double-click one to hear a 30-second, high-quality preview. That's an important step; the last thing you want is to buy a copy of "It's a Wonderful World," only to find out that you've just paid for a kids' rendition performed by Barney the Dinosaur.

But that's not the only way to find the music you want. The Music Store is loaded with clickable buttons and pictures designed to help you *browse* your way to the music you want. Here are some of the possibilities:

✔ **Browse by genre.** Use the Choose Genre pop-up menu to view the featured albums and songs, Most Popular lists, and other information related only to that kind of music (Pop, Folk, Electronic, and so on). (*Genre,* as of course you already know, is French for "style of music.")

✔ **Browse by Year.** Quick! What was the Number One song during your first year of middle school? The iTunes collection of Billboard charts should help you here. (*Billboard* is a music-industry magazine that compiles weekly lists of the most popular pop music.)

The iTunes Music Store lets you riffle through the Billboard Top 100 charts going all the way back to 1946. Just click the Charts link at the left side of the home page to open up the Browser panels, which work like this:

Click a category...then click a chart...then a year.

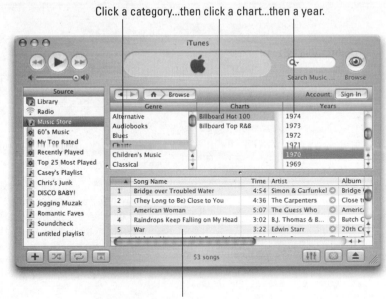

The hits for that year are listed here.

If you're old enough to remember some of these bygone years, it's amazing how listening to these sonic snapshots takes you back to those eras.

✔ **Browse by celebrity.** On the left side of the main page, the Celebrity Playlists gives you, the mere mortal, a Brush with Greatness: It shows you the "what I'm listening to these days" music lists of several celebrities. If you're ever lost to indecision, finding out what Kevin Bacon has in his copy of iTunes is always a great source of inspiration.

✔ **Submit to peer pressure.** The Today's Top Songs (and Today's Top Albums) lists show you what's hot as determined by everybody *else* who's using the Music Store.

In general, you'll find *most* of what you might be looking for on the iTunes Music Store, especially if it's a pop song. A few notables still refuse to permit their music to be sold online in any form, however — Madonna, for example, and the lawyers for the Beatles — so your searches for their stuff will come up empty.

Signing up for an account

You're welcome to listen to 30-second excerpts of any song (or 90-second excerpts of any audio book) for free. But unless you're particularly attention-span challenged, eventually, you might want to try *buying* a song — the whole thing. The minimum price is only a buck, and there's no monthly fee or further commitment.

The Shopping Cart

Usually, iTunes downloads the song you want as you click the Buy Song button. That's a quick and painless experience — *if* you have a fast Internet connection, like DSL or cable modem.

If you have a dial-up modem, though, you may not want to sit there and wait for each song to download. Each song may take several minutes, which can badly interfere with your shopping momentum.

That's what the Shopping Cart option is for. When you use it, all the songs you buy pile up until the end of the session; then iTunes downloads them all at once. This way, you can go off and do something productive (or unproductive) while the stack of tracks takes its time squeezing through the dial-up connection.

If this idea appeals to you, open the iTunes menu and choose Preferences. In the Preferences dialog box, click the Store icon, and turn on "Buy using a Shopping Cart." (You might also want to turn on "Load complete preview before playing," which prevents gaps and stops in listening to the sound clips due to slow connection speeds.) Click OK when you're done.

Now, each time you click an Add Song button, nothing happens except that the song gets added to the Shopping Cart "folder" in the Source list at the left side of the iTunes window. When you're ready to transfer all the songs at once, click that icon and then click Buy Now at the bottom-right corner of the screen.

You must, however, sign up for an Apple ID (an account, including credit-card number, so that you can buy stuff without having to type in all your information every time).

Click the Account: Sign In button on the right side of the iTunes window. You're asked to supply your account name and password.

If you've ever bought or registered an Apple product on the company's Web site, signed up for the AppleCare tech-support plan, have a .Mac membership (Chapter 6), or used another Apple service, you probably have an Apple ID already. All you have to do is remember your name (usually your e-mail address) and password.

And if you're an America Online member, you can supply your AOL screen name and password and skip the whole Apple ID business, thanks to a handy behind-the-scenes cooperative venture between Apple and AOL.

But if you've never had an Apple or AOL account, click Create Account. The software walks you through the three steps you need to follow to set up your Apple account:

✔ Agree to the terms and policies of the Music Store. (They boil down to this: *I solemnly swear that I won't download an album, copy it onto a CD, and sell bootleg copies of it in front of Tower Records.*)

> ✔ Make up a name, password, and secret question and answer. If you later have to e-mail Apple because you've forgotten your password, this is the question you'll have to answer to prove that you're you.
>
> ✔ Provide a working credit card number with a billing address.

The account creation process is complete. From now on, you can log into the Music Store by clicking the Account Sign In button in the upper-right corner of the iTunes window.

Buying music

Buying a song is as easy as clicking the Buy Song button next to a song. The Mac asks for confirmation that you really, truly want to spend money on the music. In the land of the iTunes Music Store, all sales are final.

When you click the Buy button, iTunes begins the process of transferring it to your Mac, where it shows up in the Purchased Music "playlist" at the left side of the screen. (If you've turned on the Shopping Cart option, the button says Add Song instead.)

Gift certificates and allowances

Gift certificates make perfect presents for People Who Have Everything, especially when purchased by People Who Wait Until the Last Minute to Buy a Gift. And iTunes Music Store gift certificates are available in amounts from $10 to $200. Remember that the Music Store is available for both Macintosh and Windows, so you're not even limited to shining your beneficence on fellow Mac owners. (Do inquire, discreetly, about how old your recipients' computers are. iTunes Music Store doesn't work on old PCs running Windows 98, Windows NT, or Windows Me — only the more recent Windows XP and Windows 2000.)

To buy a gift certificate, click the Gift Certificates link on the main page of the iTunes Music Store. After you click to choose delivery by either e-mail or U.S. mail, the process is like buying anything on the Web: You fill in your address, gift amount, personalized message, and so on.

Allowance accounts are similar. You, the parent (or other financial authority), decide how many dollars' worth of music or audiobooks you want to give to a family member or friend (from $10 to $200, in increments of $10). Unlike gift certificates, however, allowance accounts automatically replenish themselves on the first day of each month — a great way to keep music-loving kids out of your wallet, while simultaneously teaching the little nippers a valuable lesson in budgeting their money.

To set up a monthly allowance, click the Allowance link on the main page of the iTunes Music Store and fill out the form on the next screen. Both you and the recipient must have Apple IDs.

The songs cost 99 cents each. Most albums cost $10 to $14, which is quite a bit cheaper than the $17 or so you'd pay to buy the same album on CD (not to mention your not having to pay for parking at the mall).

Buying an audiobook

You can also buy electronic "books on tape" (spoken recordings of books, public radio programs, current newspapers, and so on) — an essential for commuters or joggers. Just select Audiobooks from the Choose Genre pop-up menu on the store's home page, and off you go to the listening library.

Selections range in price from about $3 to $16. Since you can't really flip over an audiobook to read the jacket copy, the Audiobooks section of the iTunes Music Store provides both a description of the book's contents and a 90-second sonic preview so you can try before you buy.

Signing out

If other people have access to your computer when you're not around, consider wrapping up your shopping session by clicking your name (next to the Account button on the Music Store window) and then Sign Out. You probably don't want anyone else to come along and charge up your credit card with a music-buying marathon. (Preposterous? Let's just put it this way: Apple reported in January 2004 that after six months of operation, its most ardent customer had racked up over $29,000 in Music Store charges.)

What to do with music you've bought

Once you've located the songs you've bought (by clicking Purchased Music in the iTunes Source list), the fun begins. From here, you can play the songs, drag them into other playlists, transfer them to an iPod, or burn them to a CD to play on the stereo.

These are, however, copyrighted songs, and they're not entirely restriction-free. You'd have to be a pretty dedicated music pirate to find these limitations intrusive, but they're limitations all the same:

> ✔ **Three computers, max.** Between work, home, and the family network, not everyone spends time on just one computer these days. So Apple lets you play your Music Store–bought songs on up to three computers at once.
>
> You *authorized* your first Mac (that is, designated it as one of The Three Chosen Ones) when you signed up for an Apple Account for the iTunes store. Now suppose you copy a Store-bought song to a second computer

(by e-mailing it, accessing it from across the network as described in Chapter 14, or whatever) and drag the song into *its* copy of iTunes. When you try to play the copied song, you'll be asked to type in your Apple ID and password again, thereby authorizing the second machine.

✔ **Ten CDs, max.** You can also burn purchased tracks to blank CDs, so you can listen to them in the car or on the big audio component rack in living room. Here, Apple has put in only one tiny, almost irrelevant form of copy protection: If you've made Store-bought songs part of a certain playlist, you can't burn more than ten CD copies of it in a row without making at least one change to the song list.

The iPod

The iPod is a beautiful, tiny music player whose tiny hard drive contains enough storage space to hold thousands and thousands of songs. It's available in several capacities (including a tiny model called the iPod Mini, which is available in a choice of metallic colors). Make a note to yourself: If you ever become a contestant on *Survivor,* choose one of these babies as your luxury item.

In any case, iTunes is designed to be the loading dock for the iPod. All you have to do is connect the iPod to the Mac via its included white FireWire cable. You'll see the iPod's icon show up in the iTunes Source list, as though it's a CD or a playlist. Click its icon to see what's on it.

The beauty of this arrangement is that the iPod *automatically* updates itself to reflect the music in your iTunes library. Every time you add or delete songs in iTunes, the contents of the icon are updated automatically to match.

You can also buy iPod adapters for the car radio, iPod adapters for home stereos, iPod armband holders, iPod voice-recorder microphones, iPod carrying cases — but at this point, you've probably spent quite enough already.

Chapter 10

An Eye for iPhoto

In This Chapter

▶ Putting your photos in the digital shoebox

▶ Fixing the color, the lighting, and the freckles

▶ Making hay with your photos: slide shows, Web pages, hardbound books

Digital cameras are amazing inventions. For one thing, they're incredibly economical: You never pay for film, and you never pay for developing. For another, the little built-in screen on a digital camera lets you see the picture before you actually take it — and after you press the shutter button, lets you see the picture *after* you've taken it, the better to delete it on the spot if it didn't come out well.

When you get the camera home, you can connect the camera to a computer and transfer the pictures to it. There they show up as graphics files, which you can e-mail to other people, turn into a slide show, or even edit. More than one person has erased an ex-spouse out of a favorite family picture using exactly these tools. (You think I'm kidding?)

But for years, that business of getting the pictures off the camera and onto your computer has been the hard part. Every camera came with its own software, which did very little with your pictures once the transfer was over. Sometimes you couldn't even find them on your hard drive after the transfer.

iPhoto: The Digital Shoebox

Fortunately, Apple has finally put an end to that chain of pain. The iPhoto program gives you a sweet, simple way to transfer your pictures from the camera, organize them, show them off, and send them on to other people.

Now, iPhoto comes right in the Applications folder of every new Mac, and has since 2002 or so. This chapter describes iPhoto 4, but the basics should be the same no matter which version you have. (If you don't have iPhoto at all, or you have an older version, you can buy the current version at *http://store.apple.com*.)

iPhoto meets camera

Once you've installed iPhoto, you can, of course, start up the program by clicking its Dock icon or finding it in your Applications folder. But the whole point of the program is its magical synergy with your digital camera. And that relationship begins the moment you plug the camera's USB cable from the Mac into the camera. That simple act of plugging in generally opens iPhoto automatically.

Once iPhoto is open and the camera is turned on and connected, click the Import button shown in the following figure. If the camera picture at the left side of the screen correctly identifies your camera model, you're ready to transfer the pictures. (If you don't see the camera picture there, try waiting to turn the camera on until after iPhoto has opened.)

First, however, you have an important decision to make: Do you want iPhoto to *erase the camera* after retrieving its pictures? There's very little downside to doing so — in fact, that's probably what you'll want most of the time, considering how few pictures fit on the average camera memory card. You don't have to worry about losing pictures, because the erasing process doesn't begin until *after* all of the pictures are safely transferred to the hard drive. (The only time you would *not* want iPhoto to erase the camera's memory card is if you've used the camera to take little digital *movies,* which most models can also do. iPhoto doesn't import those movies — only photos.)

If you want to erase the card after the transfer, turn on "Erase camera contents after transfer." Either way, click the Import button. The program swings into action, grabbing your pictures from the camera and displaying them in miniature on the iPhoto screen.

When iPhoto is finished importing your pictures from the camera, they show up arranged like slides on a light board. (Professional photographers, and probably professional manicurists as well, call these miniatures *thumbnails.)*

Albums

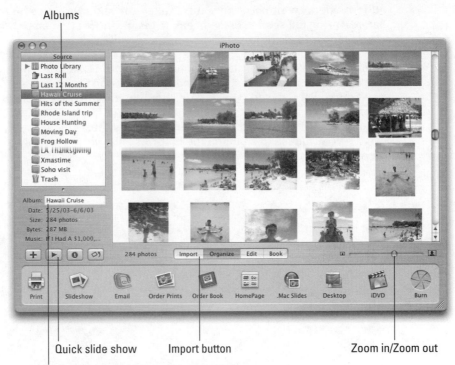

Quick slide show   Import button   Zoom in/Zoom out

Change the name of the selected photo or album

Want to try something fun? Just drag the little Zoom in/Zoom out slider at the lower-right corner of the window, identified in the picture above, and watch in amazement as all of the photos grow larger or smaller. You can drag the slider so far to the right that each picture fills the screen — or so far to the left that they become the size of molecules. The first time you see this little trick, you'll think it justifies the price of the Mac all by itself.

The post-import slide show

What's the first thing you want to do after dumping fresh photos off the camera into iPhoto?

Look at them, of course. Up until now, the only glimpse you've had of your photos is on the tiny, two-inch screen of your digital camera. (Besides looking at *real life,* that is — but what's the value of *that?*)

iPhoto offers an intoxicating feature called the slide show. It's quite spectacular, featuring full-screen, magnificent, brilliant photos that smoothly
cross-fade into each other.

Immediately after importing your photos, click the Last Roll icon in the Source
list at the left side of the screen, and then click the Play triangle underneath
the Source list (labeled "Quick slide show" in the previous illustration).

Once the slide show begins — accompanied by music, no less — you can
wiggle your mouse to summon the iPhoto 4 slide show control bar shown
here:

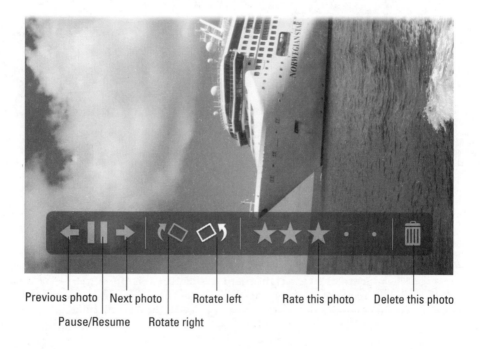

Previous photo | Next photo   Rotate left   Rate this photo   Delete this photo

Pause/Resume   Rotate right

This is the perfect opportunity to fix the newly imported batch. For example,
you can:

- **Pause the show** to ooh and aah (or laugh uproariously) at one of the
  photos.

- **Go back** to one you've already seen.

- **Rotate a photo.** If you're like most photographers, not all of your photos
  are taken in *landscape* mode, where the camera is held horizontally.

Every now and then, you may have to turn the camera 90 degrees to take a picture — of, say, a giraffe, a skyscraper, or Michael Jordan.

Unfortunately, the camera doesn't know that you turned it sideways. When you import the photos to your Mac, those vertical photos wind up displayed horizontally, which is just wrong. These buttons let you restore a photo to right-side-up orientation.

✔ **Delete a photo.** After all, even Ansel Adams took a few duds in his day.

✔ **Rate a photo.** Click within the set of five dots to turn them into stars, representing your assessment of your latest shots. Five stars means "superb"; one star means "stinker." (You may have noticed this feature in iTunes, too.)

Later, you'll be able to exploit your ratings in several ways. For example, by choosing My Rating from the View menu, you can see the actual stars, in gray, stamped beneath the thumbnails of the photos you've rated. Or if you choose Arrange and then By Rating from the View menu, you can sort all the visible pictures so that the best ones appear at the top.

When you reach the end of the new pix, click the mouse to return to iPhoto.

Editing Pictures

Over time, you'll take more and more pictures, and download each set to iPhoto. The main iPhoto display area will fill with more and more pictures. The great thing is that all of your pictures are always available in this one massive, scrolling display. You'll never again be forced to sit in the sweltering attic, opening crumbling envelopes of ancient, disorganized photos, flipping through them in a hunt for one particular shot.

Nor are you forced to just sit and *look* at your pictures. This is the electronic age, dude! Time for interactivity! Let us count the ways.

Rotating a picture

If you didn't fix rotated photos during the slide show as described in the previous section, you can also click the photo and then click the Rotate button. The photo crisply turns 90 degrees for your entertainment pleasure. (It turns counterclockwise — unless you press the Option key while clicking, which makes it turn the other way.)

Cropping a picture

Just taking the picture doesn't represent the end of the job for a real photographer. Part of the artistry in becoming a shutterbug is learning how to *crop* a picture — to trim away excess background. Sometimes, of course, you *want* the subject to look tiny and insignificant — when set against the backdrop of a building or the Grand Canyon, for example. Most of the time, though, a picture is more effective when it's a tight shot around the subject.

To trim out excess background in iPhoto, double-click the picture. It opens into a special mode called Edit (see the button beneath the picture?). At this point, grab your mouse. Start above and to the left of the subject, and drag diagonally so that the unwanted background turns faded, like this:

First, drag diagonally...

Then click here.

If you want to be sure that the photo remains photo-like in its proportions — ruling out the possibility that you'll wind up with a tall, skinny slice of the picture — use the Constrain pop-up menu at the lower-left corner of the window. Choose one of the standard photo sizes listed there, such as 4 by 6, before you drag across the picture. (If you intend to use this photo for a DVD slide show or a handsome coffee-table photo book, as described later in this chapter, you should always choose one of the "4 x 3" options from this pop-up menu.)

Once you've highlighted the portion of the picture that you actually want to keep, click the Crop button on the bottom edge of the window. Savor the way iPhoto automatically enlarges your newly cropped image to fill the window. Then click the Organize button to return to your "slides."

You'll sleep well at night, by the way, knowing that *nothing you do in iPhoto ever changes the original photo*. Even if you crop a picture, for example, you can return to it, months or years later: Click it in the iPhoto window, open the Photos menu, and then choose Revert to Original. iPhoto promptly brings back the picture as it looked the day you first imported from the camera. Safety is a beautiful thing.

Fixing the colors

The Enhance button is one of iPhoto's most magical tools. It does a spectacular job of bringing out the colors, compensating for a camera's color cast, and fixing weak contrast.

You may find that Enhance has very little effect on some photos, and actually makes some photos *worse*. But in general, it works real magic on photos that are slightly too light or dark and that lack good contrast, like the original photo shown below at left.

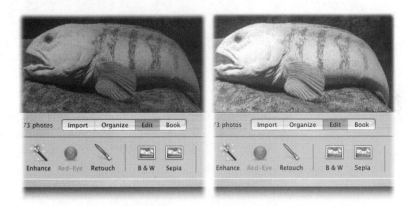

To use the Enhance button, you just click it once. That's it. Wait for a moment to see the results on your photo.

After using the Enhance button, you can hold down the Control key to see your unenhanced "before" photo. Release the key to see the "after" image. By pressing and releasing the Control key, you can jump back and forth between both versions of the photo, to gauge whether or not you like the difference.

If you go too far, remember that you can always choose Undo from the Edit menu to "take back" the change. (That goes for *any* of these edits.)

Removing the redeye demons

Redeye is when somebody in a flash photo shows up with reddish pupils. iPhoto can fix the problem quickly and efficiently, like this:

1. Magnify the picture by dragging the slider at the lower-right corner of the window. You want to be able to really see the red, as shown here at left (in the "before" picture):

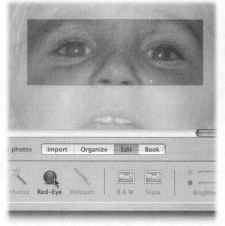 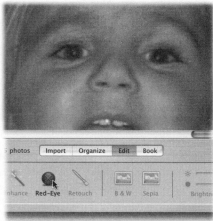

2. Drag carefully, diagonally, across the eye area with your cursor. Make sure the box encloses a decent-sized patch of skin around the eyes, too, so iPhoto can compare the light and dark areas.

3. Click the Redeye button.

Now, the truth is, the Red-Eye tool doesn't know an eyeball from an icicle. It just turns any red areas black, as you can see in the "after" photo above (right). Of course, this means that everybody winds up looking like they have *black* eyes instead of red ones — but at least they look a little less like the walking undead.

And by the way: If one particular person shows up with redeye in *all* your photos, call an exorcist.

Painting out freckles, warts, and zits

Sometimes the tiniest of imperfections can ruin an otherwise perfect portrait: a freckle, a hair, a wrinkle. Professional photographers routinely *retouch* such photos — that is, they remove those minor imperfections (or, in the case of celebrity photos, *major* imperfections) before bringing the photo to the public.

iPhoto's Retouch brush lets you do the same thing with your own photos. You can paint away minor problems like scratches, spots, hairs, or any other small flaws in your photos with a few quick strokes.

When you click the Retouch button, your pointer turns into a small crosshair with a hole in the middle. Now just "paint" over the imperfection, using short strokes to blend it with the surrounding portion of the picture. The Retouch brush blends together the colors in the tiny area that you're fixing. It doesn't cover the imperfections you're trying to remove, but *blurs* them out by softly blending them into a small radius of surrounding pixels.

Don't overdo it: If you apply too much retouching, you'll start to blur and smear the area you're working.

As you go, remember that the Retouch brush is for fixing *small* problems. It can't eliminate the grape-juice stain on your daughter's white shirt or erase the devil horns from your ex-spouse.

B & W and Sepia

With one click, the Black & White tool (labeled B&W) drains the color from a photo, converting it into moody image — a great technique if you're going for that Ansel Adams look. The Sepia button is similar, except that it makes the selected photo look old and brownish, for that old-time daguerreotype look.

If you change your mind, you can use the Undo command (in the File menu) to restore the color immediately.

Adjusting brightness and contrast

If the Enhance button described earlier is just a bit *too* automatic for your taste, you can also fiddle with a photo using the Brightness/Contrast sliders on the bottom edge of the window. These, as you can probably figure out, help you improve a photo by making it brighter or bringing out the difference between light and dark.

Organizing into "Albums"

It's nice of iPhoto to keep all of your pictures on one massive, scrolling screen. On the other hand, that's not always the most efficient arrangement. Fortunately, it's a snap to create little folders — *albums,* as they're called in iPhoto — that contain subsets of these pictures.

The trick is to click the little + button at the lower-left side of the screen. iPhoto asks you to type in a name for the album you're about to create; do so and then click OK. (If you've read Chapter 9, this concept should sound distinctly familiar: It's exactly the same idea as the little playlists you can create in iTunes.)

Now look in the list at the left side of the window: A new little book icon appears there. Above it in the list, click Photo Library (to see every photo you've ever taken) or Last Roll (to see only the pictures you grabbed from the camera during your last importing session). Your challenge now is to select the pictures that you'll want to put into the newly created album. The routine goes like this:

✔ Click one picture to select it.

✔ ⌘-click additional pictures to select them, as well. (That is, click while pressing the ⌘ key.)

✔ To select several consecutive pictures, ⌘-click the first one, and then *Shift*-click the last one. You've just highlighted all of the pictures in between, as well.

✔ Drag diagonally across a group of photos to select all of them at once.

✔ Drag diagonally while pressing the Shift key to select a separate group of pictures, without losing the ones you've already selected.

I realize that that's a lot of permutations to remember, but hey — that's why you have them written down.

In any case, once you've highlighted the pictures, drag any *one* of them on top of the album book icon. A little red circle lets you know how many photos you're dragging, like this:

Now, dragging pictures into an album like this doesn't remove them from the main photo library. The main photo library (click Photo Library at the top of the list) *always* contains every photo you've ever taken.

When you drag pictures into an album, you're neither moving them nor even copying them. You're just creating imaginary duplicates that are *linked* back to the original pictures. Thanks to this quirk, you can put a single photo into as many different albums as you like. A picture of Harold, proudly displaying the trout that he caught on your joint vacation to Mississippi, winds up in several different albums that you've created: one called Relatives, one called Fishing, and one called Vacations, for example.

Showing Off Your Photos

iPhoto provides a number of different features for showing off your pictures on the screen. Set up some folding chairs, make popcorn, and then gather the family around the Mac. Then click the Organize button beneath pictures, and get ready for some spectacular visual fireworks.

Making prints

Sooner or later, most people want to get at least some of their photos on paper. You may want to paste prints into your existing scrapbooks, to put in a picture frame on the mantle, or to share with technology-challenged friends who don't have computers. Thanks to the amazing quality of today's color inkjet printers — even cheap ones — the prints you get from iPhoto look astoundingly close to commercial drugstore prints. (If you use glossy inkjet photo paper, that is.)

When you click the Print button, you're offered a dialog box like this:

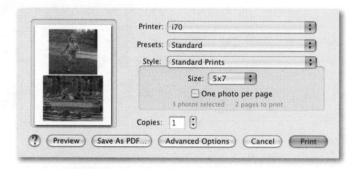

Using the Style pop-up menu, you can choose from six photo-specific printing options: Standard Prints, Full Page, Greeting Cards (which you fold into greeting-card size), Contact Sheet (prints out a *grid* of photos, tiling as many as 112 different pictures onto a single letter-size page), N-Up (tiles 2, 4, 6, 9, or 16 pictures on each sheet of paper), and Sampler (like the portrait sets you might get from a professional photographer — a sheet that contains a combination of one large photo and five smaller photos, for example).

Don't forget to click the Advanced Options button to access the standard Print dialog box for your printer. Inside, there's a pop-up menu (which starts out being called Copies & Pages) that lets you specify what kind of paper you're printing on. It's *very* important to choose the right setting here; if you've paid the big bucks for fancy inkjet glossy photo paper, and the Mac thinks it's printing on plain typing paper, the results can make your family picnic photos look like it was rained out by some kind of nuclear meltdown.

Having a slide show

Click the album icon whose pictures you want to see in the slide show, and then click the Slide Show icon at the bottom of the screen. iPhoto asks how many seconds you want to see each picture on the screen — two is usually just about right; if you click the Music button at the top, you can choose a piece of background music from the Music pop-up menu. (You'll notice that your entire iTunes music collection is available here.) Click Play to begin the show.

To stop the show, click the mouse.

Sending pix by e-mail

Start by selecting one picture, or a few. Then click the E-mail button at the bottom edge of the screen.

iPhoto asks you what size you want the photo to be — an extremely friendly gesture, because sending a *full-size* digital camera picture does your recipient absolutely no good. Thanks to a quirk of computer graphics, the *resolution* (number of dots) in a photo designed for printing is grossly overblown for the number of dots needed for viewing on the screen. That's why iPhoto offers to scale the picture down to reasonable size, such as 640 by 480 dots.

Click Compose. After a moment, you'll find yourself facing an empty piece of e-mail (Chapter 8), with the file already attached, ready for you to type in the address and any comments you'd like to include. One click on the Send command sends your picture on its merry way.

(Incidentally, iPhoto assumes that you use the Mail program described in Chapter 8 for e-mail purposes. If you use some other program, like America

Online or Microsoft Entourage, open the iPhoto menu, choose Preferences, and — from the "Mail using" pop-up menu — choose the e-mail program you *do* use. Then close the Preferences window.)

Ordering prints

Click this button if you'd like your electronic photos turned into regular old glossy prints, exactly as though they came from the drugstore. The difference, of course, is that they get transmitted to the "drugstore" (actually Kodak) via the Internet, and you have print-size options from 4 by 6 all the way up to poster size. You'll be offered a complete price list when you click the Order Prints button — and the thrilling opportunity to type in your credit-card information.

Professional bookmaking

Screen saver, schmeen saver! If you really want to see what your computer can do, turn your pictures into a *book*. We're talking about a hardback, linen-covered, acid-free, full-color, professionally-published gift book that arrives in a beautiful slipcover in about three days from an actual printing plant. It costs about $30 — more if you go beyond 10 pages — and creates an impact on the lucky recipients that neither you nor they will ever, ever forget.

Here's how you go about designing your book.

1. **Put the pictures you'll want to include into an album of their own, as described earlier in this chapter.**

   Feel free to drag them around on the screen so that they're in the right order for the book, like this:

   You can have up to 32 pictures on each page of the book, depending on the page design you've selected.

2. Click the Book button beneath the picture viewing area.

Now you find yourself in a miniature book-design program.

Theme pop-up menu   Page Design pop-up menu

Drag pages to rearrange them

3. Choose an underlying design for your book, using the Theme pop-up menu.

For example, the theme called Classic leaves plenty of margin around your pictures, but Picture Book blows up your photos so that they fill the page edge to edge. Story Book goes for a more interesting, less square look by placing the photos at slight angles, and overlapping on each page.

4. Click each page of the book and design it, using the Page Design pop-up menu to specify how many photos should appear on that page.

As you change the number of pictures on a certain page, note that the pictures on the pages *following* it slide left or right to take up the slack. For that reason, work on the pages of your book *in order,* from left to right, from page 1 to page 10 (or whatever). Otherwise, you'll drive yourself crazy.

You can also designate special pages as the cover, introduction, and final pages. You can also rearrange the pages just by dragging them horizontally. Some of the page designs feature text boxes, too, where you can type in captions and descriptions. (To choose the font and size for the type, open the Edit menu, choose Font, and choose Show Fonts from the submenu. One typeface per book, please.)

5. **When the whole book looks good, click the Organize button, and then click the Order Book button.**

The program now offers you the chance to choose the color you want for the cover. It may also warn you that some of the photos' resolution (quality) is too low to look good in your book. If you proceed without making the photos smaller, they'll look a little bit blotchy in the resulting published book — generally something you'll want to avoid, except perhaps in photo essays about skin-disease clinics.

How you wrap up your book-publishing process depends on whether or not you've created a "1-click account," a means of ordering stuff from Apple without having to type in your name and address over and over again. And to do *that,* you'll need an *Apple ID* — a name and password that you make up. The software guides you through both of these steps.

Finally, your book design is sent to the Internet, and the finished book — about 9 by 11 inches, with the photos printed directly onto the glossy, acid-free pages — arrives at the address you specify in about a week. Both the book and, by extension, you, look absolutely spectacular.

HomePage

Here's one of the all-time best ways to show off your photos to the world: Post them on the Web, where anyone who's online can see them whenever they like. It's better than e-mailing the photos, in fact, because you're not filling up somebody's e-mail box with photo files (which take a long time to send, anyway).

This feature requires that you've signed up for a .Mac account, as described in Chapter 6. You'll be offered a choice of designs for your online gallery, plus the opportunity to type in some captions for them.

Finally, click the Publish button and sit back with a magazine while your computer hangs your photos on the great refrigerator door of cyberspace. (Make careful note of the Web address you'll be shown on the screen. This is the address you need to give your friends and family — anybody who would like to actually see your photo gallery.)

Desktop or Screen Saver

Click one photo — a really, really good one — and then click this button at the bottom edge of the screen. iPhoto instantly fills your desktop background with that photo — an intoxicating and joyous feature that you'll soon wish had a physical counterpart in the world of wallpaper and house paint.

Or, if you select *more than one photo* (like a whole album), iPhoto turns them into the fodder for Mac OS X's spectacular screensaver feature, which fills your screen with animated, gently flowing photographs when your Mac is isn't in use. (After all, you have to eat and take showers *sometime*.)

Of course, you may have to wait for half an hour or so to see the effect — that's when the screensaver finally kicks in — but you're sure to be amazed and impressed.

.Mac Slides

This is perhaps the weirdest way to share your photos — electronically: publish them as a *.Mac slide show*. Once you've highlighted some photos and then clicked the .Mac Slides button, other Mac fans, all over the world, can *subscribe* to your show, displaying *your* pictures as *their* screen savers. In a minute or so, your latest photos can appear as full-screen slides on the Macintosh of a friend, family member, co-worker, or anyone else who knows your .Mac membership name. (This feature, too, requires that you have a .Mac account; see Chapter 6.)

After you've "published" your photos as .Mac slides, your fans can subscribe to the show and make it into a screen saver. They do that by opening System Preferences (see Chapter 3) and clicking the Desktop & Screen Saver icon (called Screen Effects in 10.2).

Then they click *.Mac* in the list of screen savers, click Configure, type your .Mac member name into the box, and click OK. At last, the Mac hooks up to your .Mac account and, seconds later, displays *your* slides on the little Preview screen in a miniature version of the slide show. When the screen saver actually kicks in (or when they click the Test button), the slide show will fill their screens at full size.

Backing Up Your Photos

Making a backup of your digital photos is *extremely* important. Remember that once you erase your camera's memory card, those photos — that precious record of your life — exist only in one place: on your hard drive. If anything goes wrong, the photos are *gone forever*.

Of course, you'll be sad about losing your e-mail collection and favorite recipes, too. But for many people, losing a life's worth of photos is far more devastating.

The easiest way to back up your photos is to burn them onto blank CDs or DVDs, depending on which kind of burner your Mac has. The ritual goes like this:

1. **With iPhoto in Organize mode, select the albums or photos that you want to include on the disc.**

   If your Mac can burn DVDs, your whole library might be able to fit on a single DVD (click the Photo Library icon). If it can burn only CDs, you might have to break up your library across multiple discs, choosing an album or two each time.

   To burn only a specific album or group of albums, select them in the Albums pane. Either way, the photo viewing area should now be showing the photos you want to save onto a disc.

2. **Click the Burn icon at the bottom of the iPhoto window.**

   A dialog box asks you to insert a blank disc. Pop in a CD-R or DVD-R disc (you can buy these at computer stores). After a minute, the dialog box vanishes.

3. **Check to see if your photos will fit on the disc.**

   See the Info panel just below with Albums list, shown here?

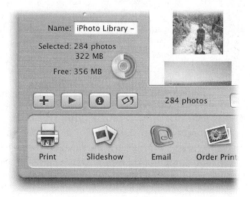

If the photos you want to burn consume less than 660 MB (for a CD) or about 4.3 gigabytes (for a DVD), you're good to go. You can burn the whole thing to a single disc.

If your photo collection is larger than that, however, you'll have to split your backup across multiple discs. Select whatever number of photo albums or individual pictures you can that *will* fit on a single disc. Then, after burning the first disc, select the next set of photos, and then burn another CD or DVD. Burn as many discs as needed to contain your entire collection of photos.

4. **Click the Burn icon again.**

   The Mac presents a confirmation dialog box, telling you exactly how many photos it's going to record to disc.

5. **Click the Burn button.**

   When the recording process is done, your Mac spits out the finished CD or DVD (named "iPhoto Disc"). Your pictures are safely backed up!

The finished disc contains not just your photos, but a clone of your iPhoto Library folder as well — all the thumbnails, comments, photo album information, names you've given your pictures, and so on.

If you ever want to retrieve the contents of your finished CD, pop the disc back into the drive. If iPhoto isn't running, your Mac opens it automatically.

Moments later, the icon for the CD appears in the Source list of the iPhoto window. If you click the disc's icon, the photos it contains appear in the photo viewing area, just as if they were stored in your Photo Library. At this point, you can drag the photos into new albums to copy them back onto the Mac.

Chapter 11

iSpielberg: Digital Movies and DVDs

Making digital movies on a computer isn't a new thing. For years, high-tech companies sold the $5,000 add-on circuit boards and $800 software programs you needed to do so. But the results weren't anything like what you'd see on TV. The finished movies played on your screen in a window the size of a Triscuit. And they were jerky. If you wanted full-screen, smooth video, you'd have had to assemble $100,000 worth of equipment. Not many people bothered.

But oh, what a difference a decade makes. You lucky, lucky soul: You're alive to see the dawn of a new era, in which ordinary mortals like you can make astonishingly high-quality movies with nothing more than a camcorder and your Mac. Everything you need — the circuitry and the software — is already built in. As you transfer your footage back and forth between the Mac and the camcorder, the film retains 100 percent of its quality, always playing full-screen, smooth, bright, and vibrant.

Got What It Takes?

This kind of moviemaking doesn't require the mountains of gear it once did, but it does require a *digital* camcorder.

Camcorders that accept only VHS, VHS-C, 8 millimeter, or Hi-8 tapes are *not* digital. True digital camcorders, which start at around $450, are very compact. Sony, Canon, JVC, and Panasonic make them. These cameras accept one-hour tapes called *Mini DV* cassettes, which record CD-quality sound and video of absolutely breathtaking quality.

If you do decide to buy a camcorder, do your shopping on the Internet. At Web sites like *www.shopping.com,* you can survey long lists of digital camcorders, read what past buyers have to say about them, and compare prices from dozens of mail-order outfits.

The last item you need is a "4 pin-to-6-pin" FireWire cable, which you'll have to buy from a computer store (or, to save money, from a Web site like *www.buy.com.*) *FireWire* is one of the built-in Mac technologies that makes all this possible. It's a high-speed cable that plugs into the FireWire jacks on the back or side of your computer. (See Chapter 20 for a picture.) Hook the tiny end up to the corresponding jack on your camcorder (this jack may be concealed by a plastic cover), and the other end to your Mac's FireWire jack.

Kinds of digital camcorders

A digital camcorder makes a pretty heady addition to your Mac. Using it and iMovie, you can edit your own home movies — a simple act that's sure to be appreciated by your fellow humans — or even produce professional-quality independent films.

You can plug either of two kinds of camcorders into the back of your Mac:

MiniDV camcorders. These are some of the smallest camcorders you can buy. The prices start at around $450, but run up into the thousands. These camcorders take tiny, matchbox-sized cassettes that hold one hour each and cost about $4 per tape (from *www.bhphoto.com*, for example).

Digital8 camcorders. This fascinating hybrid, only from Sony, accepts 8mm or Hi-8 tapes, which are much less expensive than MiniDV tapes. These camcorders are bulkier than MiniDV ones, but also less expensive.

Onto these cassettes, Digital8 camcorders record the same digital signal found on mini-DV camcorders, so the quality is just as good. But they can play back *either* digital video *or* traditional, analog video. This kind of camcorder, in other words, is a good solution if you have a library of old 8mm tapes that you'd like to edit in iMovie; your Mac can't tell which kind of tape the Digital8 camcorder is playing.

Either way, a FireWire cable connects the camcorder to your Mac. Beware, though: Editing video can put your brain into a dreamy trance. You'll look up and it'll be next week, with a pile of unread newspapers on your doorstep.

MicroMV camcorders. This kind of Sony camcorder is digital, all right, and it's *tiny;* in fact, Sony dreamed up this format, and the very expensive, very small tapes that work with it, just to make the resulting camcorder smaller. Unfortunately, this format has a lot of downsides. It's expensive, it's hard to find the tapes, and — worst of all — it doesn't work with iMovie.

Filming Your Life

Not many people actually make *films* with their digital camcorders — writing a script, getting actors together, and all that jazz. Most people wind up just editing their home-movie footage, and that's a very good thing. If you've ever spent time at a friend's house watching six consecutive hours of little Goober spitting up, you know that a *good* home movie is an *edited* home movie.

The first step in making movies on your Mac is capturing life with your camcorder. There's not a lot to it, actually: Press the red button to start filming, press it again to stop. Oh, and take off the lens cap.

But the quality of your equipment is so good, and the results are so exciting, that it's worth learning a few tricks to make your stuff look more professional:

- **Go easy on the zooming.** Yes, I know, your camcorder has a zoom in/zoom out button that's really fun to use. It's also really nauseating to watch later.

  Try to limit yourself to a single zoom — or none — per shot. Use the zoom mostly when it creates a visual punch line: There's little Timmy with a kite string in his hands, but your zoom-out reveals that the other end is, in fact, tied to the collar of a goat that's pulling him down the street on rollerblades.

- **Try a tripod.** For sure, turn on your camcorder's "image stabilization" feature, if it has one. But the biggest difference between home footage and pro TV footage is the tripod. These things are cheap — I found one for $30 at *www.amazon.com* — and the resulting stability makes an enormous difference to the quality of the finished movie.

- **For dialog, use a clip-on microphone.** The other hallmark of amateur work is the sound. The camcorder's built-in mike not only picks up its own machinery, but sounds lousy if you're more than six feet from the speaker. A tie-clip mike is about $20 at Radio Shack; pick up a couple of extension cords for it, too, plug them into your camcorder's microphone jack, and you won't believe how much better your flicks sound.

- **For iMovie movies, shoot too much.** MiniDV cassettes cost good money. If you didn't have a Mac, I'd suggest that you be very selective in what you film. But the beauty of iMovie is that it lets you *edit down* your video, and then *put it back* onto the videotape! You don't lose any quality in the process. For that reason, you may want to keep the camcorder running more liberally than you would otherwise. Doing so improves the chances that you'll catch really good stuff (especially if you're filming children, animals, or hurricanes). You can always cut the boring stuff and re-use the original tape later.

Step 1: Dump the Footage into iMovie

Once you've got some good scenes, you're ready for the fun to begin. Connect your camcorder to one of your Mac's FireWire jacks. Put the camcorder into what's usually called VTR mode (also known as VCR or Playback mode). Open iMovie — its icon looks like a Hollywood clapper board, and it's in your Applications folder (or, unless you removed it, on your Dock). Then click the Camera icon, which you can see in this big-picture view of iMovie:

Monitor window   Playhead   Clips pane

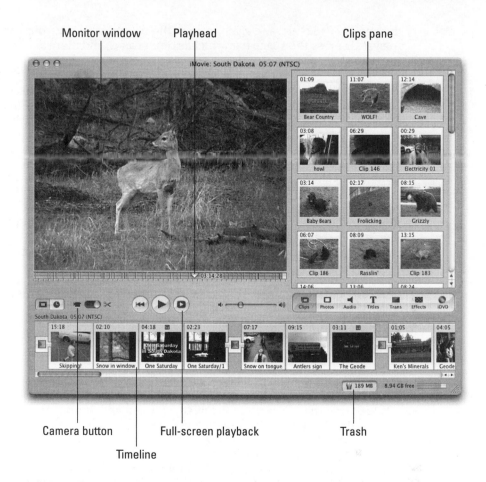

Camera button   Full-screen playback   Trash

Timeline

If all is well, you'll see a big blue screen at the upper-left with the words "Camera Connected" prominently displayed. You're ready to begin grabbing choice scenes from the camcorder for storage on the Mac.

Now you can actually control the play, stop, rewind, and fast-forward functions of the camcorder using the buttons on the screen of your Mac — an impressive and tingly feature. You do so by clicking the buttons below the big monitor screen.

Capturing clips

Here's the deal: As you watch the tape, whenever you see a piece of footage worth including in your movie, capture it! You do that by clicking the Import button once to start, and again to stop, the capturing, while your camcorder plays. Or press the space bar, which is often easier and more accurate: Press once to start, once to stop.

Each time you grab a scene from your tape, it appears on the Clips pane (see the figure at the beginning of Step 1), where it's represented by what looks like a 35mm slide. Congratulations: You've just created a *clip*. The whole business of movie editing, whether on your Mac or in $100 million Hollywood studios, boils down to rearranging clips.

The Clips pane is a waiting room, a place to store clips temporarily before you start plunking them into the storyboard thing at the bottom of the screen. (The storyboard track can hold as many clips as your hard drive can hold.) Once you've captured enough clips to start assembling your movie, you'll drag them down into the storyboard track.

How much footage can your Mac hold?

Considering that the text of this entire book consumes less than 2 megabytes of the 60,000 or 160,000 on your hard drive, you may have wondered why these models came with such enormous hard drives. You're about to find out.

Turns out that digital video, once transferred from your camcorder to your Mac, consumes a *huge* amount of hard-drive space — 3.5 megs of your hard drive *per second* of video! Do the math, and you find out that a typical Mac can hold only a few hours' worth of footage at a time.

This isn't such a big deal, however; the whole object is to edit the stuff on your Mac and then put it *back* onto your videocassettes, where you can play them for friends, family, and backers. Think of your Mac as a temporary operating table, where you work on a little bit of the patient at a time. You can transfer video between your camcorder and your Mac thousands of times; the footage will never deteriorate in quality, as it would with, for example, an audiocassette.

As you work in iMovie, watch the Free Space indicator at the bottom of the window. The graph is blue when you've got plenty of space left, yellow when things are getting tight, and red when your hard drive is nearly full. At that point, it's time to dump your movie back out to a tape, as described later in this chapter, and then delete the retired clips from your hard drive. (Each file you save from iMovie appears in a folder of its own, which contains a Media folder. To delete video files you're *certain* you won't need again, throw away this Media folder.)

Naming, playing, and trimming clips

Once your clips are on the Clips pane, you can do three things with them: Rename them, play them, and trim them.

Renaming clips

As your clips show up on the Clips pane, they take on such exciting names as Clip 01, Clip 02, and so on. Making a movie out of them is much easier if they're renamed Goober Smiles, Goober Falls Over, and so on. To do so, just click once on a clip's name, type the new name, and press the Return key.

Playing clips

To play a clip that's on the Clips pane, click it once. You'll see the first frame show up in the Monitor. At this point, you can use any of the VCR-type buttons to play this clip, just as you used them to control your camcorder earlier in this lesson.

You can also drag the tiny box called the *playhead,* shown in the previous illustration, to view earlier or later parts of the clip.

Trimming clips, method 1

Even more important is *trimming* your clips. Like pro video editors, you'll quickly learn that it's always safest to capture, from your camcorder, more footage than you need — a few seconds before and after the main action, for example. Then, later, it's a snap to trim out the dead wood.

There are two ways to go about this highly artistic sort of surgery: One that's best for trimming a clip *before* you drop it into your movie, and one that's better for trimming it *after* you've installed it into your film. (More on that second technique in a moment.)

Click the clip's icon in the Clips pane. In the Monitor window, click just beneath the Monitor scroll bar, as shown here at left:

Two triangular handles appear. Drag these handles apart, as shown above at right. The scheme is simple: Everything between them remains in the final clip; everything outside of them will be chopped out. If you find using the mouse too clunky for making fine, frame-by-frame movements of these handles, click one and then press the arrow keys on your keyboard to move it one frame at a time. (Add the Shift key to move one of these handles in *ten*-frame jumps.)

As you choose parts of a scene to crop out, keep this tip in mind: If you plan to use iMovie's cross-fades from one scene into another, leave a second or two of extra footage on the clip you're trimming. The iMovie program will do its cross-fading during this extra stuff, leaving the *really* important action un-faded.

Finally, when you've got just the good part isolated, choose Crop from the Edit menu. Everything outside your triangle handles gets chopped out.

The Trash

See the little Trash can icon on the screen? Its megabyte count increases to hint at the stuff you've cropped out. You can't double-click this Trash icon to pull stuff out of it, as you can the real Trash icon on your desktop. But using the Edit menu's Undo command, you *can* undo the last ten steps you took in iMovie — including cropping, deleting clips, and otherwise adding stuff to the iMovie Trash can.

And if you *really* mess things up, you can always click what's left of the clip and then, from the Advanced menu, choose Restore Clip. iMovie restores the clip to its original full length, just as it came from the camcorder to begin with, as long as you've haven't emptied iMovie's Trash in the meantime.

Step 2: Build the Movie

To assemble your clips into a movie, drag them out of the Clips pane and into the storyboard track at the bottom of the screen. Once there, each clip is an individual tile that you can drag left or right to make it play before or after the other clips. (You can also drag a new clip between two others; they scoot aside courteously.)

As you work with your movie, what happens when you click the Play button (or press the space bar) depends on what's highlighted:

- If a clip is highlighted in blue in the timeline, pressing the space bar plays only that clip. To un-highlight all clips, choose None from the Edit menu, or just click anywhere on the "brushed metal" of the iMovie window.

✔ To highlight a stretch of just three or four clips for playback, click the first one, and then Shift-click the second one (that is, click it while pressing your Shift key).

✔ If nothing is highlighted, the whole movie you've built plays, starting at the location of the playhead under the Monitor. Press the Home key to start from the beginning.

When no clip is highlighted in the storyboard track, moreover, you can drag the playhead under the Monitor window to jump around in the whole movie under construction. As you do so (and while you play back a clip), you'll see the tiny cursor crawl across that clip's picture in the storyboard track. Once again, you can use the arrow keys to more precisely position the playhead.

Meet the Timeline viewer

So far, you've probably been doing most of your editing work in the storyboard track in *Clips view,* meaning that each clip shows up as a little square slide. But some kinds of editing are easier done in *Timeline* view, where each clip is represented by a horizontal bar, like this:

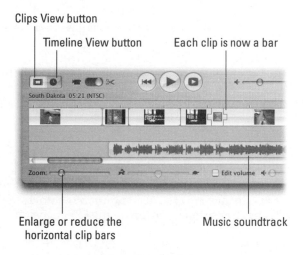

For example, you may remember reading how to *trim* the excess ends of a clip earlier in this chapter. But in the Timeline viewer, you can do that *right in place,* like this:

To shorten a clip, click carefully at its end...

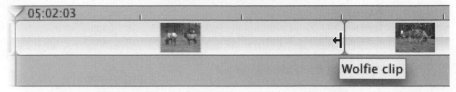

...and drag inward. The other clips slide to close up the gap.

Sharp corners indicate a shortened clip.

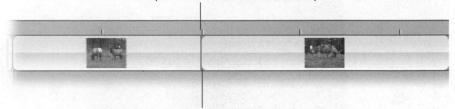

Round corners indicate that the clip length is untouched.

Instead of chopping off the ends of your clips, in other words, you're just *hiding* the ends of your clips. Later, if you change your mind about shortening that clip, you can grab its end and drag it outward again.

Adding a cross-fade

Those slick-looking crossfades between scenes, as seen every night on TV news and in movies, are called *transitions*. iMovie offers several styles; click the Trans (transitions) button on the Effects palette to make the list pop up.

Click the name of the transition you want. Use the slider above the Transitions palette to specify how many seconds long you want the crossfade to last. (One second is fairly standard.) Once you've done so, drag the *name* of the transition into the timeline window, between the two clips you want joined in this way. They'll scoot apart to make room for the new transition icon that appears.

The instant you do so, a tiny red progress line starts to crawl across the transition icon. Your Mac is now processing the crossfade — as the pros would say, *rendering it* — by melding the end of one clip and the beginning of the next. You can go right on building your movie; that little red line will keep quietly crunching its way across the transition icon in the background.

To delete a transition, click its icon in the timeline and then press Delete; to edit it (by changing its length, for example), double-click its icon, which returns you to the Transitions palette.

Adding titles

iMovie even lets you add rolling credits and opening titles to your little home flicks. It beats block lettering on shirt cardboards.

Start by clicking the Titles button. A list of title-animation styles pops up. In the tiny text box underneath the list, type the text you'll want for the credits.

Note that some of the effects, such as Scrolling Credits, let you type in *pairs* of text blobs, as shown below at left. After you've typed in a couple of pairs, click the + button to tack on yet another pair to your credits. The program automatically adds the dots and lines up the names, as shown here at right:

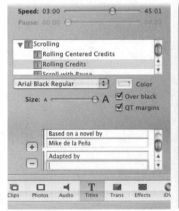

Click the Preview button to see what this effect will look like. Adjust the timing slider above the list, exactly as with transitions, and then drag the name of the title into the timeline.

If you want to insert this title *in front of* a clip, so that the text appears on a black background, turn on the Over Black checkbox. If you'd rather have the text appear *on top of* your video, leave that box unchecked. You'll soon discover that superimposing a title on a clip usually breaks the clip in half — the part with the title superimposed is now one clip, and the unaffected part is separate.

Editing a title works exactly as it does with transitions: To eliminate one, double-click the title's icon in the timeline and then press Delete; to edit, double-click its icon. You jump back to the Effects palette, where you can tweak the text, the amount of time it will stay on the screen, and so on.

Color Effects

On the Effects palette, click Effects. The various effects here (Adjust Colors, Black and White, Brightness/Contrast, and so on) change the look of whatever footage you drag them onto.

You won't be able to make, say, *Star Wars Episode 10: Jabba's Clubhouse* using these simple "special effects." And don't expect to use, say, the Brightness effect to rescue some footage that was too dark; it can't do magic. But some of them look very realistic — Aged Film, Earthquake, and Rain, for example — and may occasionally come in handy for certain comic or dramatic moments in your home movies.

Point just beneath the scroll bar to make the selection triangles appear, as described earlier in this chapter, and use them to select the region of the movie to which you want the effect applied.

Now click the effect's name, and then fool around with its sliders. The Effect In and Effect Out sliders let you ease into, or out of, an effect over the course of a clip. When it looks good, click the Apply button.

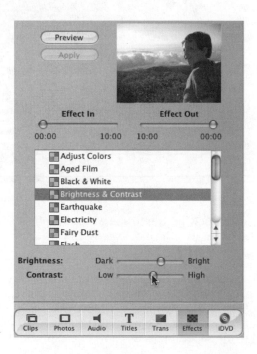

You may be surprised to discover that iMovie chops up some of the clips when you apply an effect; that's because technically speaking, you can apply these footage-changing effects only to an entire clip at a time.

What's nice about these effects, by the way, is that they're removable. At any time — even after your debut at the Cannes festival — you can restore a clip to its original, un-effected form. Switch your storyboard into Clips view; click the clip; and then press the Delete key. You're not actually deleting the *clip* — only the effect you layered on top of it.

On the other hand, if you're confident you'll never want to do so, you can reclaim some disk space by clicking the button on the Effects palette called Commit. (Great name for a button, by the way. Too bad relationships don't have a Commit button.)

Background music and sound FX

Nothing adds emotional power to a movie like music. Studies have shown that fast, driving music makes your heart beat faster. Hollywood has shown that slow, lush music makes the difference between a sad story and one that actually makes viewers cry. Virtually every professional movie has music, so why shouldn't the ones that you create?

In iMovie, click the Audio button on the Effects palette. If you inspect the pop-up menu at the top of the list, you'll find several sources of background music and sound:

- ✔ Your complete iTunes music library, complete with any playlists you've created. This arrangement makes it simple to find just the right piece of music for your movie, because you can double-click each song name to hear it.

- ✔ If you haven't yet stocked your copy of iTunes with tunes (Chapter 9), or if the song you want isn't in iTunes yet, you can also insert any music CD right into your Mac. After a moment, a list of the songs on it appears in the list. Click one, and then use the Play button on the Effects palette (the triangle) to find an appropriate snippet.

- ✔ If you choose iMovie Effects from the pop-up menu, you'll see a long scrolling list of sound effects: Cold Wind, Electricity, Jungle, Birds, Squeaky Door, and so on. (Click one of the "flippy triangles" to see your two different collections: Skywalker Sound Effects and Standard Sound Effects.)

To edit your soundtracks, you have to switch your storyboard track into Timeline view, as described earlier.

Drag a song from the Music list (either an iTunes tune, a song from a CD, or a sound effect) down onto one of the two bottom audio tracks. There it shows up as a colored stripe, as shown in the following illustration.

Narration

You can also record new sounds directly into your movie, if your Mac has a microphone. (Laptops and iMacs have built-in mikes, for example, and you can buy one for other models.) Just click the clock tab of the timeline, so that you can see your audio tracks. Click above the tracks to set the playhead where you want to begin your narration. On the Effects palette, click Audio.

Finally, click the round, red Record button, lean close to the microphone, and say what you've got to say. You actually get to watch the movie play while you narrate, which makes it ideal for "Oh, here comes my favorite part"-type narrations. Click the Stop button (formerly the Record button) to stop recording.

Your newly recorded sound appears as a colored bar in the sound track.

Editing sound in the timeline

Once you've laid a sound into the timeline, you can slide its colored ribbon right or left to align it better with the video. Click a sound, then drag the volume slider to change its loudness; or click one of the checkboxes, Fade In or Fade Out, to add a professional-sounding fade when the music begins or ends. And, of course, you can delete the sound completely by clicking it and then pressing the Delete key.

But that's just some of the fun you can have with sound. You can also:

- ✔ View the actual sound waves of an audio track, as illustrated in the next figure. (From the iMovie menu, choose Preferences, and then turn on "Show audio track waveforms." Close the Preferences window.)

- ✔ Trim an audio clip like this just as you would a video clip: by tugging inward on its starting and ending points.

- ✔ Superimpose pieces of sound. Because there are only two tracks for sounds, including narration, music, and sound effects, telling the overlapping colored stripes apart can be a challenge. But on that occasion when you want your background music to be a simultaneous playing of Carly Simon and Scott Joplin, you'll be ready.

- ✔ Make music get louder and softer over time. That's a *very* common feature of movie and TV sound tracks. For example, you can "pull back" the music whenever somebody on camera is speaking, and then bring it back to full volume in between speeches. You can also use this feature to "erase" bits of sound you'd rather make less prominent, like a swear word, a cough, or a belch. And you can use this feature to make your music (or the sound from the original video) smoothly fade in or out whenever you like.

All you have to do is turn on the "Edit volume" checkbox at the bottom of the timeline. When you turn it on, a horizontal line appears on every audio clip, stretching from edge to edge. This line is a graph of the clip's volume. When you click directly on the line and drag upward or downward, you create a small spherical handle, and the drag produces a curve in the line from its original volume level. (You can also drag this handle left or right to adjust the timing of this fluctuation.)

Drag these "rubber band" lines to make volume louder or softer   Mute a sound track

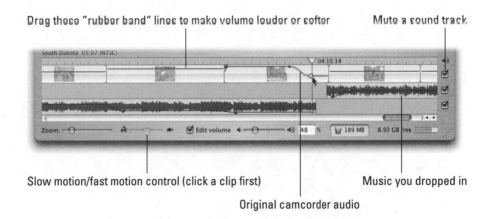

Slow motion/fast motion control (click a clip first)   Music you dropped in

Original camcorder audio

Step 3: Find an Audience

After you're happy with your movie, and you've waited for all the little red rendering lines to fulfill their destinies, check your movie. Press the Home key (to rewind to the beginning) and then the space bar (to play it one last time). For a delightful taste treat, click the Full Screen button (the button just to the right of the big triangular Play button) to play the movie so that it fills your entire screen.

If everything looks good, you're ready to show your filmless film to people. You can do so in one of three ways: by sending it back to the videotape, by creating a QuickTime movie that other computers can play, or by preserving it forever on a real, live DVD.

Sending your movie back to the camcorder

There's a lot to be said for sending your finished video back to the camcorder's tape. By connecting the camcorder to a TV, you'll be able to play your masterpiece for anyone. And by connecting the camcorder to a regular VCR, you can make and distribute VHS copies to anyone who's interested.

Begin by putting a cassette into your camcorder. *Don't record over something important!* Consider keeping a separate cassette just for your finished projects, for example, so you never risk recording over some important original footage.

Now, from the File menu, choose Share. (These instructions fit iMovie version 4. If you have an earlier version, the steps are slightly different; for example, the command is called Export Movie in iMovie version 3.)

The Share dialog box appears, as shown here. Click the Videocamera icon, and then click Share.

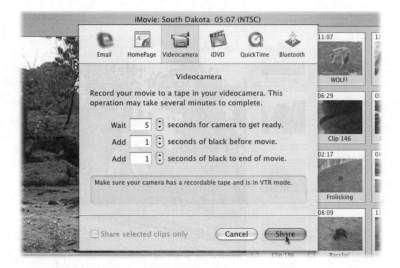

If your camcorder is correctly connected to the Mac's FireWire jack, turned on, and in VTR (VCR) mode, it now records your movie. When the recording is complete, you can prove that the transfer was successful; click the Camera button in iMovie, and then use iMovie's usual Play and Rewind buttons to control the camcorder, making it show your work one last time in its final form.

Saving your movie as a QuickTime file

A *QuickTime movie* is a movie file on your hard drive that you can double-click to watch, mail to other people, put on the World Wide Web, save onto another disk, and so on. The one big QuickTime bummer, though, is that these movies take up enormous amounts of disk space. A standard, 600-megabyte CD-ROM disc, for example, holds less than two minutes of full-screen video. Obviously, that kind of movie would be lousy for e-mailing to somebody or posting on the Web; it would take 56 *hours* to transfer by modem.

The object of creating a QuickTime movie, therefore, is to reduce the size of the file. You can do that in three ways:

- **Make the "screen" smaller.** Instead of filling your screen, most QuickTime movies play in a small, three-inch-square window.

- **Make the color fidelity worse.** Using a conversion process called *compression,* you can make the Mac describe the color of each dot of the movie using less information. The result is a smaller (but grainier) file.

- **Make the frame rate lower.** A QuickTime movie, like a movie-theatre movie, simulates motion by flashing dozens of individual still photos in sequence. The more of these *frames* that appear per second, the smoother the motion — and the bigger the QuickTime file. By telling your Mac to save the QuickTime movie with only, say, 12 frames per second instead of the usual 30, you create a file that's less than half the size (but doesn't play back as smoothly).

After wrapping up your iMovie movie, then, here's how you save it: From the File menu, choose Share. When the dialog box appears, click one of these buttons:

- **E-mail.** If you click this button, iMovie will create a movie file whose "screen" is about the size of a Wheat Thin and plays at only 10 frames per second. The resulting file *may* be small enough to send as an e-mail attachment to a friend, as long as your movie is less than a couple of minutes long.

- **HomePage.** If you have a .Mac account (Chapter 6), this button converts your masterpiece into a QuickTime file that plays on a Web page (at 12 frames per second, in a window about the size of an index card). The beauty of this system is that you don't risk clogging up people's In boxes by sending your movie via e-mail — and anybody in the world can now view your work.

  Click the Share button. The movie will take a good deal of time to post online. (If it's a longish movie, note that it might not even fit within the 100 megabytes of space you get with your .Mac account. Which is why there's a Buy More Space button right in the Share dialog box.) When it's over, you'll be told the Web address of your new Web page, so that you can send it around to your fans and groupies.

✔ **QuickTime.** If you'd like more control over the quality, frame rate, and "screen size" of your movie, click the QuickTime button. If you choose Expert Settings from the pop-up menu, and then click Share, and then click Options, you'll be offered a dialog box whose Settings buttons let you specify *exactly* how your movie is compressed: how many frames per second you'd like, what size window it plays in, how much the colors should be compressed, and so on.

Hint: Most of the time, you'll get the best results by choosing Sorenson Video, Sorenson Video 3, or H.263 from the Compressor pop-up menu. These compression methods create movies that take up a lot less disk space, without rendering the colors too grainy. Try each one to see which one produces the best size/quality tradeoff for your particular movie.

When you're finished setting up the size and quality of your finished movie, click OK. In the "Save exported file as" dialog box, type a name for the finished movie (for best results, leave *.mov* at the end of its name), and then click the Save button. iMovie begins the massive task of converting your movie into the compressed version.

When it's all over, you'll find the finished movie either on your desktop or in your Home folder, inside the Movies folder. Double-click it to open it into a program called QuickTime Player; press the space bar to begin playback.

Burning your movie onto a real DVD

All modern Macs can burn CDs. But the more expensive models go one step beyond. Thanks to an option called the SuperDrive, they can actually "burn" real, live DVD discs, which play back in any standard DVD player. (You youngsters may think this is no big deal — but until the SuperDrive came along, burning a DVD required a $5,000 burning machine and a $2,500 piece of software to run it. You, on the other hand, made out like a bandit.)

There's no better way to screen your finished movies, even for technically backward friends and family who wouldn't know a computer if it fell on their heads. Chances are good that even they own a TV, though. And both you and they will be blown away by the picture and sound quality, which make VHS tapes look like cave drawings.

You can buy five-packs of blank DVD discs from *http://store.apple.com* for $15 or less (the prices keep dropping). You can find them in computer discount stores, too, but be careful: The discs you want are called *DVD-R* discs (note the punctuation). *DVD+R discs* don't work in the Mac; if you buy them by accident, you'll have yourself a handsome collection of shiny silver drink coasters.

Adding chapter markers

If you've ever rented a DVD from Blockbuster, you know what DVD *chapters* are. They're like bookmarks for the scenes in a movie. They let viewers skip to predefined starting points within a movie, either using a Scene menu or pressing the Next Chapter or Previous Chapter buttons on the remote control. You can add bookmarks to your own iMovies markers that perfectly replicate this feature.

In iMovie, click the iDVD button to open the iDVD Chapter Markers palette. Drag the Playhead to the spot where you want the new "chapter marker" to appear. Click Add Chapter. Type a chapter title into the Chapter Title box, just as you'll want it to appear on the finished DVD menu.

Repeat until you've created all the chapters for your movie. From the File menu, choose Save. Now you're ready to hand off the movie to iDVD, where you do your menu design and DVD burning.

Exporting your iMovie

When your movie is ready for prime time, click Create iDVD Project (also in the iDVD Chapter Markers panel).

iMovie takes some time to prepare the DVD-ready file. Some time after the leaves turn, you'll find your iMovie project open and waiting — in a program called iDVD. (Apple really has a thing about the letter *i,* doesn't it?)

Setting up the DVD

As you probably know, a DVD is slightly more complicated than a videotape. When you pop a DVD into its player, you get a *menu screen* — a bunch of buttons that let you jump to any scene in the movie.

Helping you design that screen is the purpose of iDVD, which resides in your Applications folder.

The first screen you encounter looks something like a fancy DVD main menu, with a thrillingly animated screen, accompanied by music. This is, as they say, only an artist's conception of how your finished DVD menu screen will look. You're about to change it beyond all recognition.

Designing the menu screen

To design the background for your DVD's main-menu screen, start by clicking the Customize button in the lower-left corner of the screen. A tidy little drawer pops out of the side of the screen, like this:

Choose a design for your
DVD's main menu screen.

These are buttons that your audience
can "click" with their remote controls.

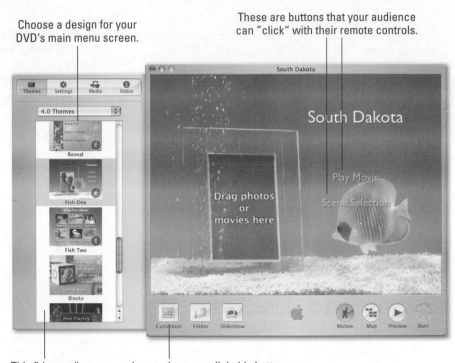

This "drawer" opens or closes when you click this button.

Try clicking each of the sample backdrops in turn, considering how each
might look as your main menu screen. Most of them have background music
or sound. Some of them (those marked by a walking-man icon) have actual
motion to them, which you may consider either astonishingly professional-
looking or cloyingly annoying.

In any case, keep exploring these canned options until you find a look that
you like for your main menu screen — a sandy background for vacation
movies, a pink or blue ribbony one for baby videos, and so on.

You might notice that some of the menu designs have big empty areas that
say, "Drag photos or movie here." These are *drop zones:* Areas where you can
use your own video, slideshows, or graphics as the backgrounds of your
menu screens.

To look over the video, slideshows, and graphics that you might use in these
situations, click Media at the top of the Customize drawer. Then choose
either Photos or Movies from the pop-up menu. iDVD shows you all the
movies (from your hard drive) and all the photos (from iPhoto) it can find.
Drag one directly into the drop zone to install it there, like this:

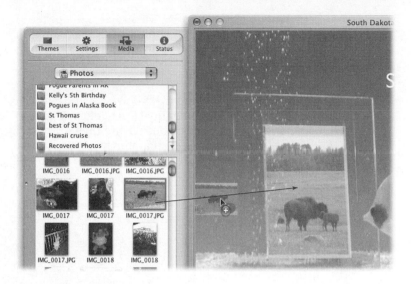

Creating movie buttons

Now, when you exported your iMovie project to iDVD, you wound up with *one* button on the main DVD menu, named after the movie. But each DVD can hold up to two hours of footage, so burning a whole DVD with nothing but a three-minute iMovie on it isn't exactly an economical use of blank discs.

More than 12 movies

All right, you prolific bigwig. So you've got more than 12 movies, eh?

The main menu on a DVD can contain only 12 buttons, take it or leave it. (And that's iDVD 4. If you use an earlier version, the limit is six.) If you've prepared more than 12 iMovie movies, you'll have to spill them over onto a second menu page.

To do that, delete the twelfth movie from the main screen, if you've added one (click it and then press the Delete key). Then click the Folder button at the bottom of the window. iDVD creates a new button for you, which you should feel free to rename.

Then double-click the "folder" button you've just created. iDVD now gives you a second empty page, which you can fill with movie buttons just as you did the first.

Well, 12 of them, anyway.

By branching out to secondary menu screens in this way, you can effectively fill your DVD with dozens of individual movies. Pity your viewer as you do so, however — remember that somebody's actually going to have to *navigate* your menu screens with their remote controls.

Fortunately, you can drag *other* iMovie projects out of the Movie panel (shown above) right onto the DVD menu screen, creating a new button for it. In fact, each menu has room for up to 12 buttons. Drag them around into a sequence you like; click their names to retitle them.

Dressing up those buttons

You can even specify which individual *frame* of each movie will appear as its button. To do so, click the movie button and then drag the tiny slider until you find a nice frame to represent that movie in this "table of contents" view, like this:

1. Click a "movie button" to see these controls.

2. Drag the slider to find just the right frame to serve as your button.

3. Turn off this checkbox if you don't want the movie button to play continuously.

While you're at it, consider the Movie checkbox (also shown above). If it's turned on, then this movie button, when selected by remote control, will actually *play* about 30 seconds of the movie hiding behind that button. If you'd rather your buttons not do anything fancy when they're highlighted, turn off the Movie checkbox.

By the way, you're not limited to the fonts, colors, and button shapes that iDVD proposes, although they do look awfully nice as Apple has prepared them. If you click the Settings tab on the Themes panel, you'll see that you can override all of these design elements.

Use taste, though. The last thing the world needs is a bunch of cheesy looking DVDs.

Previewing the work

When you've arranged the menu screen the way you like it, click the Preview button in the lower-right corner to summon a virtual remote control to the screen. You can use it to try out your simulated DVD. Click one of the miniature movie buttons, for example, to play that movie.

When the menu screens look just the way you like them, click the Burn button at the lower-right corner of the screen. Insert a blank DVD; the SuperDrive does the rest.

It can take a long time to burn a DVD — an hour or two, in fact. Do not attempt to sit and watch it happen; let it run unattended. Find something useful to do — like watching a movie.

When the burning is complete, the DVD pops out of your Mac. Label it, using magic marker on the top surface, and handle it only by the edges as you pop it into any standard DVD player. Your audience will at last get to savor your digital video in its full glory.

Part IV
Toward a New, Nerdier You

The 5th Wave   By Rich Tennant

Okay—you were right, I was wrong. F5 opens the garage door, and F6 backs the car out.

In this part . . .

Enough about turning the computer off, e-mailing tribal members half way around the world, and typing up mundane little bestsellers. Now it's time to get technical.

Not all of computer mastery is about fiddling with digital photos and listening to Internet radio stations. Sooner or later, you're going to have to confront some of the Mac's ickier, computerish aspects: How to switch back to Mac OS 9 for compatibility's sake, how to set up a small network, how to set up security and privacy, and what to do when things go horribly wrong.

Chapter 12

Back to Mac OS 9

In This Chapter

▶ Why your Mac has two operating systems

▶ How to switch back to Mac OS 9 — and why

▶ Making old programs and old equipment work with your spanking-new Mac

T his chapter is about *operating systems* — the software that actually controls your Mac and is responsible for its look and its behavior. No, this reading isn't going to be quite as fluffy as *People* magazine, but look at the bright side: You'll emerge from the other end a better person for it, and you'll finally understand a few of your Mac's most bizarre personality quirks.

A Tale of Two Systems

All the way through this book so far, you've been enjoying descriptions and pictures of the operating system called Mac OS X (that's a Roman numeral ten, and you should pronounce it that way). Mac OS X has a lot to recommend it, including the fact that it virtually never crashes, it looks awesome, and it's generally extremely easy to figure out.

Unfortunately, it's only one of *two* operating systems that you may wind up having to learn about.

From the very first day you turned on the Mac, you might have noticed something peculiar about the main Macintosh HD window: It contains *two* System folders. One is just called System, and it bears a big X to tell you that this is the Mac OS X operating system. The other is called System Folder, and the 9 on its icon tells you that this is a copy of Mac OS 9, which is an older operating system.

Mac OS X

Mac OS 9

Mac OS 9 isn't anywhere near as stable or as beautiful as Mac OS X. It does, however, have about 15,000 things going for it: All the software programs that were written in the decades before Mac OS X came along. Sooner or later, you may run across — or download — a program that looks interesting, but hasn't been adapted to be Mac OS X-compatible.

Fortunately, your Mac can run Mac OS 9 just as well as it runs Mac OS X. In fact, it may be able to run Mac OS 9 in either of two ways, both of which are described in this chapter.

The only downside to all of this is that now you've got *two different* operating systems to learn. The look, features, and locations of favorite commands are different in each one.

Two Mac OS 9 Methods

You can return to Mac OS 9 in either of two ways. Here's a quick rundown, so that you'll know what you're getting into:

✔ **Run Classic.** Your Mac came with a very special program called Classic, which you can think of as a Mac OS 9 *simulator*. It runs automatically whenever you try to open a pre-Mac OS X program.

At that point, the Classic (Mac OS 9) world takes over your screen, looking exactly like a Mac OS 9 computer. The menu now has stripes, the menu bar is light gray instead of striped, and the name of the program you're using now appears on the right side of the screen instead of the left.

At this point, you are, in effect, running two computers at once: a Mac OS 9 computer running inside your Mac OS X one. At this point, you can run most older Mac OS 9 programs without a hitch.

I'm aware that this sounds hideously technical. Remain calm, however. The upcoming discussion will make it a lot less frightening. Furthermore, a couple of years from now, none of this will be necessary, because every good piece of software will be available in a Mac OS X version.

✔ **Restart the Mac in Mac OS 9.** Depending on the model of your Mac, you may also be able to return to Mac OS 9 by *restarting* your computer with the Mac OS 9 operating system in control.

This isn't the same as running the Classic program, which still leaves Mac OS X in control. In this scenario, the only trace of Mac OS X that remains is a bunch of strangely named files and folders, which you shouldn't move or rename.

You should think of this trick as only a workaround — and an inconvenient one at that, because it involves restarting your computer between Mac OS 9 and Mac OS X, which is time-consuming. There's only one time when you'd want to do it: When you want to use some scanner, printer, or drawing tablet that requires Mac OS 9 (and doesn't work in the Classic simulator).

This trick works only on Mac models that debuted before 2003. A Power Mac G5, for example, can't do it, and neither can one of those 17-inch PowerBook laptops with a screen the size of New Zealand.

You'll find instructions for setting up both of these configurations in the following pages.

Classic: The Mac OS 9 Simulator

The way you're most likely to encounter Mac OS 9 is in the form of the Classic simulator. It starts up automatically whenever you double-click the icon of a pre-Mac OS X program. At that point, the Mac says to itself: "Well, this program won't run in Mac OS X, so I'll just go ahead and launch my Mac OS 9 impersonator."

If you want to try this for yourself, double-click the Macintosh HD icon on your desktop, double-click the System Folder (the one bearing the 9 logo), open the Apple Menu Items folder inside it, and finally, double-click Calculator. (This isn't the beautiful Mac OS X Calculator you experimented with earlier in this book; it's the old, black and white, Mac OS 9 version.)

The first sign you have that something funny is going on is the appearance of a progress bar like this:

This bar is designed to entertain you while Classic starts up, which takes a minute or so. During the startup process, you'll also see a little Classic icon (numeral 9) bouncing up and down in your Dock, bursting with enthusiasm.

If you'd like even more entertainment, click the tiny triangle to the left of the progress bar. The screen expands to show you the full-size Mac OS 9 startup screen, as shown here:

When all the bouncing stops, you'll see a number of changes on your screen. Your menu is now rainbow-striped, and the commands in it are very different. The menu bar is light gray, the fonts are smaller, and the menus and commands are different. In short, you've now gone back in time to Mac OS 9.

Once Classic is running, you're free to use the Mac OS 9 program you originally double-clicked (the Calculator, for example) — or almost any other Mac OS 9 program, for that matter.

Understanding the Classic world

The icons of open Mac OS 9 programs appear on the Dock, just like Mac OS X programs. (Well, maybe not *just* like them: Pre-Mac OS X programs usually show up with blotchy, ragged icons on the Dock. They haven't been redesigned for the graphic elegance of the newer system.)

Remember, you're now running two operating systems simultaneously. Whenever you click the icon of a Mac OS X program on the Dock, you bring forward that program *and* you switch into Mac OS X. Your menu turns shiny blue. But when you double-click the icon of a Mac OS 9 program on the Dock, you bring forward that program and you switch into Mac OS 9. The menu is now striped.

You can even copy and paste information between the programs you have running in these two worlds.

It's important to note, however, that Mac OS 9 doesn't offer any of the fancy technologies that make Mac OS X so stable. In Mac OS X, a program might crash or lock up — but all of your other programs soldier on, unaffected. In Mac OS 9, however, one buggy program can still freeze or crash the entire Classic bubble. At that point, you may have to exit the entire Mac OS 9 portion of your machine, losing unsaved changes in any of your Mac OS 9 programs.

Even then, though, you won't have to restart the actual computer. All your Mac OS X programs remain safe, open, and running.

Getting out of Classic

There's no good reason to quit the Classic simulator, ever. Once you've waited for it to open, you may as well leave it running quietly in the background, so that you won't have to wait for that long Classic startup process the *next* time you want to use an older program.

On the other hand, if some program in the Classic half of your Mac should crash or bomb, you might wish you had a way to exit Classic, if only to restart it afresh.

To do so, open the System Preferences program (the light-switch icon on your Dock). Click the Startup Disk icon to reveal this dialog box:

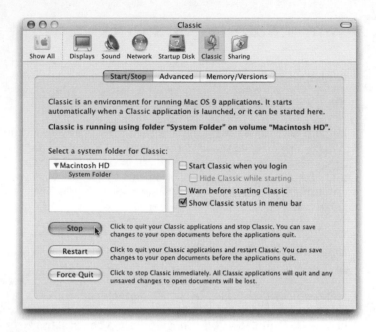

Just click the Stop button to shut down the Classic program.

Restarting in Mac OS 9

If you're lucky, the Classic program is the only trace of Mac OS 9 you'll ever see.

Unfortunately, it only goes so far. It does a very good job at tricking your older programs into thinking that they're running on a Mac OS 9 computer — but your Mac is still not *actually* running Mac OS 9. Certain older pieces of add-on equipment, notably printers, expansion cards, and scanners, don't work except on a true Mac OS 9 computer. The Classic simulation just isn't good enough.

If you want them to work properly, you have only one option: Restart the Mac *in* Mac OS 9. When you're finished using that scanner (or whatever), you can restart the Mac again, this time with Mac OS X "in charge."

(Remember, this entire discussion appears in this book for the benefit of the older generation — meaning people who've inherited older Macs with older software. These days, practically all new software and all add-on gadgets work right in Mac OS X, without this elaborate fake-out. And again, the following trick works only on Mac models introduced before 2003.)

Switching to Mac OS 9

Suppose you're running Mac OS X, and you need to duck back into Mac OS 9 to use, say, your scanner. The routine goes like this.

1. **Open System Preferences.**

   You can choose System Preferences from the menu, or you can click the light-switch icon on the Dock. The System Preferences screen appears.

2. **Click Startup Disk.**

   You now see controls that look like this:

   The icons here represent the various System folders that your Mac has found. If you're like most people, you'll find only two folder icons here: the Mac OS 9 one and the Mac OS X one.

3. **Click the icon of the Mac OS 9 System folder, and then click Restart.**

   (If the little padlock icon in the lower-left corner looks locked, you must first click it and then seek the assistance of someone with an *Administrator* account on this Mac, as described in the next chapter, for the purpose of typing in his or her name and password. You're about to make the kind of change that's off limits to ordinary underling accounts.)

   The Mac asks you if you're sure you know what you're doing.

4. **Click Restart (or press Enter).**

Your Mac restarts. When the screen lights up again after a moment, you see the startup display that was once adored — or at least endured — by millions of Mac fans before the invention of Mac OS X.

For example, you'll see a parade of little icons across the bottom of the screen. (These are little pieces of software called *extensions,* each of which adds one feature or another to the Mac. They offered a handy way to give your Mac new features — until there were so many of them that they began to fight with each other, triggering system freezes and other kinds of instability. No wonder Apple eliminated them in Mac OS X.)

You're now fully back in Mac OS 9, ready to use all your old add-on equipment and software — just without the benefit of Mac OS X's stability, good looks, and other features.

You'll find that things work quite a bit differently in Mac OS 9. For example:

- ✔ The Trash is now a separate icon sitting in the lower-right corner of the screen.

- ✔ You don't open your programs from within the Applications folder. Instead, the Mac OS 9-compatible programs are generally in a folder called "Applications (Mac OS 9)."

- ✔ There's no Dock anymore, either. When you want to open a program or document, just double-click its icon.

- ✔ The name of the program you're using appears in the upper-*right* corner of the screen, not the upper-left. Furthermore, that upper-right corner of the screen is a *menu* that lists all the programs that are currently running, just like the little triangles underneath the icons in the Mac OS X Dock. Use this menu to switch from one program to another, if you like.

Switching to Mac OS X (long way)

Once you've finished your work in Mac OS 9, the process of returning to Mac OS X is very similar.

1. **From the menu, choose Control Panels.**

   The Control Panels window opens. This is the Mac OS 9 equivalent of System Preferences.

2. **Double-click the icon called Startup Disk.**

   The Startup Disk control panel appears. After a moment, you'll see the names of both of your system folders.

3. **Click the icon of your Mac OS X System folder, and then click Restart.**

   Mac OS X starts up. After a moment, you'll be in familiar territory.

Switching to Mac OS X (short way)

The ritual of using the Startup Disk icon in the Control Panels window to switch back to Mac OS X is all well and good — if you bill by the hour.

But if your time is your own, you may prefer this sneaky shortcut. After you're finished with your Mac OS 9 work, choose Restart from the Special menu. Just as the screen lights up again, hold down the letter X key. Hold it down, in fact, until you see the smiling Macintosh icon and your cursor turns into a colorful spinning beach ball. Then you can let go of the key, confident that your computer is now starting up in Mac OS X.

(**Note to techies:** This trick works only if the Mac OS 9 and Mac OS X System folders are installed on the same hard drive.)

Chapter 13

Mono-Mac, Multi-People

· ·

· ·

*I*f you're the only one who uses your Mac, you're hereby excused from this chapter. Go out and play.

If you're not the only person who uses your Mac, though, read on.

All About Accounts

Pity the hapless Mac in a school, office, or family situation. Through the course of the day or the week, different people sit down to do their work. Each one may "bookmark" a few Web sites, create a few files, and perhaps change the desktop background.

This, if you stop to think about it, is a recipe for disaster. What's to stop one person from accidentally, or deliberately, throwing away the files of another person? How will you feel if you carefully download and install a fabulous *Finding Nemo* poster as your desktop background — and then return to the Mac the next day to find that some idiot has replaced it with a full-screen shot of SpongeBob SquarePants? And then there's the little matter of keeping your *e-mail* separate from everybody else's — how will you and your coworkers/schoolmates/family members keep from resorting to fisticuffs?

Mac OS X has a cool, collected response to all this: "No problem. I'll keep your worlds separate."

In other words, Mac OS X is a *multiple-user* system. One person, the *administrator,* is designated as the machine's owner and technical overlord; the administrator can set up individual *accounts* for each person who'll ever use the machine. Each person will have a name and, if the administrator wishes, a password.

Thereafter, each time you turn on the machine, you see a list of everyone who uses it, like this:

Using the mouse, you click your own name. (If you were given a password, you must enter it correctly before proceeding.)

And now the Mac's ready to use — except that only *your* folders, programs, bookmarks, e-mail, and documents show up on the screen. The stuff that belongs to the other students/children/workers is hidden from your eyes.

This arrangement has two benefits: convenience (because you don't have to stare at everyone else's junk and poor taste in desktop pictures) and security (because nobody can open anyone else's files or folders).

Setting Up Accounts

As noted above, in every multiple-user setup, one person is the administrator, or the Mac master — for example, the teacher, parent, or monsignor. This is the only person who's allowed to create and delete other accounts, as befits his or her exalted status. In the following discussion, let's pretend that the master is *you*.

Creating an account

Suppose, for example, that you work in a monastery, where you must share the Mac with three other people: the easily overwhelmed Brother Brian; Harold, the seven-year-old altar boy; and Giuseppe, the cybermonk who manages the group's Web site. Suppose you want to set up the Mac so that each person gets a perfect setup. Here's how you'd do it:

1. **Open System Preferences.**

   As usual, that entails clicking the light-switch icon on the Dock. The System Preferences window opens.

2. **Click Accounts.**

   Now a special dialog box appears, bearing a list of people who already have accounts on this Mac. If it's a new Mac, there's probably only one name here.

3. **Click the + button below the left-side list. Into the Name box, type** *Harold the Altar Boy,* **as shown here.**

In a family situation, the name could be Chris or Robin. If it's a corporation or school, you'll probably want to use both first and last names.

Unless you intervene, the Mac automatically makes up a *short name,* too. This is an abbreviation of the person's actual name, which can save time when people log in to the Mac or connect to it from across the network. The short name doesn't actually have to have fewer letters than the full name, but it can't have spaces or most punctuation.

4. **If you like, make up a password.**

   If security is an issue, you can require that each person type in a password before using the Mac each time. In fact, you're supposed to type it twice — into the Password and Verify boxes — to make sure you didn't make a typo the first time. (You see only dots as you type, so that nobody can discover a password by peeking over your shoulder.) Capitalization counts.

   Once you've created a password, you can also create a password *hint* in this box (like "street address, junior year in college"). Later, if you ever forget your password, the Mac will show you this cue to jog your memory.

5. **Click the Picture button. Choose a little picture to represent this account holder, if you like.**

   You'll see this picture next to your name each time you turn on the Mac to log in.

   If you like the choice of pictures that Apple has provided along the bottom of the window, just click one to select it. If there's some other graphics file on the hard drive that you'd rather use instead — a digital photo of your own head, for example — drag its icon right out of the Finder and into the little "picture box" next to the Edit button.

6. **Click the Security button. Turn on "Allow user to administer this computer," if you wish.**

   This is a biggie. Only an administrator is allowed to install new programs into the Mac's Applications folder, add fonts to the Library folder for everybody's use, make changes to the most important System Preferences panels (including Network, Date & Time, and Energy Saver), and decide who gets accounts on the Mac.

   You may want to make Brother Giuseppe, the expert, an administrator just like you. In the event you're off on a pilgrimage when one of your underlings needs to change some important Mac setting, Giuseppe will be able to fill in in your absence.

   For Brother Brian and little Harold, you might prefer to leave this checkbox turned off. They probably won't notice much difference between their worlds and the Administrator world that you see — except that they'll find their access blocked to a number of settings in System Preferences, as indicated by the padlock at lower-left in the following picture.

These are settings, such as the Mac's date and time clock, that only you (or another wise Administrator) are trusted to change correctly.

If little Harold really wants to change, say, the clock or the phone number your Mac dials to get online, you don't necessarily have to push him off the machine so that you can sign on with your special powers. Instead, you can just click the little padlock icon, type in *your* name and password when asked, like this:

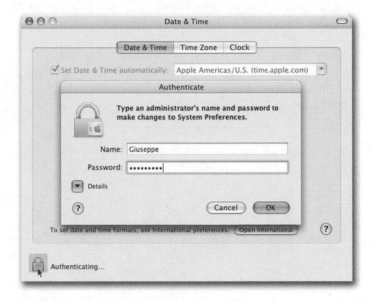

Then stand and supervise Harold as he makes the changes he wants to make.

To create a similar setup for Brother Brian, start over from Step 3.

If you ever want to modify the settings you've created, just click somebody's name in the Users list. You're once again offered the Password, Picture, and Security buttons. (You can't change a user's short name once the account has been created.)

Building a Rubber Room

If the monastery where you work (or school, family, or business) is typical, not everyone is equally technical. Somebody, inevitably, is younger, more fearful, or more mischievous than you, the all-knowing administrator.

If you're setting up accounts for young children, students, or easily intimidated adults, for example, you might want to explore one other button in the
Accounts dialog box: the one called Limitations.

Here, you see buttons called No Limits, Some Limits, and Simple Finder.

No Limits

"No limits" means that this account holder is allowed do just about anything
on the Mac that a non-administrator is allowed to do: Open any program,
change most settings, burn CDs, and so on.

Some Limits

By turning the checkboxes here on or off, you can declare certain programs
off-limits to this account holder, or turn off his ability to remove Dock icons,
burn CDs, and so on.

For example, at the bottom of the dialog box, you see a list of all the programs in your Applications folder. If you turn on "This user can use only
these applications," you can then turn the programs' checkboxes on or off. If
you turn off a certain program, it becomes invisible to this account holder —
the perfect solution to the age-old "kids playing Tomb Raider or surfing the
Web during algebra class" problem.

Simple Finder

If one of your underlings is *really* threatened by the Mac — or they're a threat to the Mac — then the Simple Finder controls are what you want. Not only does this mode let you choose precisely which programs your Simple friends are allowed to use, as described above, but when they log in, they'll find an *extremely* simplified, barren Macintosh world. There's only one window, no icons on the desktop, and next to nothing in the Dock or in the menus. They can't create folders, move icons, or do much of anything beyond clicking the icons that you, the benevolent administrator, have provided. It's as though Mac OS X moved away and left you the empty house.

Logging On

At last, you're ready to roll. From now on, whenever you turn on the Mac, you'll see the list of people for whom you've created accounts, as shown at the beginning of this chapter.

Start by clicking your own name — or, if you're a keyboard speed freak, type the first letter or two (or press the up or down arrow keys) until your name is highlighted, and then press Return or Enter.

Now type in your password, if you set one up. You can try as many times as you want to type the password in; with each incorrect guess, the entire dialog box shudders violently from side to side, as though shaking its head "No." After three wrong guesses, your hint will appear, if you had set one up.

Help! I forgot my password!

If you're an ordinary, peon mortal account holder, forgetting your password isn't a big deal. Your administrator can simply open up System Preferences, click Accounts, click your name, and then type something new into the Password box.

But if you *are* the administrator, things are a bit stickier. Still, you can get out of this scrape easily enough.

Find the Mac OS X Install CD that came with your Mac. Insert it into the machine. Then, from the menu, choose Restart. As the Mac starts up again, press down the letter C key, which starts up the Mac from the CD and launches the Mac OS X installer.

On the first installer screen, choose Reset Password from the Installer menu. When the Reset Password screen appears, click the hard drive that contains Mac OS X. From the first pop-up menu, choose the name of your account. Now make up a new password and type it into both of the boxes. Click Save, close the window, click the installer, and restart. You're saved.

If you get the password right, you're in. Enjoy your V.I.P. entrance to your private, pre-established world.

Non-administrator users will find that their worlds are somewhat limited. For example, they may occasionally encounter a message about not having enough *access privileges*. For example, Brother Brian will get that whenever he tries to open a folder belonging to Harold (in Harold's Home folder). And little Harold will find that he can't save new documents he creates anywhere except in his own Home folder or on the desktop.

Shared Folders

Ever notice the Users folder in the main hard drive window? It contains the individual Home folders of everybody with an account on this machine.

If you try to open anybody else's Home folder, you'll see a tiny red "no go here" icon on most of the folders inside, telling you: "look, but don't touch."

There are, however, exceptions. For example, two of the folders in each Home folder are designed to be distribution points for files your co-workers want you to see: Public and Sites.

These folders contain files that you're welcome to open, read, and copy to your own folders — stuff that other people have wanted to "publish" for the benefit of their co-workers. You have Public and Sites folders in your own Home folder, too, of course; here's where you should put files that you want other people to have copies of.

Within the Public folder is something called Drop Box, which serves the opposite purpose: It lets anyone *else* hand in files to *you* when you're not around. They can't open this folder, but they *can* put things into it.

Finally, sitting in the Users folder is one folder that doesn't correspond to any particular person: Shared. This is the one and only folder that everybody can access, freely putting in and taking out files. It's the common ground among all the account holders. It's Central Park, the farmer's market, and the grocery-store bulletin board.

Logging Off — Or Not

In this remarkable, time-share universe, nobody should shut the machine down at the end of a work session. Instead, learn to choose Log Off from the menu. The Mac automatically closes your programs (offering you the opportunity to save any open documents first), and then presents the list of Mac-sharers. The cycle begins anew.

What's especially cool, though, is that you don't *have* to log out if somebody else at your monastery just wants to duck in for a quick e-mail check to see if that new batch of all-weather robes has been shipped. Thanks to a feature called *Fast User Switching,* Brother B can log in and use the Mac for a little while. All of *your* stuff, Brother A, simply slides into the background, still open the way you had it.

When Brother B is finished working, you can bring your whole work environment back to the screen without having to re-open anything. All your windows and programs are still open, just as you left them.

To turn on this feature, open System Preferences again, and click Accounts again. Click Login Options, and turn on "Enable fast user switching," like this:

The only change you'll notice immediately is the appearance of your own account name in the upper-right corner of the screen.

Next time you need a fellow account holder to relinquish control so that you can duck in to do a little work, just choose your name from the Accounts menu (the name at the top right of the screen), as shown here at top:

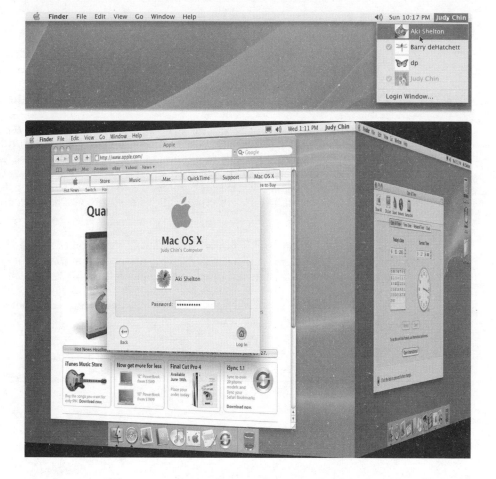

Type your password, if one is required, and enjoy the little "face o' the cube" animation as your world slides into view (as shown at bottom in the previous picture).

When you're finished, log out, or just let the next person choose from the Accounts menu.

Deleting Accounts

Sooner or later, one of your Mac's happy users may graduate, get fired, or get divorced. In short, there may come a time when you need to delete a person's account.

To delete an account, open System Preferences, click Accounts, click the appropriate name in the Users list, and then click the – button below the list. Mac OS X asks what to do with all of the person's files and settings:

- ✔ **Delete Immediately.** This button vaporizes the account and all of its files and settings forever, on the spot.

- ✔ **OK.** This button is for the less decisive type. Mac OS X will preserve the dearly departed's folders on the Mac, in a tidy digital envelope that won't clutter your hard drive, and can be reopened in case of emergency.

  (To find it, open the Users folder on your hard drive, then the Deleted Users folder inside it, then the folder inside *it* named for the deleted account. Double-click the ".dmg" file that you find there. A new, virtual disk icon appears on your desktop, named for the deleted account. You can open folders and root through the stuff in this "disk," just as if it were a living, working Home folder.)

Chapter 14

Networks for Nitwits

• •

• •

This chapter certainly won't appeal to everybody. If you're a *Survivor* contestant, for example, sitting there with a Mac as your luxury item and eating rice on some island somewhere thousands of miles from the nearest other computer, you're excused from reading this chapter. Go practice making fire by rubbing two coconuts together; learning how to connect two computers into a network is the last thing on your mind right about now.

But if there's more than one computer at your place, you might be gratified to learn that the Mac is one of the world's most networkable machines. Once you've connected it to your other computers, all kinds of joys await you:

✔ You can copy files from one machine to another just as you'd drag files between folders on your own Mac.

✔ You can send little messages to each other's screens.

✔ Everyone on the network can consult the same database (such as FileMaker Pro) or calendar (such as Now Up-to-Date).

✔ You can play games with each other over the network.

✔ You can share a single printer or high-speed cable modem among all the Macs in your home or office.

✔ You can even connect to Windows machines without having to buy any additional software.

That's a lot of payoff for just one Saturday afternoon of fiddling around, trying to get your net to work.

Two Ways to Build the Network

The first step in creating a small network is connecting your Macs. (Technically, they don't even have to be Macs — more on this later — but let's start simple.) You can string them together using either of two connection systems: Ethernet or AirPort.

Ethernet made eathy

Ethernet, a special kind of computer-to-computer connection, is fast, easy, and fun to pronounce.

It's very easy to connect your Mac directly to *one* other computer using Ethernet. It's more complicated to set up an entire *network* of Macs in an office.

Nonetheless, you paid good money for this book (or visited a good library). I won't let you down. I'll lead you by the brain, step by step, through both scenarios.

The two-Mac scenario

To connect your Mac to one other Mac, you need an *Ethernet crossover* cable. (It's not the same as a regular Ethernet cable.) You can get one for $10 or less at computer stores like CompUSA or from a mail-order joint like *www. buy.com.*

Plug your Ethernet crossover cable into each computer's Ethernet jack, which is identified in Chapter 20. It looks like an overweight telephone jack (the Ethernet jack, not Chapter 20).

That's as difficult as the wiring gets. Skip ahead to "Sharing Files."

The more-Macs scenario

Suppose you have a Mac, an iBook, a Power Macintosh, and a networkable laser printer — not to mention an office in which you'd like to wire all of this equipment together. Visit your local computer store, or a computer-stuff Web site like *www.buy.com.* Buy an *Ethernet hub,* which will set you back about $30, depending on the number of jacks it offers. Ethernet hubs usually offer between 4 and 24 jacks, or *ports.* You need one port for every gadget you hope to connect. This one, for example, can accommodate five computers or printers:

(If you have a cable modem or DSL — two kinds of high-speed Internet connections — shop for a hub that doubles as a *router*. It connects to your cable
modem or DSL box and distributes its services to four, eight, or more computers, depending on how many empty Ethernet jacks it comes with.)

Also buy enough Ethernet *cables* (also called Cat 5, 10BaseT, or 100BaseT), in
long enough lengths, to connect all your computers and printers to the hub.
The idea is that every computer and laser printer should be plugged directly
into your hub. In short, the hub is the octopus body; the wires are its arms;
your computers are its fingertips. Don't plug any computer directly into any
other machine.

Most people try to hide the hub and its ugly mass of wires by stashing it in
a closet. Some even hire an electrician to snake the Ethernet cables through
the walls, attempting to save themselves from the techno-ugliness of exposed
wires.

Once that's set up, you're ready to set up the software. Skip ahead to
"Sharing Files."

Your ride to the AirPort

You young kids today — you don't know how lucky you are! Why, when I was
your age, we used to have to connect our Macs by *plugging in wires!*

Macs are considerably less restricted. Every current model comes with a built-in *radio transmitter antenna* that gives these Macs wireless smarts. These antennas communicate through the air to an AirPort *base station* ($200), which is what's actually connected to the Internet. You know how cordless phones work, right? There's a base station that's wired to the wall, and there's the handset with an antenna. Well, an AirPort setup works exactly the same way, except that your Mac is the handset. (And the base station is the base station.)

An AirPort setup lets you perform any of these stunts:

✔ Surf the Internet without any wires attached to your computer. You can position the Mac even in a room with no telephone jack — as long the base station, up to 150 feet away, *is* connected to a phone jack.

✔ Up to 50 computers can share the same cable modem or DSL connection, if you have one — once again, from up to 150 feet away, even through walls and floors.

✔ Play multiplayer Macintosh games with other AirPort-equipped Mac owners — without having to physically connect them.

✔ Copy files between your Mac and other Macs — again, without any wires.

Setting all of this up may require some patience. Once it's set up, however, wirelessness shall be yours. It's especially wonderful on laptops, because they're designed to be *carried around,* so being free of wires just makes sense. And when you wander into an airport, coffee shop, library, or hotel that has its *own* wireless base station — an increasingly common pleasant surprise these days — you'll be ready to surf the Internet at high speed, without even having to set anything up or connect to anything physically. (Sometimes it's even free.)

Installing an AirPort card

Your Mac can't do any of those wireless stunts without an AirPort card ($100 or less), which looks like a Visa card made of sheet metal. You can buy it from an Apple store or from the Apple Web site *(www.apple.com),* either before or after you buy the computer.

If you decide to add an AirPort card to a Mac that didn't come with one, you have to install it. This is not an obvious procedure; you're well advised to consult the step-by-step, illustrated instructions that came with your Mac.

Going online with a base station

Your Mac is now ready to communicate wirelessly with the AirPort base station, which looks exactly like a shiny, six-inch flying saucer. Here it is with the actual AirPort card:

If you have a cable modem or DSL connection, plug it into the base station's Ethernet jack. If you connect to the Internet via standard phone lines, connect the modem jack on the base station to a telephone jack on the wall, using a piece of phone wire. Either way, your Mac can now get online via the base station, even through walls and floors. (Unless, of course, you're talking about the walls and floors of elevators, refrigerators, and meat lockers. The signals can't go through metal.)

Suppose your Mac is in the TV room, for example, and you launch your Web browser. Your base station, upstairs in your office, silently begins to dial. Now your Mac is on the Internet, fully connected at full speed, without actually being connected by wires to anything.

Note to teachers and small businesses: A single base station can accommodate dozens of AirPort-equipped Macs (laptops, for example), all surfing the Web simultaneously.

Setting up your base station

The key to preparing a base station is the program called AirPort Setup Assistant. It's in your Applications folder, in the Utilities folder. Run this program. One screen at a time, it will ask you for the answers it needs for the setup; for example, you'll be asked to give your base station a name and password. Note, too, that you should undertake this phase of the setup only if your Mac can *already* get onto the Internet on its own.

Going online with AirPort

Once you've installed your AirPort hardware and software, there's not much involved to getting onto the Internet with it.

Haul your Mac over to some table from which you've never before surfed the Internet. Then notice the radiating-lines icon on your menu bar, which looks like this:

From this symbolic menu, choose the name of the base station with which you'd like to connect. Most people have only one base station, so you'll see only one listed. (If it says "No AirPort Networks in Range," well, you pretty much know what the problem is.) Fill in the password, if you're asked for it.

Now try using an e-mail or Web-browsing program. As soon as you try to connect, your base station dials the number (if you have a dial-up account) or taps into the Net via your cable modem or DSL. Once the connection is complete, you should notice no difference between Web surfing wirelessly and surfing . . . wirefully.

While you're connected, you can check the strength of your radio signal to the base station by glancing again at the menu-bar symbol. The four radiating lines show you your signal strength. The farther away you go from your base station, the weaker the signal, and the slower your Internet surfing speed gets.

As advertised, the radio signal sent between the base station and your laptop isn't fazed by walls — much. Glass, paper, and wood are invisible to the signal, but concrete walls slow it down substantially. Solid metal is almost impenetrable, much to the disappointment of Mac fans on elevators, subway trains, and meat lockers.

(If you have trouble, call Apple's help line, 800 275-2273. You'll probably be advised to open the Network pane of System Preferences. There, if you double-click the AirPort line of the Network Status screen, you'll find four tabs that let you configure your apparatus to within an inch of its life.)

Most people name the base station for its location: "Upstairs Base Station," or "Mr. Mullen's Math Class." You can leave the password blank, unless you worry about the guy next door surfing the Web via your base station.

(This scenario assumes that you live in a *very* tightly packed neighborhood, that your neighbor owns a Mac with an AirPort card, and that he's smart enough to try logging onto your base station without a password. It also assumes that you *care* that your neighbor is getting onto the Internet by piggybacking onto your signal; some neighbors actually *like* sharing in this way. "You can use my cable modem, if I can borrow your snow blower . . .")

When it's all over, you'll have successfully configured your base station — and wired your network (or unwired it, depending on how you look at it).

Sharing Files

In File Sharing, you can summon the icon for a folder or disk attached to another computer on the network. It shows up on your own screen; at this point, you can drag files back and forth, exactly as though the other Mac's folder or disk is a gigantic CD you've slipped into your Mac.

Yes, it's a miracle, but you'll have to work for it.

Phase 1: Setting up the computers

These instructions assume that you've already networked your Macs, whether with wires or without (using AirPort), as described earlier.

Setting up a Mac OS X machine

Use these instructions for your Mac or other Mac OS X computers.

1. **Open System Preferences.**

   As always, you can click its icon on the Dock or choose its name from the menu. Either way, the System Preferences program opens.

2. **Click the Sharing icon.**

   The Sharing panel appears.

   Note that only administrators (see Chapter 13) are allowed to change the kinds of settings you're about to fiddle with. If the little padlock icon in the lower-left corner of the dialog box looks locked, call an Administrator over, click the lock, and prove that you have permission to do what you're doing by asking the administrator to enter the administrator's name and password.

3. **In the Computer Name blank, type a name for the computer.**

It probably has a boring computer name already — "Caseys' Computer," or whatever — but you might want to change this to a nice and descriptive name ("Front Desk Mac," say, or "Antique Kerosene-Powered iBook").

4. **Turn on the checkbox called Personal File Sharing, like this:**

The feature takes a moment to warm up. When the button to the right finally says Stop, you can quit System Preferences.

5. **In the Accounts panel of System Preferences, create an account for each person who'll be accessing this Mac from across the network.**

The previous chapter contains step-by-step instructions.

Repeat this complete process on each Mac OS X machine in your office, giving each one a different computer name.

Now you're set up. Rent a video; you've earned it.

Setting up a Mac OS 9 machine

It's entirely possible that not every Mac in your home or office is lucky enough to enjoy the good looks and smooth stability of Mac OS X. Fortunately, a Mac that's running Mac OS 9-point-whatever, if you have one, can also join the network party. You follow almost exactly the same steps as outlined above — but the locations of the controls are different. For example:

✔ **Setting up user accounts.** As with Mac OS X, nobody can connect to a Mac OS 9 machine unless they have an *account* on that machine. To set up these accounts, choose Control Panels from the menu. Open the File Sharing control panel. Click the Users tab. Then click New User to set up an account for someone.

✔ **Naming the computer.** Use the File Sharing control panel. (Choose Control Panels from the menu.)

✔ **Clicking Start.** You do this, too, in the File Sharing control panel. But there's one important additional step: Turn on the checkbox called "Enable File Sharing clients to connect over TCP/IP," as shown here.

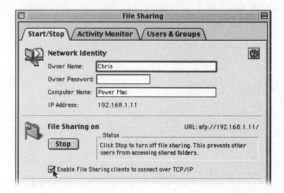

Phase 2: Connecting from your Mac

You've just turned on the File Sharing feature on every Mac. Now it's time to *use* your network.

Suppose you're seated at your iBook, and you need a file that's on the iMac down the hall. Why expend the energy necessary to get out of your chair and walk over there, when you can let your network do the work?

You'll have to follow a pretty lengthy sequence of steps — but, mercifully, you have to go through it only once for each Mac you "visit." Here's what you do (on your main Mac, the one running Mac OS X 10.3):

1. **Open any folder window. In the Sidebar at the left side of the window, click the Network icon.**

   You can read more about the Sidebar in Chapter 2.

   Anyway, for several seconds, you may not see anything at all, or maybe just a Server icon. But wait it out. After ten or fifteen seconds, more icons appear.

   If you have a simple network, these icons represent the individual computers on your network. Recover from your amazement, and skip ahead to Step 3.

   If your network is more complex, you may see a set of networky-looking folders, like this:

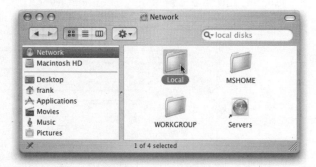

2. **Open the Local folder.**

   You might be hoping to connect to another Mac, of course. But in the hallways of Corporate America, PCs running Microsoft Windows rule the earth.

   Amazingly enough, the icons for *those* computers show up in this list, too (provided somebody has set up its folders for network sharing); the Macintosh is an equal opportunity networker. In that case, though, the folder you want might be called MSHOME or WORKGROUP instead.

   Anyway, the point is to open these folders to find the icons of every Mac that you prepared as described in Phase 1 (and every PC that's been similarly set up).

3. **Double-click the name of the computer you want to access (as shown here at top).**

The "Connect to the file server" box appears (bottom).

4. Type your short user name, press Tab, and type your password.

For details on your *short user name,* see the previous chapter. This is the name you (or your Administrator) typed in when creating your account on that computer.

If nobody has set up an account for you on that machine, on the other hand, click the Guest button; you'll have only limited access to what's on the other computer. (If the Guest button is dimmed, then someone has turned off Guest access altogether. You're completely out of luck.)

5. Click Connect, or press the Return or Enter key.

Now a list of disks and folders appears. These are the folders on the other Mac or PC that you're allowed to open (shown here at left).

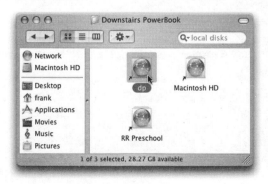

6. **Double-click the name of the folder you want to open.**

   At last, the disk or folder you've connected to appears, exactly as though it's a folder right there on your Mac (shown above at right). You can open, copy, move, rename, or delete the files you find there, exactly as though the files were on your own computer — with certain limitations, described next.

   Amazingly enough, whoever is *using* that computer can go right on using it, probably unaware that you're tapping into stuff on the same hard drive.

7. **If you think you might someday want to get at the other computer's files again, drag its folder icon onto your Sidebar, like this.**

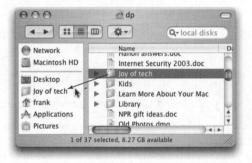

The next time you want to connect to it, you'll be able to skip almost all of the preceding steps. Instead, you'll just click its Sidebar icon, type in your password, and enjoy instant access to the disk or folder as it pops open instantly.

Phase 3: What you can do once you're in

When you tap into a *Mac OS 9* computer from across the network, you're allowed complete freedom. Once you've brought its icon onto your screen, you can trash, rename, move around, or otherwise wreak havoc with the files and folders you find there.

But Mac OS X is an extremely secure operating system that fiercely protects its System folder and the Home folders of everybody who uses it. That's why you generally can't visit another Mac OS X computer across the network unless an administrator has first set up an account for you on that Mac.

Even then, you'll be able to see only what's in certain designated folders. Precisely which folders are available depends on whether you're a *guest,* a *normal user,* or an *administrator* (see the previous chapter).

If you're a guest

If you're just a guest — somebody for whom an account hasn't already been set up — you'll be able to:

✔ **Put things into** anyone's Drop Box folder. Take a look here:

This is what you see when you connect to a Mac OS X machine as Guest — a list of everyone who has an account on it. When you double-click someone's name, you'll discover that there's nothing inside that folder except a Drop Box folder (and sometimes a Public folder, described next), as shown here:

You can copy files into a Drop Box, but can't open it. If you're a guest, you can give, but you can't take.

✔ **Open** anything that people have put into their Public folders. (If no Public folders show up, then there's nothing in them for you to see.)

The rest of the Mac is invisible and off-limits to you.

If you're a normal account holder

If you have a normal Mac OS X account, you'll enjoy Drop Box access, Public-folder access, *and* the freedom to see and manipulate what's inside your own Home folder on that other Mac. You can do anything you like with the files and folders you find there, just as though you're actually seated in front of that Mac.

All other disks and folders on the Mac, including the System and Application folders, are invisible to you. Mac OS X machines on a network, as you're by now starting to figure out, have been sanitized for your protection.

If you're an administrator

When you connect to a Mac OS X machine with a guest or normal account, you never even see the name of the hard drive on that machine. Instead, you see only the names of the *people* who have accounts on that machine. (Double-click one to get to its Drop Box and Public folders.)

But if you've been designated an *administrator,* you get to see both those user folders *and* the rest of the hard drive to which you're connecting. You're free to see and manipulate the contents of the Applications, Desktop, Library, and Users folders, too.

Chapter 15

The Book of iBook and PowerBook

*I*t's a little bit mind-blowing that today's Mac laptops, the PowerBooks and iBooks, have nearly as much computer horsepower as the most hulking desktop models. Apple makes few compromises: The speed, storage capacity, memory, and screen size on a PowerBook or iBook are almost exactly the same as those on regular Macs — but they're crammed into a book-size case that weighs six pounds and conceals dirt.

iBook versus PowerBook

Apple makes two kinds of laptops:

✔ **The iBook.** It's shiny, white, and made of bulletproof plastic. You could get a lot of mileage out of your iBook, socially speaking, by simply parking it on your coffee table during parties.

Despite all of that overwhelming coolness, the iBook is extremely inexpensive, on the grand scale of laptops: $1,100 and up. That's because it isn't quite as fast as the PowerBooks, and it lacks a couple of high-end features. (For example, if you connect another screen to it, or a projector, both screens show the same thing. On the PowerBook, the second screen can act as an extension of the first one.)

In other words, it's not the laptop you'll see in corporate board meetings — but that's just fine for the hundreds of thousands of students, creative people, and rugged individualists who've snapped up this machine.

✔ **The PowerBook.** This laptop is the real business machine: It's faster than the iBook; comes in three models, including two with much bigger screens than the iBook; comes only in silver; and costs about $500 more than the iBook.

They're both absolutely thrilling machines. And they work essentially alike, as you'll see in this chapter.

Laptop Care and Feeding

Working on a Mac laptop is so much like working on a desktop Mac that a separate chapter is almost unnecessary. *Almost.* A few weirdnesses remain, largely pertaining to these diminutive Macs' screen, battery, and portable nature.

Sleep is good. We like sleep.

Do you have a PowerBook or iBook? Don't tell me you shut it down at the end of each day!

Yes, alas, thousands of people shut their laptops off unnecessarily each day or — horrors! — even more than once a day. Don't do it!

Instead, put your machine to *sleep* — that is, just *close the lid.* The thing instantly blinks off.

Sleep is almost like Off. You're not running down the battery; nothing moves; all is calm, all is dark. But the advantages of letting a sleeping laptop lie are considerable. For example, when you want to use it again, you can just *touch any key* to wake it up. And when the thing wakes up, it doesn't go through the usual 45-minute startup process — instead, it takes you instantly right back to whatever you were doing. If you were typing up a letter, you wake up to your half-finished letter, still onscreen. Great timesavings.

You don't have to shut your laptop down for travel, either. The only time you need the Shut Down command is when you'll be storing the computer for more than a few days. Much more than that, and your battery will run out of juice, even asleep.

Battery positives and negatives

Of course, it's perfectly possible to work for years on your laptop with its power cord firmly attached to a wall outlet, happily ignoring its capacity for running on battery power. Plenty of people do just that — people who bought a laptop for its compact size and one-piece construction, not because they travel on airplanes a lot. In fact, keeping your laptop plugged in whenever possible is a great idea.

But if you *do* plan to use your laptop in the back seats of taxis, in hot-air balloons, and on Grand Canyon promontories, you'll be running on battery power. In that case, every time you move the mouse or type something, you wince, wondering if you just unnecessarily sped closer to your battery charge's demise. It's a strange feeling, running a Mac on battery juice; in no other circumstance do you feel time's winged hoofbeats beating so loudly at your back. *(Is that your best simile? — Ed.) (Keep out of this. — Auth.)*

At the end of this chapter, you'll find out how to milk the most minutes from each charge. Frankly, though, if you find yourself going crazy worrying over your battery, spending the $90 for a second battery might be a worthwhile expenditure.

Aside from making it last longer, here are some fun and interesting battery facts to help you better understand your little square electrovoltaic friend:

- Your battery is recharging whenever the laptop is plugged in.

- Laptop computer batteries don't last even close to the number of hours advertised. Not Macs, not IBMs, not any. You'll be lucky to get 3.5 hours out of the standard "five-hour" PowerBook battery. It's a fact of life. Or advertising. Or something.

- Even when your laptop is sleeping or completely off, your battery is still slowly being drained. That's why you may return to your laptop, which had had a full battery, after a week away, only to find the battery empty.

- Notice the little battery gas-tank gauge that's on your menu bar, like this:

Battery gauge (time remaining)

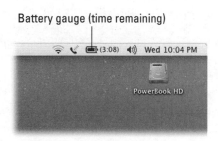

While not quite as accurate as, say, an atomic clock, this little gauge is the best indicator you've got as to how much longer you can work on your current battery charge.

✔ When you're recharging the battery, the numbers next to the battery gauge stop indicating how much time the battery has left to *run*, but rather how much time it needs to finish *charging*.

✔ Running out of battery juice at 39,000 feet with six hours to go before Paris may be inconvenient, but it really doesn't endanger whatever you've been working on. You get two warnings — increasingly urgent messages on the screen — stretching over a 15-minute period. And then the laptop goes to sleep.

Even if you hadn't saved your work, whatever is in memory is completely safe for another few days, even after the laptop has gone to sleep. Just plug your laptop in at the next opportunity, wake it up, save your masterpiece, and go see the Eiffel Tower.

✔ Laptop batteries are good for about 500 chargings. That, as well as common sense, should be your cue to use the laptop plugged into the wall whenever possible. You'll know when it's time to retire a battery when it just won't hold a charge anymore. At that point, unless you've got some psychotic grudge against the neighborhood raccoons, don't chuck this lethal chunk of toxic chemicals into the garbage. Instead, return it to an Apple dealer, who will send it back to Apple's battery-recycling program.

Trackpad Proficiency Drill

A laptop works great with a mouse — when you're home at your desk. Finding a place to lay down your mouse pad can be a challenge, however, when you're using your laptop in a telephone booth or while whitewater rafting.

The one extended-warranty deal that's not a scam

Just a word of advice about Apple's extended-warranty program, known as AppleCare. In general, as with those ridiculous $600-a-year service contracts they try to sell you with your $250 television, I don't believe that these contracts ever pay off. Macs in general are built like bricks.

It's different with laptops. You carry them around, you put them to sleep and wake them up, attach and unattach equipment constantly, shove them into overhead racks, and set down your orange-juice glass on them. With this kind of treatment, *you* would be more prone to failure, too. As a bonus, AppleCare gives you the right to call Apple's toll-free help line for free.

In short, getting AppleCare for a laptop is an excellent investment.

That's why iBooks and PowerBooks come with a *trackpad,* the flat plastic square between you and the keyboard, across which you run your fingers to simulate mousing. You need to know just a few fun factoids about the two-inch Teflon square that's about to become your best friend:

✔ When you first buy your laptop, all you can do with your trackpad is slide the arrow cursor around the screen. But the trackpads on all modern laptops actually offer many additional features — if you know how to unlock them!

The secret is in System Preferences. Open it (click the light-switch icon on the Dock), click Keyboard & Mouse, and click the Trackpad button. Here, you'll find a few more trackpad features worth trying out (click each checkbox to turn the feature on).

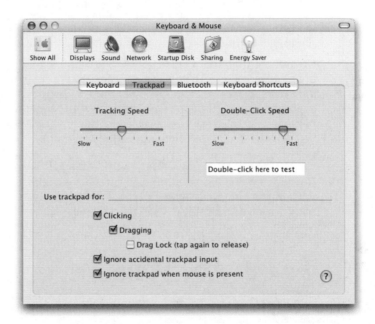

Clicking means that you can tap the trackpad surface itself (instead of clicking the big thumb button) to "click the mouse button," and even double-click on the pad to "double-click." *Dragging* lets you "drag the mouse" by tapping down-up-down (and moving your finger once it's down for the second time); you can even continue a long drag by lifting your finger between scoots.

And then there's *Drag lock,* the most useful option, since it helps with pulling down menus and moving icons around (which is difficult to do if you're working while, say, riding a camel). When this third checkbox option is on, you can double-click the trackpad — but if you begin moving your finger after the *second* click, the Mac won't "release the mouse button" when you lift your finger — even if you lift it *forever*. You must tap the trackpad again to release the drag lock.

No doubt about it, some people loathe these newfangled behaviors, preferring to do all their clicking, dragging, and drag-locking by pressing the big plastic clicker below the trackpad. But give them a try, in the name of becoming a more skilled laptopper.

✔ Does the cursor seem to leap around as you type, making you wind up putting words WRONG PLACE in the? That's because as you type, one of your fingers is softly, accidentally brushing the trackpad and "clicking" it. The solution is the "Ignore accidental trackpad input" checkbox in the System Preferences panel illustrated above. This ingenious option somehow tells the laptop to ignore the wayward clicks.

✔ Laptops show up in a lot of big action movies. Can you spot the whopping implausibility?

No, no, not that Tom Cruise gets safely off an exploding helicopter chasing a bullet train at 160 miles per hour. No, I'm referring to the fact that *the trackpad doesn't work if you're nervous*. If your hands are damp, sweaty, or lotioned in any way, the electronic sensors inside the pad get confused. Yet even as aliens were blowing up Los Angeles, Jeff Goldblum seemed to have no problem operating his laptop.

Personally, that glaring gaffe ruined *Mission: Impossible* for me.

Anyway, several easy solutions await. For example, if you've just washed your hands and are in a hurry to use the laptop, you can put a piece of paper (such as a Post-It note) over the trackpad as a temporary measure.

The Keyboard: Not Your Father's Typewriter

If you've spent much time staring mindlessly at the translucent keys of a modern Apple laptop — during the final hours of a plane flight, for example, after your battery has died — you may have noticed something unusual about the keys. Each key on the right half of the keyboard has *two* labels painted on it: the normal letters (J, K, L, and so on) plus, in a different color, a bunch of numbers and other labels.

If you've ever used a standard desktop computer's keyboard, you'll immediately recognize these color-labeled keys: They're the *number pad* that's usually a separate bank of keys off to the right of the alphabet keys.

On a non-laptop computer, the number-pad keys do exactly the same thing as the number keys across the top of the keyboard. But after some practice, typing stuff like phone numbers and prices is much faster using this number pad than using the top keyboard row.

Some people like to plug in a regular keyboard and mouse to use when they're not traveling, and that's totally okay by the laptop.

But when you're on the road, your laptop doesn't have a separate bank of number keys, jutting off into space beyond the laptop's right edge; if it did, you'd give the airline passenger to your right one helluva thigh bruise. Instead, the number pad is *superimposed* on the normal alphabet keyboard. You turn the right-side keys *into* a number pad whenever you press the *Fn* (Function) key, which is in the very lower-left corner of the keyboard.

Look, for example, at your letter U key. If you press it normally, you type the letter U. But if you press it while the Fn key is down, you get a number 4. (See the color-coded labels on the keys?) What's especially clever is the way the 7, 8, and 9 keys of the regular keyboard and the "Fn" keyboard *overlap*. These keys type 7, 8, and 9 whether you press Fn or not!

Here are some other keys that spring to life when you press Fn.

Home, End

"Home" and "End" are ways of saying "the top or bottom of the window." You trigger this function by pressing the left-arrow or right-arrow key (at the lower-right cluster of the keyboard) along with the Fn key.

If you're word processing, the Home and End keys jump to the first word or last word of the file, respectively (in most programs). If you're looking at a list-view window full of files in the Finder, they jump you to the top or bottom of the list.

Pg Up, Pg Down

In most programs, these keys mean "Scroll up or down by one screenful." Once again, the idea is to let you scroll through word-processing documents and lists without having to use the trackpad. To trigger this function, press the up-arrow or down-arrow keys in the lower-right keyboard cluster — along with the Fn key.

Clear

Clear means "get rid of this text I've highlighted, but don't put a copy on the invisible Clipboard like the Cut command would do." To trigger this phantom key, hold down the Fn key, and then press 6.

Have Laptop, Might Travel

Okay. You've figured out how to work your laptop. Now you want to show it off — somewhere other than your living room. Who can blame you? A few pointers, if I may.

X-ray machines and you

Airport X-ray machines can't hurt your laptop.

Airport X-ray machines can't hurt your laptop.

Airport X-ray machines can't hurt your laptop.

Okay?

Desperate for a fix

Now look, I don't want to get angry letters from spouses and significant others, blaming me for converting their beloveds into power-nerd hermits. What I'm about to tell you should be socked away in the back of your mind and used only in emergencies.

The tip is about airplanes and airports. You know that laptops and airplanes were made for each other. What you may not know is what to do when the dreaded warning messages pop up, letting you know that you have only a few minutes of battery power remaining, while you're in the middle of a brainstorm.

First of all, you can find publicly-available power outlets at almost every gate of almost every airport (and at every bus and train station, too). The outlets are there, actually, for the benefit of the cleaning staff's vacuum cleaners; as such, the outlets are sometimes concealed on the side of a pillar. Unfortunately, the outlets are *never* convenient to a seat, so if your Mac habit is stronger than your pride, you'll have to sit on the floor.

What's more, when you run out of juice *on the plane,* let me call to your attention the electric-razor outlet in the bathroom of almost every plane in America. You feel like an absolute idiot, of course, wedged in there on that toilet with your adapter cord snaking up to the plug above the doll-size sink while your laptop recharges.

Well, that's what I've been *told*, anyway. Naturally, I would never do anything that pathetic.

Insta-Printer

Okay, so you bought the laptop. But what do you print on? Painful experience has demonstrated that few airlines accept a 45-pound laser printer as carry-on.

There *are* portable printers, of course; they're generally expensive, fragile, and slow. But here's a better idea: Use your built-in fax modem. Thus equipped, just *fax* whatever-it-is that you want to print *to yourself.* (Chapter 18 has instructions.) For example, fax it from the laptop, while sitting in your hotel room, to the same hotel's front desk. Ingenious, fast, and free.

No need to thank me.

Top Tips for Maximizing Battery Power

Many new laptop owners are devastated to find that instead of getting "up to five" hours of life out of each freshly charged battery, they get only two and a half. These tricks can help.

1. The lighting for the screen uses up *half* the power. The more you turn brightness down, the longer your battery lasts. (On modern PowerBooks and iBooks, you control the brightness by pressing the F1 and F2 keys at the top left corner of the keyboard.)

2. Another enormous battery-drainer is your hard drive. Keeping those platters spinning at 4,500 rpm would drain *your* battery, too.

   It might seem silly to suggest that you try to avoid making your hard drive spin, but actually it's possible. First, visit your Energy Saver panel of System Preferences and make sure the "Put hard drive to sleep" checkbox is turned on. This setting makes your hard drive stop spinning sooner when it isn't really needed.

3. Every little appliance you attach to the laptop takes little sips from each battery charge. That especially includes external monitors, the built-in CD-ROM, USB scanners, and the mouse.

4. If you have an AirPort wireless card (see Chapter 14), turn it off when you don't need it. To do so, use the menu-bar control shown here:

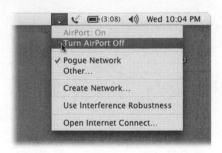

5. If you're not going to use the machine, even for five minutes, put it to sleep. (Choose Sleep from the Special menu, or just close the lid.)

6. Whenever you plug the machine into the wall, make sure it is, in fact, getting power. There's nothing worse than heading to the plane for your flight to Australia, only to discover that the battery is dead because it was plugged into a dead outlet all night.

   Checking this is easy: Look at the ring around the power-adapter jack, where the power cord goes into the laptop. If this ring is glowing, you're getting power; if it's not lit up, you're not getting juice.

7. This isn't actually a battery-saving tip, but I had nowhere else to put it: What's great about PowerBook batteries is their *built-in* fuel gauges. Have a look at the four little LED lights on the outer panel of your battery; when you push the tiny button beside them, they light up. The more lights turn on, the more juice your battery has.

Chapter 16

When Bad Things Happen to Good Macs

Introduction to Computer Hell

Let's face it: Computers are appliances. As such, they have minds of their own. And like other expensive appliances (cars, homes, pacemakers), they tend to get cranky at the worst possible times.

Now, when that happens, most beginners immediately suspect the circuitry. I understand the instinct. I mean, when VCRs, lawnmowers, or electric razors go on the fritz, you're right — you need a repair shop.

But a computer's different; it has *software*. When your Mac starts behaving oddly, it's probably a software problem, not a mechanical one. That means that you can fix it yourself, for free. Almost always.

This chapter reveals the steps you can take to restore your Mac's software to health.

Frozen Programs

The old Chinese curse used to be, "May you live in interesting times."

The modern curse should be, "May you be visited by the Spinning Beachball of Death." That's a reference to the colorful, spinning cursor that appears whenever the Mac decides to lock up, becoming utterly unresponsive to your clicks or keystrokes.

First resort: Force quit

Usually, you can escape the SBOD by *force quitting* the program you're in, which has somehow gotten stuck.

To do that, open the menu and choose Force Quit. (If you can't even open the menu, there's an alternative way: Hold down the Option and ⌘ keys. While they're down, press the Esc key at the upper-left corner of the keyboard.)

Either way, this box appears:

Click the name of the program you've been using, click Force Quit, and click Force Quit in the confirmation box. That program immediately departs the scene, without even giving you a chance to save any unsaved work. You should feel free to keep using your other programs, or even to re-open the program you just quit. Having had its little time-out, it should be ready for action.

Last resort: Restart the Mac

Very, very rarely, even force-quitting all your programs doesn't help the Mac out of its funk. If the machine is truly locked up, and even the force-quit method does nothing for it, you can always force-*restart* the Mac.

You can do that in a number of different ways. Try these methods in this order:

- ✔ **Press the Restart button.** It's on the front of Power Mac models: a tiny button bearing a left-pointing triangle. It makes your Mac restart.

- ✔ **Hold in the Power button.** About six seconds usually does the trick. Your screen goes black. Now you can turn the Mac on again normally.

- ✔ **Press the restart key combination.** It's Control-⌘-power. That is, while pressing the Control and ⌘ keys on the bottom row of your keyboard, push the power button. This tactic, too, generally restarts the computer.

> ✔ **Cut the cord.** If your Mac is so profoundly frozen that even these tactics don't restart it, you can always unplug the thing (and, if it's a laptop, remove the battery). *That* method always works.

Things Are Too Slow

If your Mac starts seeming to run more slowly than it once did, the #1 favor you can do for it is *installing more memory*. You can get it from any mail-order company, such as *www.chipmerchant.com*. When you call, tell them that you have a Mac; they'll tell you what kind of memory chips you need and in what quantities they're available.

Installing memory isn't especially difficult, but it does entail opening up the machine. For instructions, choose Mac Help from your Help menu and do a search for "installing memory." Or check the pamphlet that came with your Mac. If it looks too hard, get an Apple dealer to do it for you.

Having lots of memory to kick around in is a joy. Your Mac runs faster and generally acts like a new machine. It's a situation I heartily recommend.

Startup Problems

Problems that you encounter when you turn on the Mac are especially disheartening when you're a new Mac user. It does wonders for your self-esteem to think that you can't even turn the thing *on* without problems.

No chime, no picture

Chances are very, very, very good that your Mac simply isn't getting electricity. It's probably not plugged in. Or it's plugged into a power strip whose On/Off switch is currently set to Off. Or it's plugged into an outlet that's controlled by a wall switch.

Picture, no ding

Every Mac makes a sound when you turn it on. The speaker-volume slider (in the Sound panel of System Preferences) controls the sound of the startup chime.

First resort: Press the Louder button on your keyboard a couple of times (see Chapter 3) to make sure that you haven't muted your speaker.

Last resort: When headphones or speakers are plugged into the Mac, no sound can come out of the Mac speaker. Unplug the headphones, in that case.

Some crazy program opens itself every time you start up

In the words of programmers everywhere, "It's a feature, not a bug."

As you can read in Chapter 19, you can set up a certain program or document to open automatically every time you log in or turn on the Mac. This feature is supposed to be a time-saver for people who work on the same documents every day.

If you'd rather stifle this gesture, open System Preferences (click its Dock icon). Click Accounts. Click the name of your account. Click the Startup Items button. In the list, click each program or document listed there and press the Delete key on your keyboard, as shown here.

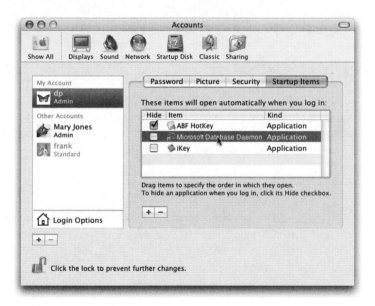

Kernel panic

When a strange error message appears on your screen in six languages — the United Nations of error messages — you've got yourself a *kernel panic,* the computer version of a nervous breakdown. No wonder a kernel panic quickly leads to an *owner panic.*

Kernel panics are rarer than Bigfoot sightings in New York City. But if you actually get one, it's probably the result of a hardware glitch: some memory board, accelerator card, graphics card, SCSI gear, or USB hub that Mac OS X doesn't like, for example.

Simply restarting the computer usually solves the problem. If it doesn't, detach any gear that didn't come from Apple. If you're able to pinpoint the culprit, seek its manufacturer (or its Web site) on a hunt for updated drivers, or at least try to find out for sure whether the add-on is compatible with Mac OS X.

Freezes during startup

If the Mac locks up during the startup process, you need to run Mac OS X's disk-repair program, as described at the end of this chapter.

"I don't want to have to log in every day — it's my own Mac!"

The whole idea of the name-and-password system described in Chapter 13 is to keep everybody's files and settings separate.

But if you're the only person who uses your Mac, it might seem a bit silly that you have to log in each morning. And it *is* silly — and you can bypass it.

Open System Preferences. Click the Accounts icon. Click the Login Options button. Turn on "Automatically log in as," choose your name from the pop-up menu, and type in your password when the Mac asks for it. Click OK.

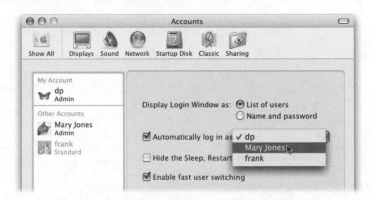

From now on, the Mac won't display the usual list of account holders at startup. It will assume that you're you, and it will take you straight to the desktop. Of course, this means that anybody else in your house, office, or school has full access to your files, without having to know a password — but then, you're only reading this if there *isn't* anyone else who might use your Mac.

"I can't log in! I'm in an endless startup loop!"

If your Mac uses the user-accounts feature described in Chapter 13, you might one day find that the usual list of account holders doesn't appear when you turn on the machine, thus preventing you from getting access to your own stuff. Even if you shut down or restart the Mac, it keeps taking you into one particular person's account each time it turns back on.

The reason: Somebody has turned on the Automatic Login feature described in the previous paragraphs. The solution: Either turn off Automatic Login or choose Log Out from the menu.

Forgotten password

If you or one of the other people who use your Mac have forgotten the corresponding account password, no worries. Anyone with an administrator account can type in a new password (using the Accounts panel of System Preferences). And even if you, the all-mighty administrator, have forgotten *your* password, your Mac OS X Install CD offers you a handy Reset Password command. It's described in Chapter 13.

Viruses? What viruses?

You hear an awful lot about viruses these days — malevolent little programs written by malevolent little creeps who get kicks from gumming up people's computers. Fortunately, 99.9999% of all viruses are written for Windows PCs, not the Mac. In fact, at this writing, there isn't even *one* virus that works in Mac OS X.

For some people, this freedom from the viruses that make life miserable for Windows fans is a key reason for switching to the Mac.

A special kind of automated software robot called a *macro virus* may still affect you if you regularly download Microsoft Word and Excel files by e-mail. Even then, there's not much to worry about: When you open such a file, a big fat dialog box will warn you if it contains macros. Simply click the Disable Macros button, open the file, and get on with your life.

Sleep well!

Software Situations

Every Mac model is one beautiful piece of hardware: sleek, made of gorgeous materials, and awaiting its rightful place in the technology museums of tomorrow.

But what really makes the world go 'round is *software*. Programs are what make your time go by, make your checkbook balance go down, and make your pulse race as you visit the Web — and they're the most likely things to go wrong.

Minor eccentric behavior

All kinds of weird little software glitches may befall you. Maybe a program won't open when you click its icon on the Dock — its icon just bounces a couple times and then stops. Maybe a menu won't open. Or maybe the program freezes whenever you click a certain icon on its toolbar.

All of these are typical computer hiccups, and all of them are pretty easy to fix. When a single program is acting up, try the following steps, in this sequence:

First resort: Restart the program

If one particular program starts exhibiting one eccentric behavior or another, the first step to take is simply to quit the program and start it up again. Restarting the flaky program lets it load from scratch, having forgotten all about its previous problems.

Second resort: Toss the preference files

Take this simple test. Log in using a different *account* (see Chapter 13), maybe a dummy account that you've created just for testing purposes. Run the flaky program. Is the problem gone?

If so, then the glitch exists only when *you* are logged in — which means it's a problem with *your* copy of the program's preference files. These are tiny files in your Home folder, in your Library folder, that memorize the way you like to have each program: where you've parked its toolbars, your preferred font settings, and so on.

Return to your own account. Open your Home folder, open the Library folder inside it, and open the Preferences folder inside *it*. Here you'll find preference files for all of the programs you use. Each ends with the file name suffix *.plist*. Find the one that bears the name of the problem program, and throw it into the Trash.

Now try opening the program again. If the glitch has gone away, you're home free. (The program creates new, fresh, virginal preference files automatically.)

If that didn't work, also visit the Preferences folder (a second one) in the Library folder in the hard drive window. Once again, throw away the .plist files for the offending program. (You'll be asked to provide the password for an administrator's account, as described in Chapter 13.)

Third resort: Repair the permissions

Confusion is responsible for an amazing number of software glitches. Not your confusion; the Mac's.

Remember from Chapter 13 how different account holders on a certain Mac aren't allowed to discard, change, or even see the files belonging to *other* account holders? Behind the scenes, your Mac keeps straight who is allowed to open which folders using an elaborate system of *permissions* — software switches that say who's allowed to open, change, or even see which folders and files. These software settings govern not only what *humans* can do, but also what *other software* is allowed to do.

Over time, the Mac might accidentally flag some important file as off-limits to one of your programs, which reaches for the file in the heat of battle and finds it unavailable. A glitch is the result.

Fortunately, your Mac came with a magical little program that fixes *all* permissions glitches on *all* of the tens of thousands of files on your Mac. When something just doesn't seem to be working right, therefore, open your Applications folder, open the Utilities folder inside it, and open the program called Disk Utility.

Click your hard drive's name in the left-side list; click the First Aid tab; click Repair Disk Permissions; and then go make lunch while the Mac checks out your disk. If the program finds anything amiss, you'll see messages like the cryptic codes displayed here:

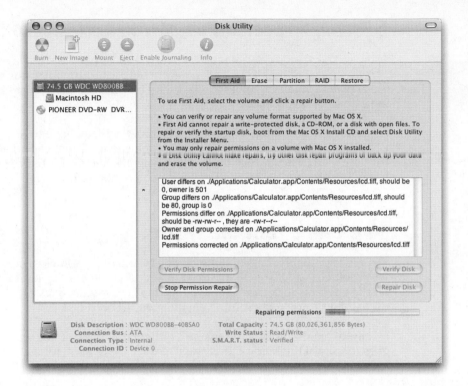

This is a *good* thing. Your Mac is fixing stuff.

You'll come to love Disk Utility, because it clears up the *weirdest* and most apparently random little problems. Many Mac gurus, in fact, believe in running this Repair Permissions routine after running *any kind of installer,* just to nip nascent problems in the bud. (Software installers are notorious for fiddling with the invisible permissions settings.) That includes both installers of new programs and of Apple's own Mac OS X updates.

Last resort: Trash and reinstall the program

Sometimes reinstalling the problem program clears up whatever the glitch was.

First, you should throw away all traces of the program. Just open the Applications folder and drag the program's icon (or its folder) to the Trash. In most cases, the only remaining piece to discard is its .plist files (the preference files) described in the preceding paragraphs.

Then reinstall the program from its original CD or installer — after first checking the company's Web site to see if there's an updated version, of course.

System Preferences controls are dimmed

Many of Mac OS X's control panels are off-limits to people who have normal *accounts* (see Chapter 13). That is, only people with Administrator accounts are allowed to make changes, as indicated by the padlock icon at the lower-left corner of such panels.

As described in Chapter 13, though, you don't actually have to have an administrator account *yourself* to make such changes. Just call an administrator over to your desk, click the padlock, and ask him or her to type in his or her password and supervise the change you're about to make.

You can't rename a file

The file is probably locked. Does its icon bear a tiny padlock symbol in the lower-left corner? If so, click it, choose Get Info from the File menu, and turn off the Locked check box. Or maybe the file is on a locked *disk*, such as a CD-ROM disc. You *can't* rename anything on a locked disk.

Finally, of course, you can't rename anything that doesn't belong to *you*. That goes for any of the Mac's own system files (in the System folder, for example) or any files that belong to other people's accounts (see Chapter 13).

Well, at least you can't *at first*. See "You do not have sufficient access privileges," later in this chapter, for the clever backdoor.

Can't empty the Trash

It's enough to drive you buggy: There's something in the Trash that refuses to be deleted. One error message after another tells you that the Trash can't be emptied.

First resort: Bypass the lock

In general, a file that's been *locked* (as indicated by the tiny padlock on its icon) can't even be moved to the Trash. Still, locked files sometimes make their way Trashward; somebody who's had a few beers, for example, may have locked a file *after* putting it into the Trash, for example.

The solution is to press Option as you click and hold on *the Trash icon itself*. Now, when you choose Empty Trash from the pop-up menu, Mac OS X empties the Trash without complaint, locked files and all.

Second resort: Close the file

You're not allowed to trash a file that's still open — one you're editing, for example. Close it before emptying the Trash.

Last resort: Check the permissions

If emptying the Trash gives you "Could not be completed because this item is owned by Arnold," you're trying to move or delete another Mac account holder's stuff. As you know by now, that's a big no-no in Mac OS X.

Still, there's a workaround. See "You do not have sufficient access privileges," later in this chapter.

Hardware Headaches

These glitches aren't as common as software problems, but they're just as frustrating.

Your mouse is jerky or sticky

The beauty of the Mac's mouse is that it's an *optical* mouse. Unlike old-fashioned mice, it doesn't have a little ball on the underside that rolls around collecting grit and crud like some kind of sticky toddler.

Instead, it has a tiny electronic eye that watches the ground beneath the mouse as you move it around, passing its movement information along to the cursor on the screen.

This ingenious system breaks down only when it's on *glass or mirrored* surfaces. If yours is, slip a piece of paper or a mouse pad underneath.

Until that trouble strikes, here are two fun facts about your mouse:

- You can turn the ring on the bottom of it, if your mouse has one, to adjust the clicking "tension."
- If, in the middle of dragging something across the screen, you run out of desk surface, squeeze the rounded flaps on the sides of the mouse. While you're squeezing, you can pick up the mouse and set it back down without "letting go" of whatever you clicked.

Double-clicking doesn't work

You're probably double-clicking too slowly, or you're moving the mouse a little bit during the double-click process.

A CD won't come out

Some Macs have only a *slot* for inserting CDs and DVDs. Others have a *drawer* or *tray* that slides out to accept a disc. (And while we're on the topic: Don't insert those cute novelty mini-CDs, which sometimes come in specially marked packages of breakfast cereal, or "business-card CDs," which sometimes come from specially marked annoying salesmen, into a slot-loading Mac. They'll break it.)

To make the drawer open, or to make the slot spit out a disc, the trick is to hold down (not just tap) the Eject button at the upper-right corner of your keyboard.

But if the drawer won't open when you press the button, something's jammed. The solution: Shut down the Mac (choose Shut Down from the menu). Turn it on again — but as it lights up, press the mouse button continuously until the CD pops out.

The screen is too dim

On most Macs, you can find a Brightness slider by opening System Preferences and clicking the Displays icon.

There's a shortcut, though: Tap the brightness *key* on the top row of your keyboard (it's usually F2 or F15). (F1 or F14 is the Dimmer key.)

The Wrong Program Opens

As noted in Chapter 4, the Mac generally does something very courteous when you double-click a document icon: It automatically opens the program that created it.

But what if the *wrong* program opens? What if you double-click, say, a graphics file, and it opens up in Preview instead of Photoshop?

File name extensions

When you double-click a document icon, the Mac inspects its three-letter *file name extension* — a suffix following a period in the file's name, as in *Madonna Hairstyles Master List.doc* or *family finances.cwk.*

"That's strange," you must be saying, glancing back and forth between this page and your Mac screen. "I don't *see* any of those extensions."

That's because the Mac comes set to *hide* most file name extensions, on the premise that they make the Mac look technical and threatening. If you'd like to see them, however, open the Finder menu, choose Preferences, click Advanced, and, in the resulting box, turn on "Show all file extensions," like this:

Before (extensions hidden)   After (extensions showing)

Now examine a few of the files in your Home folder's Documents folder. You'll see that their names now display the previously hidden suffixes.

You can hide or show these suffixes on an icon-at-a-time basis, too. Just high-light the icon or icons you want to affect. From the File menu, choose Get Info. Click the "Name & Extension" triangle to make it point down, and then turn on "Hide extension," as shown here.

The point is that the Mac has memorized which suffix "belongs" to which parent program. Files ending ".doc" open in Microsoft Word. Files ending ".cwk" open in AppleWorks. And so on.

Reassigning documents to programs

So how does all these geeky knowledge pay off in troubleshooting terms?

The problem with file name extensions is that they aren't always sure-fire in pinpointing which parent program should open a particular document. Suppose, for example, that you've downloaded a graphic called Barney.JPEG. Well, almost any program these days can open a JPEG graphic — AppleWorks, Word, Preview, Safari, and so on. How does your Mac X know which of these programs to open when you double-click the file? And what if it opens the *wrong* program?

Reassigning a single document

Double-clicking a downloaded graphics file generally opens it in Preview, the graphics viewer included with Mac OS X. Most of the time, that's a perfectly good arrangement. But Preview can only *display* graphics — it can't edit them. What if you decide you want to edit a graphics file? You'd want it to open, just this once, into a different program — Photoshop Elements, for example.

To do so, highlight the file's icon and then, from the File menu, choose Get Info. The Get Info window for that file appears.

Click the Open With triangle to expand its panel. From the pop-up menu, choose "Open with application." The pop-up menu just beneath it tells you what program *usually* opens this kind of document. From this pop-up menu (below, left), choose the name of the program you'd rather open this particular file, like this:

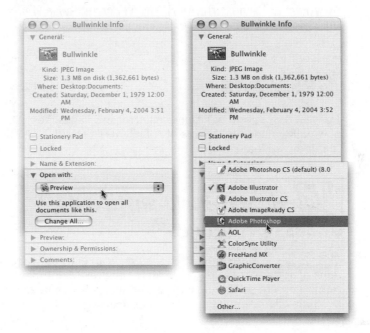

Reassigning all documents of this type

So much for the one-shot, one-document procedure. What if you're the editor of, say, a book called *Wallpaper For Dummies,* and the author has sent you 400 photographs to use in the book — all of them in the TIFF graphics format? Mac OS X comes set to open *every* TIFF file in its little Preview program, where you can only look at pictures, not edit them.

Sure, you could reassign all of these files, one at a time, to a different program, but you'd be 135 years old before you'd finished. What you really want, of course, is to tell the Mac: "For heaven's sake, make *all* TIFF files open in Photoshop Elements from now on!"

To make it so, repeat the "Open with application" ritual described above. But this time, follow up by clicking Change All at the bottom of the window.

(This button is dimmed until you've actually selected a different program from the pop-up menu.) In the confirmation box, click Continue.

You've just taught Mac OS X to open *all* TIFF files from now on in Photoshop Elements. (Or, rather, all files whose names end *.tif.* You might have to repeat the process for *.tiff* files, which are also TIFF files.)

You can, and should, use the same technique to reassign other kinds of documents to your favorite programs — either because you *prefer* those other programs or because the Mac's been opening those kinds of documents in the *wrong* program from the beginning.

Error Messages

Ah, yes, those good old American error messages. Yes, kids, these are the new-millennium equivalents of "DOES NOT COMPUTE." These are messages that indicate that something's wrong.

"You do not have sufficient access privileges"

Mac OS X, the Mac's operating system, is an extremely stable and secure hunk of software. As you can read in Chapter 13, it hides or protects itself rather fiercely, so that no clueless or malevolent human winds up moving, deleting, or renaming important files, causing a computer meltdown as a result.

Therefore, you get this message whenever you try to mess with the files in, for example, the System folder.

But you also get this message when you try to open or move files that belong to *other account holders* on this machine. (See Chapter 13 for details on accounts.) What's yours is yours, and those are the only files and folders you're allowed to move, open, trash, rename, and so on.

People with *Administrator* accounts (again, see Chapter 13) have slightly greater freedom. These blessed souls are at least allowed to add to, or remove icons from, the Applications folder, for example. Everybody else, though, gets the old "Not enough privileges" door slammed in their faces when they try to open *any files at all* that aren't in their Home folders, or that they didn't create themselves.

In short, Mac OS X is like a tough-love parent who says, "I'm grounding you because I love you."

Nonetheless, you paid a lot of money for this computer, so it's your right to do what you like with its files. Using the following technique, you can tell the Mac, "Hey, you're *my* Mac, and I can do anything I like with the files I find here! I am the ALL-MIGHTY ADMINISTRATOR!"

(Tell it that only if you do, in fact, have an administrator account.)

Click the file that's giving you trouble. From the File menu, choose Get Info. In the Get Info panel, click the Ownership & Permissions triangle to expand its panel, and then do the same for the Details triangle.

You should see something like this:

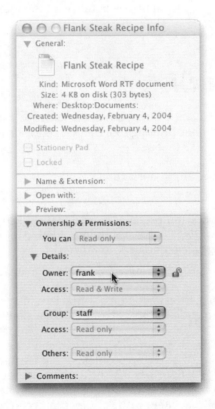

Click the little padlock icon, if it looks closed. Then, from the Owner pop-up menu shown here, choose your own account name. The Mac asks you to prove your worthiness by entering your administrator password. Make sure the top Access pop-up menu says Read & Write.

Then you're in. The file or folder belongs to you. You can trash it, open it, or do whatever the Mac previously told you was against policy. (Avoid seizing this kind of control over files in the System folder, though. Those are the files that run your Mac, and you wouldn't like the Mac when it's angry.)

"DNS Entry not found" or "Error 404"

You get these messages when using your Web browser (see Chapter 7). It says that the Web page you're trying to visit doesn't exist. Usually this means you've made a typo as you typed the Web address (sometimes called a *URL*), or the page's address has changed and you don't know it, or the computer the Web page is on has been taken off the Internet (for maintenance, for example).

Fixing the Disk

Mac OS X comes with a powerful disk-repair program called Disk Utility. It's a useful troubleshooting tool that can cure all kinds of strange ills, including problems like these:

- ✔ Some program is acting flaky
- ✔ The Mac freezes during startup
- ✔ The startup process interrupts itself with the appearance of the *command line* — a text-only, intimidating-looking screen where only programmers dare to tread
- ✔ Your programs show up as *folders* instead of double-clickable icons

One of Disk Utility's features — the awe-inspiring *Repair Permissions* button described earlier in this chapter — is available to you at any time.

Its other repair feature, *Repair Disk,* can fix more serious problems with your hard drive (like startup problems). But like a painter who can't paint the last corner of the floor because he's standing there, Disk Utility can't check the disk it's *on.* That's why you have to restart the computer from the Mac OS X Install CD that came with your Mac, and run Disk Utility from there. Proceed like this:

1. **Start up the Mac from the Mac OS X Install CD.**

   The best way to do that is to insert the CD and then restart the Mac while holding down the C key.

   After a minute or two, you wind up at the Mac OS X Installer screen. Don't be fooled — installing Mac OS X is *not* what you want to do here. Don't click Continue!

2. **From the Installer menu, choose Open Disk Utility.**

   After a moment, the Disk Utility screen appears.

3. **Click the First Aid tab. Click the icon for your hard drive at the left side of the window, and then click Repair.**

   The Mac whirls into action, checking a list of very technical disk-formatting parameters.

   If you see a note that says, "The volume 'Macintosh HD' appears to be OK," that's good news. That's as upbeat and confident as Disk Utility gets. (The message's last line says "Repair completed" whether or not any repairing was done at all.)

   Disk Utility may also tell you that the disk is damaged, but that it can't help you. In that case, you'll have to call Apple's help line (see the next chapter) or buy a more heavy-duty disk-repair program like Disk Warrior (*www.alsoft.com*).

Reinstalling Mac OS X

If some troubleshooting effort has left you exhausted and panting on the beach of desperation, and Mac OS X continues to act up, you may have to make the ultimate sacrifice: reinstalling Mac OS X.

The following instructions guide you through a *clean install,* which is considered an essential troubleshooting technique. You're about to install a *second* copy of Mac OS X: a fresh, clean one, uncontaminated by whatever lint you and your various software programs have gotten into the works.

Find the Mac OS X 10.3 discs that came with your machine (or that you bought for your machine). Ready?

1. **Insert the Mac OS X CD. Double-click the icon called "Install Mac OS X" in the CD's main window. When the Restart button appears, click it.**

   The Mac starts up from the CD and takes you directly to the first Installer screen.

   The installer screens always follow the same a pattern: Read some information, make a couple choices, and click Continue to advance to the next screen.

2. **Work your way through the Select Language, Welcome, Important Information, and Software License Agreement screens.**

   Finally, you arrive at the Select a Destination screen.

3. Click the disk icon where you want to install Mac OS X.

For most people, there's only one hard drive icon here: Macintosh HD, the one inside your Mac.

4. Click Options.

Now you're offered four kinds of installation.

5. Turn on "Archive and Install." ("Preserve Users and Network Settings" should be on, too.)

This option will leave all of your files and settings *untouched* (Home folders, documents, pictures, movies, Favorites, e-mail, and so on). It's just going to give you a fresh copy of the operating system itself.

6. Click OK.

You arrive at the Easy Install screen. The easiest way to proceed here is to click Install. But you can save an *enormous* swath of hard-drive space if you take the time to click Customize.

The Installer shows you a list of the software chunks that make up Mac OS X. If you turn off the checkboxes for, say, Additional Asian Fonts, Language Translations (for Japanese, German, French, and so on), and the printer models that you don't own, you save *1.1 gigabytes*. That's a *lot* of room.

7. Click Install.

Now you're in for a 25-minute wait as the Installer copies software onto your hard drive.

Eventually, the Mac restarts itself and spits out the first CD. Insert Disc 2. When that's done, insert Disc 3, if you're asked for it.

When the installer's finished, a message lets you know that your Mac will restart in 30 seconds. If you haven't long since wandered off to take a shower, click the Restart button to end the countdown and get on with it.

When all of this is over, you'll find a new folder on your hard drive called Previous System Folders. It contains your *old* copy of Mac OS X, which you can safely drag to the Trash. You have a new, fresh, glitch-free copy now, which was exactly the point of this exercise.

Alas, you may not be quite finished with your homework here. Remember that Apple continues to hone Mac OS X with successive versions — 10.3.1, 10.3.2, and so on. Chances are pretty good that the newly installed copy of Mac OS X is not, therefore, the very latest version.

Fortunately, when you connect to the Internet, your Software Update program (described in Chapter 3) will notice the discrepancy and offer to download and install the updates you're lacking.

Chapter 17

Beyond the Mac: Where to Go from Here

The first 16 chapters of this book are the crash course. Now, Grasshoppa, it's time for you to venture forth into the world by yourself. Go for the gold. Do the right thing. Use the Force.

But first, a few parting words of wisdom.

Where to Turn in Times of Trouble

You own the world's most forgiving, self-explanatory computer. But things will go wrong. And not even this astoundingly complete book can anticipate the problems you may encounter while running BeeKeeper Pro or No Namo Scanner Doodad Plus. Fortunately, the world is crawling with help possibilities.

Your 15 minutes of free help

TIP

During the first three months you've owned your Mac, you can call Apple's delightful toll-free hotline at (800) 275-2273 and ask your questions of the gurus there. (Hint for the budget-conscious: Apple doesn't know when you bought your Mac. They measure your 90 days, therefore, from your first *call*, not really from the day you bought your machine.)

Beyond those 90 days, Apple charges you nosebleed-inducing fees for your use of their experts (unless the computer actually turns out to need fixing, in which case the fee is waived). The number for this service is (888) 275-8258 (toll-free, again), and you can choose to have your wallet milked in either of two quantities: One problem solved for $50; ten for $290.

The bottom line: Try to have all your problems in the first 90 days.

$150 for three years

If you anticipate needing phone help at least three times, you're far better off buying AppleCare. It's an extended-warranty program that covers all Mac troubles for three years, including mechanical problems. Keep in mind, however, that you must sign up for this program during the first year you own your Mac. (The price depends on which model you bought.)

AppleCare is an especially good idea if you have an iBook or PowerBook, because laptops get banged around a lot. If something goes wrong with yours, Apple actually sends a padded FedEx box to your house, picks up the patient, fixes it in a day or so, then overnights it back to you.

But even if you have a less mobile Mac, AppleCare buys you the right to call that 800 number and ask all the questions you want, without paying another nickel.

Free help sources

If spending money isn't your way of problem solving, consider these all-expenses-paid avenues:

- ✔ **Apple Knowledge Base:** The mother of all troubleshooting resources. This is the collection of 50,000 individual technical articles, organized in a searchable database, that the Apple technicians themselves consult when you call for help.

  If you like, you can visit this library using your Web browser; the address is *www.apple.com/support.* You can search it either by typing in keywords or by using pop-up menus of question categories.

- ✔ **Apple's Web page:** Also at *apple.com/support,* you can find downloadable manuals, software updates, frequently asked questions, and many other resources.

✔ **MacFixIt Web page:** You get hundreds of discussions of little tweaky specific Mac problems at *www.macfixit.com.*

✔ **Bulletin boards online:** The other great source of help is an electronic meeting place like America Online, where you may get your question answered instantly — and if not, you can post your question on a bulletin board for somebody to answer overnight. Try keyword MOS, for example. (See Chapter 6 for details on keywords.)

If you're Internet savvy, you can visit a newsgroup called *comp.sys.mac* for similar assistance. (See Chapter 6 for information on newsgroups.) If you're polite and concise, you can post questions to the multitudes here and get more replies to them than you'll know what to do with.

Otherwise, your next resort should be a local user group, if you're lucky enough to live in a pseudometropolitan area. A user group, of course, doesn't exist to answer *your* personal questions; you still have to do some phoning and hobnobbing and research. But a user group *is* a source of sources. You can call up and find out who will know the answer to your question. (To find the nearest user group, call Apple's referral service at (800) 538-9696.)

As for your continuing education — after you spend four figures on a computer, I'll bet you can afford $30 more for a subscription to *Macworld, MacAddict,* or *MacHome Journal* magazine. Agreed, huge chunks of these rags may go right over your head. But in every single issue, you'll find at least one really useful item. You can learn all kinds of things just by reading the ads. And if you're not in touch with the computer nerd world at least by that tenuous thread — via magazine — then you might miss stuff like free offers, recall notices, warnings, and other consumer-oriented jazz.

Where to Get the Inside Dirt

The Web sites listed in the previous paragraphs are great for Mac troubleshooting. But when the computer is running *smoothly,* consider visiting these sites for news, rumors, and commentary:

✔ **MacSurfer** *(www.macsurfer.com):* A daily roundup of articles about the Mac from newspapers and magazines around the country. Click a listing to read that article.

✔ **MacCentral** *(www.maccentral.com):* News, updates, tricks, and product announcements — all about the Mac.

✔ **Think Secret** *(www.thinksecret.com):* One thing you'll find out pretty quickly is that Mac fans are an exciting, creative, *very* enthusiastic group. They — that is, *we* — love our Macs, and tend to obsess over Mac developments, news, and rumors much more than, say, Windows fans.

Lots of Web sites are devoted to Mac rumors (Will there be an Earlobe Mac? Will Apple unveil new see-through iPods?). Think Secret.com happens to have a better track record than most at predicting Apple and Mac news. Check it in late December, for example, to find out what Apple might be unveiling at its annual Macworld Expo show in San Francisco the first week of January.

Upgrading to Mac OS 10.4 — and Beyond

Apple never stops tinkering with its crown jewel, the Mac operating system. From time to time, you'll connect to the Internet and encounter a Software Update dialog box like the one shown in Chapter 3, notifying you about a free upgrade to an even better version of Mac OS X. It's almost always a good idea to click Install.

Apple has even bigger plans for Mac OS X, though. Every year or so, it adds some *very* big new features — and changes the version number. This book assumes that you're using Mac OS X 10.3 (code-named Panther), but before it was version 10.0 (Cheetah), 10.1 (Puma), and 10.2 (Jaguar). And before you've filed two more tax returns, Apple will be offering version 10.4 (Bobcat? Cougar? Ocelot?).

Most of the advice in this book will still be sound — but you'll have a few additional features designed to make the Mac faster, easier, and trouble-freer. And your wallet will be about $130 lighter.

Whenever you upgrade your operating system in this way, however, you run the risk that any *add-on* programs — that is, software that didn't come from Apple — might develop quirks and tics. Your big, everyday, came-with-the-Mac programs like AppleWorks and Microsoft Word probably won't be affected. But other stuff you've bought, or downloaded from the Internet, may occasionally behave oddly after a system-software upgrade.

In that event, contact whoever made the software in question — or visit the corresponding Web page. Check to see if an upgrade is available. (It almost always is.)

Finally, if you do decide to upgrade your Mac to the next version of Mac OS X, you'll have a much smoother time of it if you choose the *clean install* option. Never mind what that means right now; just remember that when it comes time to upgrade your Mac to Mac OS X 10-point-whatever, follow the "Reinstalling Mac OS X" instructions in Chapter 16 for the smoothest sailing.

Save Changes Before Closing?

If you decide to get more into this Macintosh thing, use the resource list at the beginning of this chapter as a starting point.

But wait a minute — the point of this book wasn't to convert you into a full-time Mac rabbit. It was to get you off the ground. To give you just enough background so you'll know why the computer's beeping at you. To show you the basics and help you figure out what the beanie heads are talking about.

Don't let them intimidate you. So *what* if you don't know the lingo or have the circuitry memorized? If you can turn the thing on, get something written up and printed, and get out in time to enjoy the sunshine, you qualify as a real Mac user.

Any dummy knows that.

Part V
The Part of Tens

The 5th Wave   By Rich Tennant

"I tell you, it looks like Danny, it sounds like Danny, but it's NOT Danny!! I think the MAC has created an alias of Danny! You can see it in his eyes - little wrist watch icons!"

In this part . . .

Here's what we *For Dummies* book authors often refer to as "the chapters we can write in one day apiece" — a trio of top ten lists, for your infotainment pleasure.

Chapter 18

Ten Cool Things You Didn't Know Your Mac Could Do

● ●

*I*t's fast, it's hip, and it complements any décor. But the Mac does more — much more. Try *these* some lazy Saturday afternoon.

Type Across the World

If your Mac has Mac OS X 10.3 (the "Panther" operating system), it came with an ingenious little program called iChat AV. It lets you conduct typed *chats* with other people on the Internet. You type messages to friends and colleagues in a chat window, in real time, and they type replies back to you, just like millions of teenagers before you. This delightful conversational forum, also called *instant messaging* (as in, "He I.M.'ed me last night") offers the privacy of e-mail with the immediacy of the phone.

Get a chat account

When you open iChat for the first time (it's in your Applications folder), you see the "Welcome To iChat" window, where you're supposed to type in your *chat name*. (People who conduct typed, spoken, or video'ed chats on the Internet don't have phone numbers; they have chat names. They're free.) You can get one in any of the following ways:

✔ **Use your .Mac name.** If you signed up for Apple's .Mac Internet service as described in Chapter 6, you already have a chat account. You can just use that account name as your chat name.

✔ **Get a free .Mac account.** Apple charges $100 for an annual .Mac subscription. But if you don't care about the iDisk and other .Mac perks, you can get an iChat-only account for free.

When the "Welcome To iChat" window appears, click Continue. You arrive at the "Set up a new iChat account" screen shown here:

Click the "Get an iChat Account" button, proceed to Apple's iChat Signup Web page, type in your name and e-mail address, and make up a chat name and password for yourself. Once that's done, return to this dialog box, fill in your freshly minted iChat address (which ends with "@mac.com") and password, and click Continue.

✔ **Use an AOL Instant Messaging account.** The .Mac network is only one of the *two* chat networks that iChat can navigate. It can also hook into the much larger AOL (America Online) Instant Message network, also known as AIM.

From the Account Type pop-up menu on the Welcome to iChat screen, choose AIM Account. From here, type in your America Online screen name and password, if you're already an AOL member, and click OK.

If you're not an AOL member, you can get an AOL chat account name and password for free. Open your Web browser and go to *my.screenname. aol.com*. Click "Get a Screen Name" to make up an AOL screen name.

The rest of the setup process offers you the chance to fine-tune your video camera, if you have one, and join an in-office network (a Rendezvous network), if you have one. Finally, you're ready to chat.

The Buddy List

All you need now is what's known as a *buddy* in instant-messaging circles — somebody to talk to. You'll choose this lucky person's name from your Buddy List, as shown here:

Sending a file during a chat

If you open the Buddies menu and choose Send a File, you can select a file from your hard drive to send to your chat partner.

This is a fantastic way to transfer a file, for two reasons. First, there's no size limit (unlike e-mail, which sometimes refuses a file because it's too big or because the recipient's mailbox is "full").

Second, sending a file this way cuts the transfer time in half. Your recipient gets the file *as* you send it, rather than waiting 15 minutes for you to *send* the file, and another 15 minutes to download it.

(If you don't see it, open the Window menu and choose Buddy List.)

Of course, your Buddy List is probably empty the first time you use it. It's up to you to find out what your colleagues' chat names are. (You might have to use a lower-tech method of asking them — like calling them up on the phone.)

Once you know somebody's chat name, click the + button in the Buddy List, then click New Person. Fill in the blanks, like this:

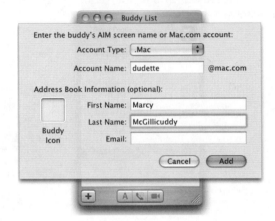

Now your buddy's name appears in the Buddy List. To begin a chat, wait until a buddy's name shows up in dark type, which means he or she is online.

Then double-click the person's *name,* type a quick invite ("You wanna tawk?"), and press Enter.

(And if you see a window like this —

— then they're inviting *you* to chat. Type a response in the bottom text box if you like, and click Accept.)

Now the chat has begun! Each time you type something and then press Enter or Return, your masterful prose appears on *both* your screen and your buddy's, like this:

As the conversation bubbles along, your witticisms roll up the screen like a screenplay being written in real time.

Make Free Phone (and Video) Calls

If your Mac has a microphone, and so does your chat partner's, the two of you don't have to *type* to communicate; that's so 1990! Instead, you can talk to each other *out loud,* using the Internet as a free long-distance telephone.

Better yet, if your Mac has a camcorder attached (or a pocket-sized video cam like Apple's $150 iSight camera), you can *watch* each other, as though you're both on each other's TV. Yes, baby, this is *videoconferencing,* minus the $50,000 worth of fancy equipment. It's the perfect way to keep in touch when you're on the road, or to show somebody else on the Internet your new idea, new house, or new baby. (This feature requires a high-speed Internet connection like a cable modem or DSL.)

To begin a "free phone call," click the telephone icon next to a buddy's name (if there is one), or highlight someone in the Buddy List and then click the microphone icon at the bottom of the list. (The microphone icon means, "This person has a mike set up.")

Once your invitation is accepted, you can begin speaking to each other. You hear the other person's voice from your Mac's speaker. Talk as long as you like, call any country you like; it's all free! Better yet, you don't run the risk of waking up some European pal in the middle of the night by ringing the phone. If they're online, they're obviously awake.

To begin a video chat, click the camera icon (if there is one) next to the buddy's name, or highlight someone in the Buddy List and then click the camcorder icon at the bottom of the list.

A window opens, showing a live video image of *you*. This Preview mode is intended to show what your buddy will see. (Hint: More light on your face can make a huge difference.)

Once your buddy clicks Accept, the chat can begin. It's as though you're both on TV at once, like this:

When you're finished with any kind of chat, close the window or quit iChat — after first saying goodbye, of course. And be grateful that you were alive to see the day.

Talk to You

It's been said that we spend the first year of a child's life trying to get it to talk, and the next 18 years trying to get it to shut up. Well, with the Mac, getting it to talk is fantastically easy.

Start by opening your System Preferences program (click the light-switch icon on the Dock). Then click the Speech icon; on the Speech control panel, click Default Voice, as shown here.

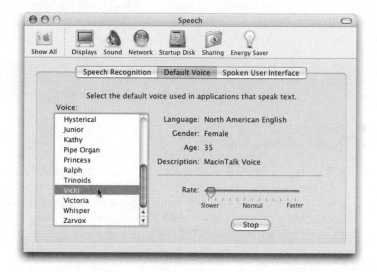

Now is your chance to choose a voice for your particular Mac. The voice menu lists about two dozen different voices. They're great: male, female, kids, deep voices, shaky voices, whispered voices. Click each one to hear it say a funny sentence in its own voice. And don't miss the Rate slider, which governs how fast each voice talks.

When you're happy with your Mac's voice, the next step is to give it something to say. Click the Spoken User Interface button.

Turn on "Selected text when a key is pressed." The Mac invites you to press a certain key combination (like Option-S) that will serve as your "start talking" Keystroke. Press the keys, whose names appear in the box like this —

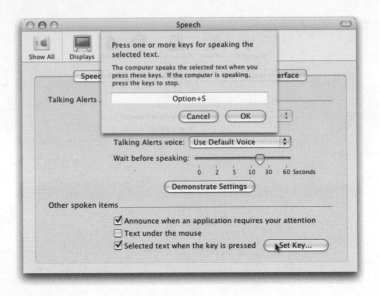

— and then click OK.

You've just turned on an amazing feature that's not available in Windows or any other operating system: The Mac can now read aloud *any text in any program*. You can hear any Web page read to you, any e-mail message, any Sticky note. Furthermore, if you do any kind of writing at all, you'll discover the value of having your material read back to you out loud; it's a proofreading technique that reveals all kinds of typos and wordos that you wouldn't catch just by reading.

To make it happen, go to the program where you'd like the reading to take place. Highlight (drag through) the text you want to hear. Then press the keystroke you specified.

Amazingly, the Mac begins reading it aloud immediately. To interrupt the playback, press the same keystroke again.

Sing

Although it's a little humbling that your Mac may be more talented than you are, it does indeed sing. It has a somewhat limited repertoire — in fact, it knows only four songs — but it can use any lyrics you want, and it never even stops to take a breath.

To make your Mac sing, you simply need to get it talking, as described in the preceding section. Then choose one of these voices in the Speech panel of System Preferences:

- **Pipe Organ:** Sings to the tune of the Alfred Hitchcock theme.
- **Good News:** Sings to the tune of "Pomp & Circumstance," otherwise known as the graduation march.
- **Bad News:** Sings to the tune of the funeral march.
- **Cellos:** Sings to the tune of "In the Hall of the Mountain King," from *Peer Gynt*, by Edvard Grieg. Such culture!

Punctuation marks make the Mac start over from the beginning of the melody. Sample lyrics for the Good News graduation-march melody, for example, should look like this:

You just won the jackpot good luck and God bless

Too bad you owe half to good old IRS!

Listen

The Mac wouldn't be much of a conversation partner if all it did were talk to *you*. Believe it or not, your little machine can also *take spoken commands*. You can't exactly say, "Answer my e-mail, compose my report, and change the oil in the Subaru," but you can open programs by voice and even exchange knock-knock jokes with your machine.

All you need is a microphone. (It's built into the screen of iMacs, iBooks, eMacs, and PowerBooks; for a Power Mac, you can buy a cheap USB plug-in microphone.)

Turning on speech recognition

Open System Preferences and then click the Speech icon. Click the Speech Recognition button. See where it says "Apple Speakable Items Is"? Click On.

The first time you do this, a small instructions window appears. Read it if you like, and then click Continue.

Now a weird, round, UFO-like floating window appears. The word *Esc* in its center indicates the "listen" key — the key you're supposed to hold down when you want the Mac to respond to your voice. (You wouldn't want the Mac listening all the time — even when you said, for example, "Hey, it's cold in here. *Close the window.*" Therefore, the Mac comes ready to listen to you only when you're pressing that key.)

What the Mac can understand

You can't exactly chat away in conversation with your Mac; it is, after all, only a hunk of plastic, glass, and metal. In fact, the only commands it understands are the utterances listed in the Speech Commands window (below, right). To see this list, click the bottom tip of the little round window (below, left) and choose Open Speech Commands Window:

When you start talking, you'll also see the Mac's interpretation of what you said written out in a yellow balloon just over the Feedback window. Here are a few examples of the kind of thing you can say:

- **Open Sherlock.** Say this to open Sherlock, the Web-searching program described in Chapter 7.

- **Go to my home directory.** That's a fancy way of saying, "Open my Home folder."

- **Make a new folder.** Just what it says.

- **Close this window.** Closes the frontmost window instantly.

- ✓ **Empty the trash.** This one works only when you're in the Finder and there is, in fact, something in the Trash.

- ✓ **Switch to AppleWorks.** Actually, you can say "switch to" and the name of *any* running or recently used program.

- ✓ **Quit all applications.** Saves you the trouble of switching into each program and choosing Quit.

- ✓ **Show me what to say.** This command opens the Speech Commands window that you're probably looking at right now.

- ✓ **What day is it?** Tells you the date.

- ✓ **Tell me a joke.** Begins a pathetic knock-knock joke. You've got to play along, providing the "who's there?" and "so-and-so *who?*" answers. (You don't necessarily have to say, "Who's there?" You can also say "Stop," "Go away," or even "Stop with the jokes!")

When you switch from one program to another, the list in the Speech Commands window may change, so that you see whatever special commands work in the new program.

Speaking to the Mac

When you're ready to try talking to your computer, hold down the Esc key. Begin speaking normally. Try one of the commands in the Speakable Commands list, like "What time is it?"

If all goes well, a few things should happen. First, the lines in the little round Feedback window change color, indicating that the Mac is hearing you. Second, a balloon above the Feedback window tells you what the Mac *thinks* you said. Finally, the Mac *does* whatever you told it to do. In the case of the knock-knock jokes, you'll actually hear it converse with you using whatever voice you selected in the Speech panel of System Preferences.

Play DVDs

The Mac can't just dish out DVDs, as described in Chapter 11; it can also take them. Unless you have a very elderly machine, it can play back standard DVD discs you've rented from Blockbuster, rented from online DVD clubs like *www.netflix.com* and *www.DVDovernight.com,* or made yourself using iMovie and iDVD.

To play a DVD movie, insert it just as you would a CD (either slip it into your Mac's slot, if it has one, or press the ▲ key at the upper-right on your keyboard to make the sliding tray open).

The very first time you insert a DVD, you wait about a minute, and then you get a strange dialog box that asks what *Region* you're in.

As an anti-illegal-copying system, your Mac requires that you tell it where you are in the world — and you can only change your mind about that five more times. If you're not especially interested in becoming a software pirate, this shouldn't be much of a limitation; just click Set Drive Region and get on with your life. (You have to do this using an Administrator account, or with an Administrator supervising you, as described in Chapter 13.) Click OK in the confirmation box, too.

Now you're in a program called DVD Player, and the DVD movie starts playing automatically. Put the popcorn in the microwave; it's showtime.

You might have wondered, by the way, how, in the absence of a remote control, you're supposed to pause a flick when nature calls. Simple: Just move the mouse. Doing so makes the Mac's virtual remote appear, which looks like this:

Now you can control the Mac like a VCR, using a combination of buttons on the remote and keys on your keyboard. For example:

- ✔ Click the triangle to play, the square to stop, or the | | button to pause. You can also press the space bar to play and stop.

- ✔ Hold down the Forward or Backward button to fast-forward or rewind through the movie, watching in fast motion. You go at 4 times regular speed using this method (or whatever speed you've selected in the Scan Rate submenu of the Controls menu).

  You have much greater control, though, if you learn the ⌘-right arrow and ⌘-left arrow keystrokes. They let you switch between 2x, 4x, and 8x speeds (press repeatedly to cycle through these speeds) — and don't even require the remote control.

- *Click* the Forward or Backward button (without holding down the button) to jump to the next "chapter" of the movie.

- Adjust the volume by pressing ⌘-up arrow and ⌘-down arrow, or by dragging the volume slider on the remote.

- Full-screen mode is by far the most satisfying one (choose Enter Full Screen from the Video menu). But when you're trying to show off, choose Half Size or Normal Size from the Video menu. Now you've got the movie playing in a window of its own, which continues to play away even as you use other programs to surf the Web, reply to e-mail, or whatever.

Once your DVD disc is playing, the Menu button brings up the disc's special features. They may include foreign-language sound tracks, director's narration, subtitles for the hearing impaired, and a list of "chapters" (scenes) in the movie.

In DVD Player, choose Apple DVD Player Help from the Help menu to read about even more fancy stuff you can do with DVDs. After a certain point, though, you'll probably decide that just *watching* Hollywood movies on your computer is fancy enough.

Send Faxes

Because your Mac has a built-in fax modem, you're in for a delicious treat. Faxes sent by a Mac come out looking twice as crisp and clean when a real fax machine receives them. You save all kinds of money on paper and fax cartridges, and may even spare you the expense of buying a physical fax machine. And sending faxes couldn't be more convenient for you — no printout to throw away, no paper involved at all. Your Mac sends the thing directly to another fax machine's brain.

Just make sure you've connected the Mac's modem jack (see Chapter 20) to a phone jack on the wall.

You can fax anything you can print — like a Web page, an e-mail, or something you've written. Here's how the faxing process goes:

1. **Type up (or open) whatever it is you want to fax.**

   Usually, this means a letter you've written in, say, Word or TextEdit.

2. **From the File menu, choose Print.**

   The Print dialog box appears.

3. Click Fax.

You see a dialog box like this one:

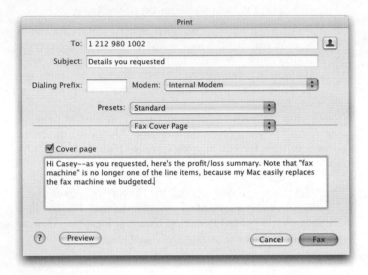

4. Type the fax number into the To box.

Type the complete phone number, complete with 1 and the area code, if necessary.

Or, if you keep your little black book in the Mac's Address book program, click the little silhouette-of-a-guy button in the upper-right corner. In your list of addresses, double-click the name of each person you want to receive your fax.

Incidentally, if you turn on "Cover page," you're allowed to type a little message into the box. Your note here ("Casey — here are those numbers you asked for concerning the profits from my organic lettuce farm") will appear on a separate page before the rest of the fax. (Watch out here, though; you can type only a single paragraph. If you press the Return key, thinking that you're creating a new paragraph, you'll trigger the Fax button, and you'll send your message before it's complete.)

5. From the Modem pop-up menu, choose Internal Modem. Then click Fax.

Although it may look like nothing is happening, the icon of a program called Internal Modem appears on your Dock. If you click it, you'll see a dialog box that indicates the progress of your fax. Here you can pause the faxing, or delete it.

Otherwise, you don't get much feedback on the faxing process. The only indication you get that the fax was successful is a call or e-mail from the recipient saying "Hey, thanks for the fax" (and maybe not even that).

Receive Faxes

If you promise not to tell anyone, here's a little secret: Your Mac can *receive* faxes, too, provided that.

- The Mac is turned on.
- It's not asleep.
- You treat your Mac like a fax machine: that is, you dedicate a second phone line to it — or live with having to plug it into your phone jack (thus blocking normal voice calls) every time you're expecting a fax.
- You've made the proper sacrifices to the technology gods. (Faxing is not, ahem, Mac OS X's most reliable feature. But if it works for you, you've got a friend.)

To set this up, open System Preferences (click the light-switch icon on your Dock). Click Print & Fax, so that you see this:

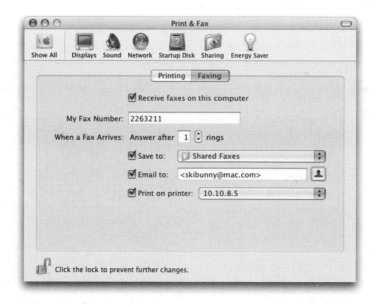

Turn on "Receive faxes on this computer." Then specify how you want to handle incoming faxes by turning on the checkboxes. For example, when your Mac answers the fax line, there are three things it can do with the incoming fax:

- ✔ **Save it as a PDF file** (a graphics file) that you open with Preview. (The Mac proposes saving these files into the Shared Faxes folder, which is in the Shared folder, which is in the Users folder on your hard drive. But you can set up a more convenient folder by choosing Other Folder from the pop-up menu here.)

- ✔ **E-mail it to you,** so that you can get your faxes even when you're not home.

- ✔ **Auto-print it,** just as a real fax machine would.

When a fax call comes in, the Mac answers it after the number of rings you've specified. Then it treats the incoming fax image in the way you've specified: by sending it to your e-mail program, printing it automatically, or just saving it as a PDF file in a folder that you've specified.

There. I just saved you $200 (or whatever fax machines cost these days).

Take Pictures of the Screen

Not just anybody can be a computer-book author. If possible, the candidate should have years of technical training, a PhD in computer programming, and the ability to take apart a computer and put it back together blindfolded.

Of course, I don't have any of that. But I do know how to take *screenshots*.

Screenshots are printable illustrations of the Mac screen. They appear everywhere in this book. If you can make screenshots, you're halfway home to being able to write computer books of your own.

To capture your screen image, press Shift-⌘-3. You hear a satisfying camera-shutter sound, and a new graphics file appears on your desktop called *Picture 1*. Each time you press Shift-⌘-3, you get another file, called Picture 2, Picture 3, and so on. You can double-click one of these files (they're PDF files, if you're scoring at home) to open it in Preview, in readiness for editing or printing.

If you're interested in capturing only *part* of the screen, though, you press Shift-⌘-4. Your cursor becomes a tiny + symbol. Now drag diagonally across the screen to capture only a rectangular chunk of it. (Or, if you're trying to take a picture of just one window or dialog box, press the Space bar to turn the cursor into a little camera, and then click the window you want.)

When you release the mouse, you hear the camera-click sound, and the Picture 1 file appears on your desktop as usual.

Run Windows Programs

It's true: Never again must you feel game-deprived. The Mac can run almost any Windows program alive. All you need is a program like VirtualPC for Mac OS X *(www.microsoft.com/mac)*. Your Windows programs won't run quite as fast as they would on the fastest actual Windows *computers* — but they'll run.

Chapter 19

Ten Tricks That Didn't Quite Fit the Outline

● ●

*T*his chapter is filled with miniature Mac lessons. It reveals Mac features you'd be unlikely to discover on your own, unearths shortcuts and slick tricks, and shows you how to tailor your Mac so that it perfectly fits your personality.

In short, the following discussions are useful, surprising, delightful — but utterly random. They just didn't fit tidily into any other chapter. That's a syndrome we writers try to avoid, but greatly prefer to writer's block. May you find enlightenment even in randomness.

Closing All Windows at Once

Suppose you've opened a gaggle of folders. Their windows are lying open all over the screen. And suppose that the niggling neatness ethic instilled in you by your mother compels you to clean up a bit.

You could, of course, click the close button of each window, one at a time. But it's far faster to click only *one* window's close button while pressing the Option key. Bam, bam, bam — they all close automatically, one after another, all of the windows in the program you were using. (You can perform the same trick, by the way, on the yellow Minimize button. Option-click it in one window to send *all* open desktop windows scurrying down to the Dock, out of your way.)

Multitasking Methods #1

As you discovered early on, the Mac lets you run more than one program simultaneously. (Remember when you tried some tricks with both Stickies and the Calculator open on the screen at once?) You can switch from one program to another by clicking the program's icon in the Dock.

So how does the Option key play into all this? When you switch from one program to another, you can make the program you're *leaving* hide itself, and all of its windows, automatically. Just press Option while clicking the new program's icon on the Dock (or while clicking in its window). That way, you always keep nonessential programs hidden.

Multitasking Methods #2

Efficiency fans eschew the mouse, a little fact you've probably picked up on by this point in the book. Anything that's worth doing, goes the thinking, is worth doing with the keyboard alone.

To that end, Apple has equipped you with a handy keystroke that lets you switch among your various open programs without your having to click the Dock — or even use the mouse at all. It's ⌘-Tab.

That is, hold down the ⌘ key. While it's down, keep tapping the Tab key. With each tap, you highlight a different icon in a secret "dashboard" of open programs that appears in the middle of your screen, like this:

When you've highlighted the icon of the program you want to jump to, let go of all keys. The Mac responds by bringing that program to the front, ready for action.

(You can also call up the dashboard with a quick ⌘-Tab — and then use the mouse to click the program you want.)

Make an Alias of a File

The File menu has a command called Make Alias. Although you might expect this command to generate names like One-Eyed Jake or "Teeth" McGuire, the term *alias* in the Macintosh world represents something slightly different — a duplicate of a file's *icon* (but not a duplicate of the file itself). You can identify the alias icon because of the tiny, tiny arrow that appears on its icon. (The word *alias* sometimes appears, too.)

Spy Photos

Spy Photos alias

What's neat about aliases is that, when you double-click an alias icon, the Mac opens the *original* file. If the 1980's were your formative years, you might think of the alias as a beeper — when you call the *alias,* the *actual* file responds.

So who on earth would need a feature like this? Well, there's more to the story. An alias, for one thing, requires only a tiny amount of disk space (a couple of K) — so it's not the same as making an actual copy of the full-sized, original file. (And you can make as many aliases of a file as you want.) Therefore, making an alias of something you use frequently is an excellent time-saver — it keeps the alias icon readily accessible, even if the real file is buried somewhere four folders deep.

Trash, aliases, and a word of caution

If you trash an alias, you're deleting only the alias. The original file is still on your disk. If you delete the *original* file, however, the alias icons will remain uselessly on your disk, rebels without a cause, babies without a mother, days without sunshine. When you double-click an alias whose original file is gone, you'll just get an error message. (The error message offers you the chance to attach this orphaned alias to a *different* "real" file — but the original file is still gone forever.)

Likewise, if you burn your inauguration speech file's *alias* onto a CD, thinking that you'll just print it out when you get to Washington, think again. You've just copied the alias, but you *don't* actually have any text. That's all in the original file, still at home on your hard disk.

Here's the drill:

1. **Click the real icon once.**

2. **From the File menu, choose Make Alias.**

Or, as a shortcut, just drag any icon out of its window while pressing Option and ⌘.

You can put that alias anywhere you like, confident that it serves as a handy elevator button that takes you to the real file that spawned it. The *real* file can be anywhere on your hard disk, or even on a different disk. You can move the real file from folder to folder or even rename it, and the alias still opens it correctly.

Self-Launching Programs

If your daily routine begins with the same program each morning — your e-mail and word processor programs, for example — you can tell your Mac to fire them up automatically, saving you a couple of manual mouse clicks.

To specify what you'd like to auto-open, open the System Preferences program (the light-switch icon on your Dock) and click the Accounts icon. Then click the Startup Items button.

As shown here, you can now build a list of programs or documents that will auto-open each time you log in.

You can add the icons of programs or documents you'd like to auto-open in either of two ways:

✔ Click + to open a dialog box showing the contents of your Applications folder. Double-click the icon of the program you want to self-open. Or, if you want to open a certain *document* each morning, navigate to your Documents folder and select the file there.

✔ Find the icon of whatever it is you want to self-open, in whatever folder contains it — and drag it directly out of the Finder and into the list illustrated in the previous figure.

You can also specify the order in which your startup items auto-open just by dragging them up or down in the list. To remove an item, click it in the list and then click the – button.

The Secret Life of a Scroll Bar

You may remember from Chapter 1 that the little square box inside a scroll bar lets you view what's hidden in a window — what's above or below what you're seeing, for example. (Man, I sure *hope* you remember — otherwise, you've been using your Mac all this time without ever writing a memo taller than three inches.)

The trouble with scroll bars, though, is that you have to use them one at a time. If you want to move diagonally to see a different part of a window, you have to scroll first horizontally, then vertically.

But in the Finder, you can use a secret trick: Press ⌘ and Option in any icon view or list view. Now drag *inside* the window, marveling that you can now scroll up, down, or diagonally in one smooth move. Notice how your cursor becomes a butler's white-gloved hand, as though to say: "Your wish is my command, master."

An Instant "You Are Here" Map

See the tiny folder icon in the title bar of any window? You may already realize that it's a *handle*. If you click it (and hold down the mouse button until the icon darkens), you can use it to drag the open window to another place, such as your backup disk or (in the case of perfectionist computer-book authors) directly to the trash.

But when you're lost in the sea of your hard drive, and you're examining the contents of some window and you've forgotten how you got here, a handy navigational trick awaits you. While pressing the ⌘ key, click the name of the window, like this:

A menu drops down, listing the disks and folders that this one is *inside* of. If you're looking at the Seattle window, for example, you can backtrack to its parent folder — called Washington, let's say — just by choosing it from this very secret menu.

Folder Burrowing in the Dock

As Chapter 3 makes clear, you should consider the Dock the primary nesting grounds for the programs, files, and folders you use often. Whenever you click something on Dock, you open that something.

But here's a trick worth putting into practice right this very minute. Try dragging a *folder* onto the right side of the Dock — your Applications folder or Home folder, for example.

Now you can open anything *inside* those folders without leaving a messy trail of windows behind you. The trick is to click the Dock folder *and hold* the button down for a moment. (Or, if you can't wait for that extra second, Control-click the Dock folder icon.)

Either way, a pop-up menu of the folder's contents sprouts at your cursor tip, like this:

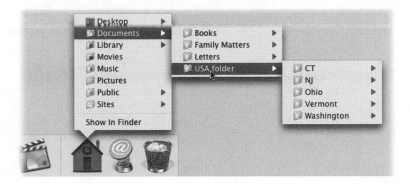

Choose anything from this menu, or even choose something that's in one of the *folders* in this list, to open it.

It shouldn't take much of a leap for you to figure out how you might put your *entire hard drive* onto the Dock, thereby gaining quick access to anything on it, in any folder at all.

Adding folders to your Dock has another handy benefit, too: They still work as folders. That is, you can still drag files and other folders on top of them, even though they're in the Dock.

The Secret Program's Dock Menu

Speaking of secret pop-up menus in the Dock, here's another one. If you click-and-hold the Dock icon of a *program* (or Control-click it), you get a handy pop-up menu of commands. The beauty of this menu is that it lists all of the documents that are currently open *in* that program — in this case, TextEdit:

Choose the name of a document to jump right to it. You can also choose Quit (to quit the program without actually switching to it first), Show In Finder (to jump to the program's icon, in your Applications folder or wherever it happens to be), or Keep in Dock (to ensure that the program's icon will remain on the Dock even after you've quit out of it). That's a lot of power that most people never even discover!

Redesigning the Finder Toolbar

At the top of every Finder window is a row of navigation buttons called the *toolbar*. Here's where you find the three buttons that switch a window between icon, list, and column view, for example.

If you'd rather do without this toolbar, just click the little white-glob-of-toothpaste button in the upper-right corner. (That's a shortcut for choosing Hide Toolbar from the View menu.) The toolbar disappears. To bring it back, choose Show Toolbar from the View menu.

Different buttons, smaller buttons

But you don't have to do without the toolbar altogether. You might simply prefer that it take up less screen space.

To make it so, open the View menu and choose Customize Toolbar. The dialog box that appears, shown here at bottom, offers a Show pop-up menu at the bottom, which lets you choose picture-buttons only (Icon Only) or, for the greatest space conservation, Text Only, shown here at top:

While this window is open, you might want to survey the optional, alternative buttons that Apple has provided for your toolbar enjoyment. There's an Eject button that makes the Mac spit out whatever disk is currently highlighted, a Burn icon that records a blank CD or DVD, a New Folder button, and so on.

You can add these to the toolbar just by dragging them into place from the gallery before you. Remove icons from the toolbar by dragging them up or down off the toolbar, or rearrange them by dragging them horizontally.

Click Done to make your changes stick.

Adding your own stuff

As useful as some of Apple's toolbar-gallery icons may be, the toolbar really takes off only when you add your own icons. You can drag *any icons at all* onto the toolbar — files, folders, disks, programs, Web sites, or whatever — to turn them into one-click buttons. Just drag them right up onto the brushed-metal area from any window, or the desktop. (You can do this at any time, even when the Customize Toolbar window isn't open.) Wait for the dotted-line rectangle to scoot out of the way, as shown here, and then release the mouse:

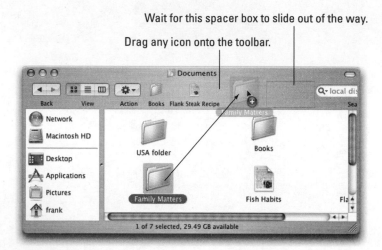

Wait for this spacer box to slide out of the way.

Drag any icon onto the toolbar.

To drag toolbar icons around, rearranging them horizontally, just press ⌘ as you drag. And to take an icon off the toolbar, ⌘-drag it clear away from the toolbar. (Watch your Trash on the Dock turn into a pair of snipping scissors as you do it. Cute!)

Chapter 20

Ten Back-of-the-Mac Jacks

*N*o Mac is an island. A computer just isn't a computer if it doesn't have some way to hook up with a printer, scanner, digital camera, speakers, and other goodies — and the back, front, or sides of your Mac is just the place to make these connections.

You may not need all of these jacks today, or even tomorrow — but you'll certainly need some of them. Here's how to identify them, and what to plug into which.

(These photos show the jacks on a PowerBook and an iMac, but you'll find pretty much the same assortment on the other Mac models.)

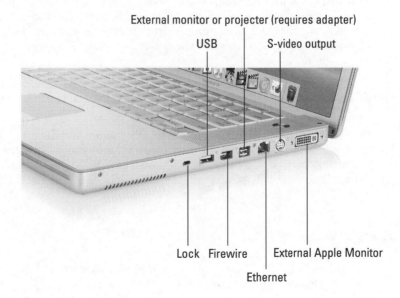

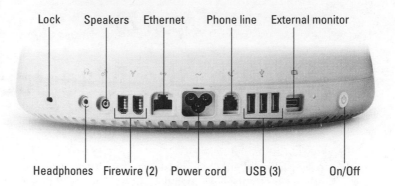

Lock   Speakers   Ethernet   Phone line   External monitor

Headphones   Firewire (2)   Power cord   USB (3)   On/Off

Lock

Just because bad guys are hardened and immoral doesn't mean they don't also have good taste in computers. The truth is, the Mac's sleek lines, high horsepower, and easy portability make it a prime target for theft, especially when the machine sits in public places like schools and businesses.

This little oval jack accommodates something called a Kensington Security cable *(www.kensington.com),* which provides a way for you to lock down the machine. Your Mac is then immune from theft — except perhaps by crooks who are also prepared to steal the desk it's attached to.

Headphones

Plug in your favorite Walkman-style headset when you need to listen to music or games without disturbing those around you — or without them disturbing you. (If you buy a headphone-jack Y splitter, two people can even listen simultaneously.)

Speakers

Oh, yes indeedy: The Mac is more than hi-tech — it's hi-*fi,* capable of churning out gorgeous stereo sound.

The cheap little speakers built into your Mac are okay, I guess, although there's very little chance you'll mistake your living room for Carnegie Hall.

But the real fun begins when you attach a pair of miniature speakers designed for computers. (Some iMac models, for example, come with Apple's own

globule-shaped, transparent ones.) If you play Mac games, particularly
CD-ROM discs, you won't believe what you've been missing; the sounds
are much richer and deeper.

Just be sure that you buy speakers that are especially designed for computers. They must be *self-powered,* and they must be *shielded;* the magnets
inside normal stereo speakers are enough to distort the image on your monitor like the Sunday comics on Silly Putty.

On the other hand, you'll get the same extremely rich sound by popping a
pair of Walkman headphones into the headphone jack on the back of the Mac.
(When you do so, the Mac's built-in speakers automatically shut up.)

FireWire

FireWire is an especially lovable jack. The three things most people plug
here are:

- **A camcorder.** This is where you plug a digital camcorder when you want
  to edit your home movies (Chapter 11).

- **An iSight.** Apple's $150 iSight is a pocket-sized video camera with built-
  in microphone. It's perfect for conducting video chats using iChat AV.

- **Another hard drive.** You can plug in external hard drives here, including
  little pocket drives — a convenient option if you're the kind of person
  who needs a little more space, or who'd like to haul around a lot of data
  from place to place.

- **The iPod.** The iPod is the world's most popular portable music player,
  although it probably belongs in an art museum. It's part mirror-finish
  stainless steel and part white acrylic, and it fits in your hand like a deck
  of cards whose edges have been laser-rounded for your comfort.

  The iPod has enough capacity for the average person's entire music
  collection — the songs of hundreds of CDs can fit on this thing.

  The iPod needs only a single cable — a white FireWire cable — to mate
  with your Mac. Over this cable, it draws both the power to recharge its
  battery and the music, which it copies automatically, and *quickly* (about
  9 seconds per album) from your iTunes music library (see Chapter 9).

  The FireWire cable also permits the iPod's hard drive to show up on
  your Mac's screen as, well, a hard drive icon, which is precisely what it
  is. At this point, you can drag data files and folders to or from the iPod,
  which is now a very fast, extremely chic-looking backup disk.

You may see the occasional scanner or digital camera that has a FireWire
cable, too.

What's so nice about FireWire is that, first of all, it's extremely fast, which is why speed-intensive gadgets like camcorders and hard drives are such a natural for it. Second, FireWire is easy to plug and unplug. It's nothing like the balky jacks of the 90s that preceded it, which required that you shut down the Mac completely before attaching or disconnecting your add-on gear.

Ethernet

This is your networking jack. You'll be very happy to have it when a second or third Mac joins your household, because this is where you plug the Ethernet cable that will connect your Mac to the network. (Details in Chapter 14.)

One important caution: This jack looks and works almost exactly like a telephone jack. It's actually slightly larger — but it's still possible to snap a phone wire into this jack. In fact, many a hapless computer owner has done just that by accident, and then spent days trying to figure out why their machines couldn't dial up to the Internet. Don't plug anything in here except an Ethernet cable.

Phone Line

This is where you plug the wire that goes to a phone jack, for faxing and dialing-the-Internet purposes. (A Mac-matching white one even came in your Mac box.)

USB

USB stands for *Universal Serial Bus* ("bus" meaning "connector"), which you'll never need to know.

You will, however, become intimately familiar with USB. Apart from camcorders and hard drives, almost everything worth connecting to the Mac plugs in here. For example:

- **Printers.** Most inkjet printers (see Chapter 5) connect to your USB port. Even some laser printers do.
- **Scanners.** If the point of a printer is to take something on the screen and reproduce it on *paper,* a scanner, then, is the opposite — its function is to scan an image on paper and throw it up on the Mac *screen.* After the

image has been scanned and converted into bits and bytes that the Mac understands (meaning that it's been *digitized*), you can manipulate the image any way that you want. Erase unwanted parts, make the background darker, give Uncle Ed a mustache, shorten your brother's neck — whatever.

The more dignified use for a scanner is grabbing real-world images that you then paste into your own documents, particularly in the realm of page layout and graphic design. Got a potato-industry newsletter to crank out? Scan in a photo of some fine-lookin' spuds, and you've got yourself a graphic for page one.

A middle-of-the-line color scanner costs around $100 — which sometimes even includes software that can do a decent job of converting scanned articles into typed-out, editable word processor documents. (When shopping, be careful to buy a scanner that's *Mac OS X compatible*.)

✔ **Digital cameras.** Ordinarily, the concept of paying $300 for a camera that lacks any way to insert film would seem spectacularly brain-dead. Yet that's exactly the point of *digital cameras,* like those from Canon, Kodak, Casio, Olympus, Sony, Nikon, and others. They store photos without film — actually, on a memory card — and when you get home, you can dump the images into iPhoto (Chapter 10), thereby freeing your camera's memory card for another round of happy-go-lucky shooting.

If the camera you buy has a resolution of at least three *megapixels* (millions of dots per shot), you can print out spectacular eight-by-tens that look every bit as sharp as traditional photos.

✔ **Musical keyboards.** *MIDI,* pronounced like the short skirt, stands for Musical Instrument Digital Interface. What it *means* is "hookup to a synthesizer." What it *does* is let your Mac record and play back your musical performances using a synthesizer attached to it. When you record, the Mac makes a metronome sound — a steady click track — and you play to the beat. Then, when you play back the music, your keyboard plays *exactly* what you recorded, complete with feeling, expression, and fudged notes; you'd think that Elvis's ghost was playing the instrument, except that the keys don't move up and down. Then you can edit your fudged mistakes and wind up sounding like [insert your favorite musician here].

All you need is either a MIDI piano keyboard (about $100) or, if you have a full-blown synthesizer, a little adapter box called a MIDI interface (about $50) that connects it to your Mac's USB jack.

You also need a program that can record and play back the music, called a *sequencing program,* like GarageBand (see the end of Chapter 3). Or, for making sheet music, investigate Nightingale, Sibelius, or Finale. Check out a music store, or read some reviews on the Web, and get jammin'.

✔ **Joysticks.** The Mac, with its superb graphics, makes a great game-playing machine. But how can you get the feeling of soaring over the fields of France in a fighter plane using a *mouse* to control the action? You can't. You need a joystick. It works just like a real airplane joystick, controlling your movement in flight simulation, driving simulators, shoot-'em-ups, and other games. They cost between $20 and $50, and you can find them on a Web site like *www.buy.com* by searching for "Mac joystick" or "Macintosh joystick."

The USB port also accommodates your keyboard, your mouse, microphones, and many other kinds of doodads.

But not, alas, all at once. On a desktop Mac, your mouse plugs into the USB jack at the end of the keyboard, and the keyboard uses up one of the Mac's USB jacks. That leaves at least one more USB jack free, at the other end of your keyboard.

Still, that may not be enough USB jacks. Maybe you've plugged in your printer and scanner — great — but now where are you supposed to plug your digital camera?

Easy: Buy an adapter box that gives you more USB jacks. Those so-called *USB hubs* multiply your USB jack so that you wind up with four, eight, or even more jacks. Connect enough of these hubs to one another, in fact, and you can have up to 127 USB gadgets connected to your Mac all at once.

The only thing that could conceivably go wrong with USB has to do with *power.* Many USB gadgets draw power from the Mac itself, sparing you the ugliness and hassle of power cords and plugs for all your external equipment. It turns out, however, that the back-panel jacks provide more power than the keyboard jacks do.

You can take away two lessons from this. First, if you ever plug in some USB gizmo to the end of your keyboard and discover that it doesn't work, try plugging the gizmo into one of the back-panel USB jacks instead. Second, when you buy a USB hub, shop for a *powered* one (one that requires its own electrical plug), so that you won't run into the same trouble as you did with the keyboard-end jack.

External Monitor (Adapter)

If you use your Mac to give slide shows or classroom lectures, you may sometimes wish you could project images onto a big screen.

That's exactly the purpose of a *video-output* jack. Depending on your Mac model, you may have one or both of two types.

First, there's the kind that requires a little white adapter cable (which came with your computer). If you have a laptop, you probably have this tiny connector. Don't lose the three-inch adapter cable that came with your laptop. One end of this little adapter connects to the back of your Mac; the other end connects to the standard *VGA connector* of the sorts of projectors and PC monitors found in schools, businesses, and presentation halls.

If you've ever been to a user-group meeting and seen a Mac demonstration projected onto a huge screen, now you know how it's done.

External Monitor (Apple Only)

This wide, grille-like connector is designed to plug straight into Apple's own monitors.

Why does Apple require its own, nonstandard cable design? To save you cable clutter. This connector transmits not just the screen-image signal, but also power — so you don't have to plug the screen into an outlet — and even USB signals, because most Mac monitors have USB jacks right on them.

S-Video Output

Some Mac models offer this round jack, which is designed to mate with an *S-video cable* — a standard jack on modern DVD players, DVD recorders, TVs, and VCRs. The chief benefit here is playing a DVD on the Mac and watching it on your TV.

Index

• *Q* •

• *R* •

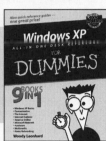